English Primary Education
and the Progressives, 1914-1939

English Primary Education and the Progressives, 1914-1939

R. J. W. Selleck

School of Education
University of Melbourne

London and Boston
Routledge & Kegan Paul

First published 1972
by Routledge & Kegan Paul Ltd
Broadway House, 68-74 Carter Lane,
London EC4V 5EL and
9 Park Street,
Boston, Mass. 02108, U.S.A.

Printed in Great Britain by
Northumberland Press Ltd
Gateshead
© R. J. W. Selleck 1972
ISBN 0 7100 7208 2

THE STUDENTS LIBRARY OF EDUCATION has been designed to meet the needs of students of Education at Colleges of Education and at University Institutes and Departments. It will also be valuable for practising teachers and educationists. The series takes full account of the latest developments in teacher-training and of new methods and approaches in education. Separate volumes will provide authorative and up-to-date accounts of the topics within the major fields of sociology, philosophy and history of education, educational psychology, and method. Care has been taken that specialist topics are treated lucidly and usefully for the non-specialist reader. Altogether, the Students Library of Education will provide a comprehensive introduction and guide to anyone concerned with the study of education, and with educational theory and practice.

J. W. TIBBLE

The English primary school—or at least its most advanced section—is probably unique in the world, and is certainly arousing widespread interest, perhaps particularly in the United States. Its main features include flexible grouping systems, especially the rapid shift towards non-streaming, together with, in many cases, vertical grouping; a new approach to the curriculum, or rather, to the content of pupils' activities, based on enhancing the child's activity in variously structured (or sometimes unstructured) learning situations; the promotion of artistic, aesthetic and musical activity with the emphasis on creativity; new approaches to the teaching and learning of mathematics and science, and many other features. Although the extent of this advance should not, perhaps, be exaggerated (the Plowden Committee claimed to have identified the 10 per cent 'best' schools), there can be no doubt that, in spite of all the well-known material difficulties, primary education in Britain today presents features which are historically quite new.

What is the background to this development? Why is it that the ideas of the 'new' education have penetrated so deeply into the primary field? What are the origins of the ideas now being brought into practice on so wide a scale? These questions are often asked, but less often answered with any conviction.

In this book, R. J. W. Selleck explores the ideas and faith that gripped the prophets of the 'new' education during and after World War I, relates this movement to its social background and explores its development. He shows how 'progressive' ideas in education, 'a barely respectable doctrine' held only by a group of outsiders in 1914, had by 1939 'captured the allegiance of the opinion-makers' and had in fact become the 'intellectual orthodoxy'. So the stage was set for their breakthrough into the schools following World War II.

This book indicates clearly how historical study illuminates contemporary educational practice, and adds a new dimension to our understanding.

BRIAN SIMON

Contents

CONTENTS

Preface

This book is concerned with 'progressive education' and its effect on the English primary school in the period from 1914 to 1939. The limitations of the study need emphasis.

First, it is concerned with England only. Comparisons which could be made with other countries, and especially with the United States, have not been attempted.

Second, the study is focused on the primary school—this differentiates it from previous work, such as W. A. C. Stewart's. (I should like, however, to acknowledge the stimulus and the help his book has been.) It was necessary to study progressive education as a whole, not just its relation to the primary school, and this has been done in chapters 2 and 3 (the first chapter prepares the ground by examining the effect of World War I on English education). But no attempt has been made to examine every aspect of the progressive movement. Thus the discussion of 'progressive schools' concentrates on those started before 1925, not necessarily because they were more important or more interesting than later foundations, but because they provide sufficient insight into the progressive movement to enable its effects on the primary school to be studied. The term 'primary', it should be noted, is used throughout with the meaning which Hadow made official in 1926.

The third limitation is the period of the study. This has been chosen partly because it permits the continuation of previous work which I reported in *The New Education 1870–1914*, but mainly because this period saw vital changes made in English primary education. In 1967 the Plowden Committee began the main part of their report, *Children and Their Primary Schools*, with a statement which would have greatly gladdened the first progressives: 'At the heart of the educational process lies the child.' Much else the Committee had to say showed a similar regard for 'progressive' attitudes. Studying these attitudes in the period of their formation, the inter-war years, assists an understanding of today's primary school.

Acknowledgments

I wish to acknowledge the assistance of some of my colleagues at the School of Education, University of Melbourne, particularly Professor A. G. Austin, Peter Gill, Imelda Palmer, A. V. Robinson, and Miss Olive Battersby and Mrs C. Gigante from the Education Library. Two other librarians were of great help : Miss D. M. Jepson at the Department of Education and Science, London, and Mr D. J. Foskett, of the Institute of Education, University of London. I am grateful to Mr Lionel Elvin, the Director of that Institute, for granting me the privileges of a Visiting Scholar in 1968. Special debts are owed to my wife, to Professor A. C. F. Beales, King's College, London, to Don Miller, Political Science Department, University of Melbourne and to Miles Maxwell of Welwyn, Herts; I learned much from talking to them and gained from their encouragement. My principal debt is to the Nuffield Foundation who, by awarding me a Dominion Travelling Fellowship in 1968, made it possible for me and my family to visit England. To David Yonge and Margaret McGill I am especially grateful, for their friendliness made our stay all the more memorable.

Abbreviations

C.E.A. Conference of Educational Associations
C.N.I. Conference on New Ideals in Education
E.M.   Education Miscellany (Library, Department of Education
        and Science, London)
N.E.F. New Education Fellowship
P.R.O. Public Record Office, London

I

The state, the school
and war, 1914-1918

Bertrand Russell was upset by the outbreak of war in 1914. 'And
all this madness,' he wrote,[1]

> all this rage, all this flaming death of our civilization and our
> hopes, has been brought about because a set of official gentlemen,
> living luxurious lives, mostly stupid, and all without imagination
> or heart, have chosen that it should occur rather than that any
> of them should suffer some infinitesimal rebuff to his country's
> pride.

Of course, others were upset too:[2]

> Already we have suffered in a greater or less degree, and we
> schoolmasters not least. Business and professional men have
> some choice as to when they will take their yearly outing, but
> for teachers August is *par excellence* the holiday month, and for
> many an overworked man and woman it has been worse than a
> disappointment or inconvenience to find long-laid plans upset and
> holiday courses cancelled; to be turned back from the station,
> or, still worse, from a foreign frontier, or, as in the case of
> elementary teachers, to be docked altogether of half their
> holiday.

Not for them the 'flaming death'; 'business as usual', even though
the business was holidays, could hardly have received a more
emphatic endorsement. In the years that followed many teachers
passed the frontiers of foreign lands, although, as they were pawns
in the not so long-laid plans of official gentlemen, their sight-seeing
was often confined to examining the mud of trenches. Others
were never to have a holiday again but to crowd back into the
schools they had left as entries on honour boards, where in shining

gold letters they admonished the future generations not to forget. Others again returned determined to create a new world so that the future generations should be able to forget; while some, who could not forget, found that a loss of faith in the old world prevented them from hoping for a new.

But in the beginning it was different. England might not have gone willingly to war but some were almost relieved that the long-threatened storm had finally broken and a few, who saw in war a means of redeeming the Empire, rejoiced. In any case, as the lamps went out all over Europe on a bank holiday weekend, cheering crowds sang patriotic songs in Trafalgar Square and Whitehall. It would be, most believed (but not Kitchener), a swift and brief encounter, a 'war of tradition' where 'cavalary charged at the foe' and where, 'when death came, it was a heroic death brought about by heroes on the other side.' After a brief panic business continued and Lloyd George noticed that 'something infinitely greater and more enduring' was emerging—'a new patriotism, richer, nobler, and more exalted than the old.' Volunteers flocked to the colours, 750,000 of them by the end of September, though there were not enough qualified men to train them nor enough barracks to house them. As the battalions of war gathered the once vociferous anti-war and pacifist groups dissolved, leaving a few resolute souls to face the wrath of the righteous. The government put through the Defence of the Realm Act on 8 August and took such emergency measures as it considered necessary, believing apparently that nothing more far-reaching was required. The fourteen Territorial divisions were left to protect the country against invasion and the British Expeditionary Force dispatched to France from where its commander-in-chief, Sir John French, began sending optimistic reports.

Then everything went wrong. Despite the assistance of the angels of Mons the British forces were retreating before the end of August and when, on 5 September under Joffre's orders, they began to counter-attack, they could find no Germans. After they found them, there followed the first battle of Ypres which, according to A. J. P. Taylor, marked the end of the old British army. It also marked the end of the old type of war for by November the trenches had already been dug. 'I don't know what is to be done,' Kitchener said; 'this isn't war.'[3]

The next four years were to show that it was war and that, like Kitchener, few knew what to do. 'Open' warfare did not come;

instead of brilliant victories in the dusty field there was the pro-
tracted frustration of trench warfare, desperate sallies through
mud and barbed wire and gas to gain more trenches (which
might be lost next day), and a growing sense of bitterness and
futility. At the start of the war Rupert Brooke wrote of a soldier
who, when he died, would be 'a pulse in the eternal mind' giving
back the thoughts 'by England given':

> Her sights and sounds; dreams happy as her day;
> And laughter, learnt of friends; and gentleness,
> In hearts at peace, under an English heaven.

The soldier of whom Wilfred Owen wrote at the end of the war
had no vision of an English heaven.

> I am the enemy you killed, my friend.
> I know you in this dark: for so you frowned
> Yesterday through me as you jabbed and killed.
> I parried; but my hands were loath and cold.
> Let us sleep now ...

Reluctantly the military authorities faced the fact that they
were fighting a new kind of war and the civil leaders came to
realize that, if victory were to be theirs, English social and political
life would need profound alterations. Apart from the passing of the
Defence of the Realm Act their first measures were essentially *ad
hoc*, emergency steps. The espousal of 'business as usual', the first
two budgets and the enthusiastic but indiscriminate recruiting
which filled the army but crippled industrial life showed that
(understandably enough) they had not seen that this war was, in a
sense that no other had been, a national affair, that the country
as a whole and not just the front-line soldier was required to
play a part. Gradually, even if haphazardly, the hand of government reached out until it had brought the country within its
control and attuned it to the purposes of war. English drinking
habits and financial practices, prices, rents, manpower, shipping,
the purchase, supply and distribution of the raw materials for
industry and much else were organized (not always efficiently)
so that they contributed to the war effort. The Englishman's news
was censored, his food rationed, his sons conscripted. Ministries
(for the blockade, for labour, shipping, food and pensions) appeared,
and day-to-day living came under the direction of officials and
boards with strange names: the Coal Controller, the Cotton Control Board, the Royal Commission on Sugar Supply, the Fat and

3

Meats Executive, the Oil and Seed Executive. If men were to be transported to the trenches, their bodies fed, the guns kept loaded and their dead replaced, the old amateurish ways had to go. Success depended upon the organization of all the nation's activities. Once a civilian had contributed adequately to the war effort if he sent his son to fight and his daughter to attend the wounded; he could then be left to worry with a clear conscience. Now he too had to be organized—war had attained the dignity of a full-time activity.

Schools and the war effort

Many teachers immediately volunteered for service and what happened in schools in the next four and a half years was not of much interest to them. When they returned, if they did, the most important change could not be seen; it was the absence of the dead and disabled. But the schools to which the soldiers came back, no less than the soldiers themselves, had been profoundly altered.

The first reaction of educational administrators mirrored that of the other civil authorities—business as usual. It was very undesirable, in the Board of Education's opinion,[4]

> that the unrest, to which the present crisis in the affairs of the Nation naturally gives rise, should be intensified by any avoidable interruption or dislocation of the public educational service of the Country.

J. A. Pease, then President of the Board, addressed an open letter to 'my colleagues in the national service of education' which received wide publicity. Drawing on his words the *Journal of Education* argued, 'The first duty of teachers ... is to keep the system of education going; to fill up the gaps in our ranks; to contrive makeshifts; and be ready to work double spells when called upon.'[5] Of course, business could not go on as usual. Expenditure on school buildings was frozen; schools and training colleges were taken over for military purposes despite the Board's successful protest against the over-enthusiastic requisitioning that marked the early days of the war; teachers volunteered in large numbers (over twenty thousand had served in the forces by the end of the war) thus making staffing problems critical; specialists, such as doctors in the School Medical Service and physical education instructors, were withdrawn from the schools.[6] The Board was forced to admit that 'the system, as a whole, undoubtedly

4

has suffered ... the war has ... imposed on educational resources a continual and increasing strain as regards both personal and material conditions, and has entailed many sacrifices.'[7]

However important they were for the war effort, these sacrifices do not represent a specifically educational contribution, that is, a contribution made by an education system which could not, or could not so easily, have been made by other parts of society. Stopping expenditure on schools, handing buildings over to the military or allowing teachers to enlist was evidence of a willingness to co-operate with the national policies; but, important though this co-operation might have been and gladly given though it was, it did not involve the use of professional skills or exploit the teacher's greatest asset, influence over children. But this influence was put to work when teachers and the Board encouraged children to participate in the home front's voluntary war effort. Children knitted, made socks and mufflers, sent parcels to prisoners of war, collected eggs (the Board spoke with pride of the thirty children in one small village school who collected 2,542 eggs in 'a short period'), dispatched candles and food to the trenches, made sandbags, bed-tables and crutches, bed-rests and clinical chart carriers.[8] These and the many similar activities were not confined to the classroom but they were often organized there and sometimes, as the produce of the manual training rooms testifies, actually carried out there. Their importance was not their contribution to the improvement of conditions in the trenches—sandbags, food and clothes would have come in any case and the voluntary activities were often as inefficient as they were enthusiastic. They were important because they involved children and the community at large in the war effort and, by giving them the opportunity to contribute, assisted national solidarity and assured everyone that the cause was just.

Children were involved more completely with the war than these peripheral activities indicate. In July 1915, for example, the Board sent a circular to local education authorities asking for their support in the war savings campaign. Later they sent a leaflet which gave details of the activities of the National War Savings Committee and throughout the war they stressed the importance of this kind of saving.[9] Their efforts were most successful: the schools formed more than one-third of the 36,316 War Saving Associations which were set up and the Board pointed out that 'a very large number of teachers are secretaries of local committees and have done most valuable work on "propaganda" '.[10] Thrift had always been encouraged by the public elementary school and penny banks were a long-established institution; but the savings campaign aimed to make thrift contribute to the war effort. The teacher, it was claimed,

> can easily lead the older scholars to see that great expenditure of money is necessary for the successful prosecution of the War and that in order to defray it, the State must rely on the savings of individuals. There is no need for him to go into details which are beyond the comprehension of children; but he should give them some account of the War Loan and the advantages which it offers.

Saving, the child should know, was 'a service due to his country'.[11]

There were other services he could render. In December 1916 a worsening in the food situation led to the appointment of a Food Controller. In May 1917 Lord Devonport, who then held the office, made it known through the Board that he 'would be glad if Local Education Authorities and Teachers in all schools would take special steps to impress upon children the urgent need for the prevention of waste'.[12] Special lessons were given to all children, the instruction in Domestic Economy Centres was to emphasize economy, mothers and 'other adults' could attend the classes in which children were taught cooking, and special classes in cookery for adults were run by the women inspectors of the Board. Exhibitions were arranged to demonstrate the best and most economical methods of cookery and housecraft. A pamphlet, *Economy in Food*, was printed, discussed with children and distributed to their parents by school nurses and other suitable people. School gardens (which, like penny banks, had been introduced before the war) were encouraged and flourished; teachers were specially trained to give instruction to their colleagues in school gardening and in some cases the supreme sacrifice was made of turning playing-fields into school gardens.[13] Horse-chestnuts were gathered by children and delivered to the Director of Propellant Supplies at the Ministry of Munitions because, as the Board explained, 'The experiments prove that for every ton of horse-chestnuts which are harvested, half a ton of grain can be saved for human consumption.' When increasing the supply of jam became a matter of 'urgent national importance' children were asked to help in the 'systematic picking and collection of blackberries'.[14]

It is not important to decide how much this campaign assisted the war effort. In any case it would be difficult as the Board contributed to the war economy by cutting back on the statistics it gathered and as a result the number of school gardens or the value of their produce is not known. But even if grossly inefficient, the school gardens illustrate (as does the whole food economy campaign) how the education system was used to further governmental policy. The teacher was in a favourable position to assist the Food Control Committee, and by helping them he contributed to the cause of national solidarity. 'Scholars, teachers, and parents,' wrote *The Times Educational Supplement* when discussing the problem of food supply,[15]

> must be made to feel that each and everyone is concerned in this vital matter. It is not that our armies are waging war; *we* are at war—*we*, scholars and teachers, students and professors, country folk and city people! 'Every sack of food is worth a gun.' The words are not mere rhetoric, but a forcible statement of fact.

Less rhetoric was needed to justify another of the school's contributions, its assistance in meeting the labour shortage. Some technical schools trained pupils in the making of munitions and the Board asked the local authorities to arrange for school holidays to fall at a time which would least interfere with the work of parents in munition factories.[16] Of more value for the war effort was the willingness of local authorities to allow use of the exemption clauses which permitted children to leave school, either permanently or on a part-time basis, before they had reached the leaving age. The system of exemptions was complicated but broadly speaking it meant that children could get 'time off' or be excused school altogether (usually at thirteen, but often at twelve and, in agricultural districts, sometimes at eleven) if they had made a required number of attendances or reached a certain standard of work. The Board, while recognizing the need to supplement the labour force (children's time, a Departmental committee said in 1917, 'was worth its weight, not in gold but in blood'), endeavoured to control exemptions. It met with little success and by January 1918, *The Times* calculated, six hundred thousand children had been withdrawn prematurely from school to meet the needs of industry.[17]

The problem was particularly acute in rural areas and arrangements were made to permit the employment of children who previously would not have qualified for exemption. Asquith remarked on 4 March 1915, 'I do not think we ought to be bound in a great national emergency like this by any pedantic regard for rules and conventions and usages which have prevailed, and rightly prevailed, when circumstances were normal'.[18] Others found a more elaborate justification:[19]

> The work will, in fact, have a high moral value. The school teachers in organizing this work will be performing national service of the first moment, and we do not doubt that it will be so organized throughout the land as to be of direct educational value.

As the numbers doing this national service increased, and suggestions were made that farmers were capitalizing on the emergency to get cheap labour, the Board increased its efforts to keep control; but it was forced in February 1916 to allow girls of thirteen, or even twelve, to be excused from school so that they could look after the home and thus free their mothers to work on the land.[20]

The Board's efforts to keep the labour pool full were indirect: they involved the removal of impediments which kept the young worker in the school. Its contribution to the solution of the problem caused by unemployment was more direct. For a short time early in the war there had been fears of unemployment among young people and the Board encouraged the organization of special day and evening classes which, had they got under way, would certainly have proved futile. However the necessity for them was removed by the increasing demand of industry for labour[21] and until the end of the war, as the speed with which the school leavers were absorbed by industry shows, there was no unemployment problem. Yet long before the war ended many had begun to worry about the peace-time fate of the young wage-earners. Peace might slow the growth of many of the industries (munitions, for example) which had absorbed them; and even if work could be found elsewhere there would at least be a period of dislocation which, if not properly handled, might have unpleasant consequences. They would be competing with returned soldiers who might not easily understand how the country which had paid them to fight could not find them jobs when the war was over. And it was recognized that the young were owed a debt. They had been permitted, if not encouraged, to leave school early and take up work which, though vital to the war effort and well paid during the war, left them with no skill or trade and made them vulnerable to changes in the pattern of employment. H. A. L. Fisher, whom Lloyd George had called to the Presidency of the Board of Education in December 1916, expressed this view clearly:[22]

> Though they are earning wages, and in some cases high wages, let us make no mistake about it, these children are incurring a real sacrifice, the effects of which, in many cases, will be felt to the end of their lives. I ask the House to consider whether the nation has not incurred a special responsibility towards these children who have been brought in to help in the War, often in circumstances most adverse ...

If this appeal to conscience failed, the chance that the bitter labour disputes of the pre-war years might flare again provided a motive for action.

Once more education was pressed into the national service. When the 1918 Education Act provided for continuation schools, fixed the leaving age at fourteen and abolished exemptions and the part-time system, it was certainly influenced by the desire to control the flood of young workers into the labour market. It had more in mind, of course, but it had this. As Fisher, its architect, said:[23]

> you cannot extend popular education without to some degree contracting the quantity of juvenile labour in the market, and ... seeing that we have reason to apprehend that upon the demobilization of our army at the conclusion of peace there will be a large mass of adult labour seeking employment which the labour market will have difficulty in absorbing, it would clearly be a wise step to effect part at least of our change in time to assist the process of demobilization.

A departmental committee ('on juvenile education in relation to employment after the war') came to a similar conclusion:

> a strong effort ought to be made, by teachers and all other persons capable of influencing children and their parents, to explain to them the difficulties of obtaining suitable work during the process of demobilisation, and the great advantages, both personal and national, of prolonged attendance at school.

This committee, whose existence testified to the concern over juvenile unemployment,[25] produced that rarity among official educational documents, a vigorous and moving report. They were deeply disturbed by the need to use juvenile labour, concerned by the demoralization unemployment was causing and were determined to create a new and better world. They recommended a leaving age of fourteen and the establishment of continuation schools, thus anticipating Fisher's Act. They were so impressed by the need for action that they produced an interim report which urged local education authorities to act immediately to strengthen the juvenile employment bureaux. These institutions had had a chequered history. The exchanges set up after the Labour Exchanges Act of 1909 had included juvenile departments though, of course, they were primarily concerned with finding work for adults. Advisory committees chosen by the Board of Trade, who administered the exchanges, were also organized; they contained people with some knowledge of education and, though not officially members, H.M.I.s could attend their meetings. This arrangement was not satisfactory and the Education (Choice of Employment) Act in 1910 allowed local education authorities to establish juvenile employment committees which were empowered to advise on employment and to assist in finding jobs for young people.[26] Thus, in consecutive years, there were established competing agencies for juvenile employment between whom rivalry rapidly grew. Despite a joint memorandum by the Boards of Trade and Education setting out the relationship between the agencies, neither their rivalry nor the overlap of responsibility was fully removed.

The details of their uneasy development need not be discussed; what has to be noted, however, is the emphasis placed on the local authorities' committees by the report of the departmental committee on juvenile education and employment after the war. It praised the labour exchanges and their advisory committees and did not want them duplicated, but it urged the local education authorities to fill the gaps in areas where these institutions had not been established.[27] The Board immediately asked local authorities to follow this advice and as soon as the war was over it urged those authorities who had not complied with the earlier recommendation to ensure that their junior employment committees were put into 'thorough working order without delay'.[28] Improvements were made and useful work done, though the bureaux were not as effective as had been hoped.

Where the bureaux failed to find work for the unemployed the Board had made other arrangements. Juvenile employment centres were to be established so that those out of work could receive some instruction while waiting for a job. The scheme was announced the day after the Armistice and some centres started immediately. They had a fitful existence, though they were revived in the winter of 1920-1 and during the depression.[29] They aimed to console the unemployed with informal instruction, guidance in the use of the library and reading room, recreative handwork and 'occasional lectures of a useful and attractive kind'.[30] At least they kept some adolescents off the streets and slightly diminished their chances of earning the title of juvenile delinquent.

This title was frequently employed during the war years. There was a marked increase in hooliganism and crime, though the extent of the increase is difficult to estimate. The number convicted of indictable offences before the age of sixteen rose from 14,325 in 1913 to 24,407 in 1917, a very marked rise; but Cyril Burt considered that these figures (of a kind always liable to collapse if too much weight is put on them) exaggerated the increase, though that there was an increase he does not deny.[31] Contemporaries had no doubts—and no hesitation in making their concern obvious. When *The Times* lamented the existence of

a good deal of rowdyism, in some cases passing into hooliganism, and a notable increase in what may be called minor crime, such as stealing fruit from orchards, and some increase in serious crime, such as robbery from the person,

it was expressing the thoughts of many, not all of whom were as concerned with offences against property.[32]

Many reasons for the delinquency were found: lack of parental control, the increased independence given by high wages, the sudden lifting of school's restraints from a large number of adolescents, the general strains of war, the cinema. Remedies were harder to find and the education authorities, both central and local, were asked for assistance. It was thought that a cure or at least a palliative might be found if children, instead of wandering the streets at night, were gathered into supervised groups. Evening classes still continued but not even the most sanguine expected that the potential delinquent would voluntarily come to school at night. The evening play centres, started by Mrs Humphry Ward in London in 1905, seemed a better hope. In these centres children could be kept busy with a mixture of games, singing, dancing, lantern talks, handwork and reading. The 1907 Education (Administrative Provisions) Act had enabled local authorities to spend money on the centre but relatively few had. However, in December 1916 the Home Office wrote to the Board drawing attention to the increase of juvenile delinquency and suggesting that, outside the usual school hours, of course, schools might be lent to voluntary organizations who were trying to cater for the needs of youth. After all, the Home Office pointed out, the school buildings had been erected 'at a great expenditure of public funds'.[33] A month later the Board offered to assist the financing of evening play centres, stressing that the work done in them was valuable in its own right but making clear that 'the immediate occasion of ... action in this matter is the need for preventing and remedying deterioration arising out of war.'[34] There was an immediate and dramatic increase in the number of play centres. Before the grant nineteen had been established in London, by March 1919 there were thirty-two; outside London only one local authority had established play centres before the grant was offered (though a few had been set up by voluntary bodies), yet by March 1919 there were forty-seven authorities operating 167 centres.[35]

This system of government support for voluntary bodies was used in another attempt to combat juvenile delinquency. Whatever their limitations, the numerous youth organizations (the Boy Scouts, Girl Guides, the Church Lads' Brigade, the Boys' Own Brigade, the Girls' Friendly Society, for example) could be expected to make some contribution. For most of the war they made it alone but as the concern over juvenile crime increased an effort was made to co-ordinate their activities: a Juvenile Organizations Committee was set up by the Home Office in 1916 to improve co-operation between the voluntary bodies working among juveniles. This central committee encouraged the formation of numerous local versions of itself, committees whose effectiveness, it was hoped, would be increased by their knowledge of local problems. There was never much promise in this arrangement but there was more promise than achievement for, in the immediate post-war years particularly, the local committees suffered severe financial restrictions. The co-operation of the educational authorities had always been sought and the responsibility for the central Juvenile Organizations Committee was transferred to the Board in October 1919.[36] Probably the activities of the potential juvenile delinquent were not seriously curtailed by the evening play centres and the juvenile organizations committee, though no doubt some were persuaded to adopt respectable pursuits. In any case their importance for us lies not in their achievements but in the example they provide of efforts to use the educational authorities to solve social problems resulting from, or at least exacerbated by, the war.

A more successful use of the educational system for a similar purpose came when the war drew attention to another problem, the health of the nation's youth. A concern with this had been obvious before the war and, as the introduction of school meals and medical inspection shows, had been acted upon. The war increased the concern, though the first suggestions to emerge were not promising. 'Military or Naval training,' it was declared, 'should form a part of every boy's education, just as nursing and housewifing should form a part of every girl's training.' Military drill, which had been gradually losing popularity as a means of physical training, found new advocates, though the Board insisted that it would not re-introduce it. Those interested in military drill were not quietened but no action was taken.[37]

In 1914 the Education (Provision of Meals) Act was passed, empowering local authorities to supply meals during the holidays and lifting the restriction which had prevented them from spending more than the proceeds of a halfpenny rate on school meals. The Act cannot be attributed to the war as it had been prepared before its outbreak; however, the war speeded its passage for it was envisaged as one of the 'defensive measures against any economic distress which may be caused by war conditions.'[38] This statement, made by the Board when announcing its intention to help local authorities with the financing of school meals, was not mere rhetoric—the number of meals supplied in the early years of the war increased and fell off later when unemployment ceased and wages became higher. Once more the school had been used to take up the slack in the national war effort, this time in the cause of the children's health. It is clear that the Board's intention had been quite deliberate. J. A. Pease, its President, remarked when the war began: 'If we can keep the schools open and effective, and have ready against the hour of distress our organization for feeding school children, we shall have done much to guard a vital point.'[39] Of course when there was a conflict between the war's requirements and those of child health the war's received preference: although the School Medical Service continued throughout the war, it was seriously handicapped by the loss of staff to the services whose need was considered more pressing.

But despite the struggles of the School Medical Service the Chief Medical Officer of the Board, Sir George Newman, did not become despondent about the war's effect on his work. He had every reason to remember that war often resulted in an increased interest in national health, and particularly in child health, for the Service which he administered had grown partly out of the disquiet fanned by the Boer War. Never reluctant to turn his reports into an impassioned lecture (which he liberally spiced with statistics), he seized the opportunity to stress the importance of physical fitness.

> In no direction are the ravages of war more serious or more difficult to replace than in the loss of human lives. Whatever degree of success may attend the nation in the present European war, the cost in life must inevitably be heavy. Consequently, the question of the preservation of the rising generation, and care for its physical fitness and equipment, is of more than ordinary importance. Apart from the grave disadvantage that much of the value of the education of children will be lost unless they are physically fit both to profit by the instruction they receive and to perform the industrial tasks which await them in the future, it is a matter of grave national concern to secure that physical unfitness and inefficiency in all its forms, due to ill-health or lack of vitality, are reduced to the smallest possible dimension.

And when, as had happened during the Boer War, many recruits had to be rejected because they were physically unfit, Newman was swift to point the moral. 'We profess', he said, 'to be astonished and depressed by the magnitude of the sickness claims or the large rejections of recruits, but there is, in fact, insufficient grounds for this surprise.'[40]

Physical education, which Newman wanted for its own sake and not just for its contribution to national ends, received more attention. The evening play centres were used but trust was placed mainly in the public elementary schools. In February 1917 the Board announced that it had received funds which would enable local authorities to employ organizers of physical education in elementary schools. The number of such organizers rapidly increased and where the Board was dissatisfied with the progress of local authorities it did not hesitate to threaten the withholding of the grant. For most of the war scholarships were offered to teachers who, after intensive courses, could specialize in physical education. Finally the Fisher Act and a new syllabus, issued in 1919, expressed a wider conception of physical training in which medical inspection, school meals, systematic 'exercises' (but not drill), open-air schooling and holiday and school camps were closely integrated.[41]

Probably the efforts to improve child health had more success than others which the schools made, but they were not different in kind. Whether they were asked to advertise the need for recruits, to check on state expenditure (teachers were to report if the children of those in receipt of Army Separation Allowances appeared unduly neglected), or to fight against the inadvertent disclosure of military information, the schools were being treated as cogs in the war machine.[42] Whether they encouraged the child to knit or make sandbags, to collect eggs or send parcels to prisoners of war, to give to national savings or start a school garden, to make munitions or gather in the harvest, whether they struggled against unemployment or juvenile crime, they were contributing, to an extent never before attempted, to a national purpose. They were not always efficient, and were sometimes quite ineffective (the same could be said of industry, commerce or the army), but their intentions were always good.

'Propaganda'

Nowhere was the contribution of the school more evident than in its efforts to form attitudes and beliefs favourable to the war effort. This is the most obvious task which schools can take up during war-time and almost certainly the most important. Horse-chestnuts have their place, and if schools can collect them so much the better; but the most vital task they were given was one they were well equipped to discharge: the formation (as far as was in their power) of a belief in the rightness of the nation's cause and a willingness to assist it. As the war progressed the importance of this task increased for it became evident that if the new kind of war were to be waged successfully it required the co-operation of the whole community. Morale had to be kept up, triumphs celebrated and defeats explained away or made the cause of greater efforts; the enemy had to be shown to be wrong and his leaders evil and stupid; the fervour needed to meet war's insistent demands had to be developed, the patience to meet its inconveniences encouraged.

The schools accepted their task so enthusiastically that the Board had no need to prod them. Like most of their countrymen teachers shared a belief in the justice of their cause which propaganda could feed and sustain but did not have to create. They flocked rapidly to the colours and those left behind contributed willingly to the war effort—lecturing, partaking in the numerous voluntary activities, writing propaganda.[43] Their journals did not, on the whole, descend to the demagogic depths which some others plumbed —the *Journal of Education* in particular, maintained an unswerving attachment to the national cause with a dignified refusal to hate all things German. But neither did they allow a moment's doubt to disturb their pages: they were confident that 'No one in England, except a few cranks or professional jesters, like G.B.S., now needs convincing that our cause is just.' And sometimes, especially as the war dragged on and the early enthusiasm and expectation of swift victory disappeared, they expressed more bitter thoughts: 'We must treat Germany and all Germans as we would mad dogs and should incarcerate every German or Austrian, man or woman, and make them earn their living.' They compared 'the howling of the German wounded under treatment of a dressing station' with 'the quiet stoicism of the British soldier'. They described the German susceptibility to propaganda: 'The German has an unbounded faith in newspapers, and his Government is unusually clever in its conduct of press propaganda.' They argued about teaching the German language; 'we know at last, what we did not know before the war, that we have nothing to learn from it [German philosophy]. We know what it is by practical experience, and there is no reason why our children should have to study it at second-hand in books.'[44] In comparison with the hysteria of the fervid patriots or the demagoguery of Horatio Bottomley these are mild comments. Yet there was no doubt that educationists generally and teachers in particular were, from the government point of view, sound. Not many had prickly consciences. And they carried their soundness into the classroom and displayed it to their pupils.

It was not strange that they did this for, like everyone during World War I, they were exposed to the blasts of the propaganda furnace, which was lit at first by a sort of patriotic spontaneous combustion but by the end of the war required a more systematic fuelling. The fuelling was not as competently organized as it would now be but it kept the furnace going. Assured by their politicians, press, intellectuals and businessmen that they fought for freedom, and by their clergy that they had God on their side, they set themselves to overthrow a power-crazed and brutal enemy (*Once a Hun, always a Hun*, the title of a propaganda film reminded them). Throughout the war, but especially in its early stages, this was the belief of most Englishmen (as its reverse was for most Germans) and the few pacifists who remained to have the white feather thrust upon them were, rightly most people thought, scorned or imprisoned.[45]

Believing this themselves, teachers set about getting children to believe it; because they were sincere (they may even have been right, but that is not the point) they worked with enthusiasm. The war was brought into the classrooms of the land so that the young would know what their fathers were fighting for. They were thoroughly taught. Apart from the activities already discussed which, because they were indirect were probably the most valuable, there were lessons on the causes of the war ('what are we fighting for?') and on patriotism generally; subjects such as history, literature and geography were related to the war; abundant patriotic poems were recited, and tales of brave deeds done for the country narrated; music was asked to play its part (something had to be done, an indignant teacher protested, to remedy 'the paucity of the English soldier's musical repertory'); reading lessons were devoted to issues raised by the war ('Our en-e-mies made War! It was their war, not God's war', declared an infants' reader reducing the message to its essentials); rolls of honour appeared in school after school; letters were written to the trenches and came from them; old boys returned and spoke 'stirring words about their experiences to the assembled classes' who were probably not as bored by their stories as others were to be in the future; Haig wrote thanking children for their good wishes on Empire Day (first celebrated in May 1916) and assured them that they were 'the heirs of everything we are fighting to preserve'.[46]

Yet while every effort was made to encourage beliefs and behaviour favourable to the war there was not a cool and calculating effort to brainwash a potentially rebellious population. Rather there was a channelling and directing of a population which in the beginning was almost hysterically co-operative and which, when it tired, suffered more from war-weariness and disenchantment than from a spirit of opposition. The Board were speaking truthfully, not writing propaganda, when in the course of discussing 'the great stir of national feeling' in the elementary schools they said: 'The manifestations vary greatly in form; they are largely spontaneous in character, springing from the initiative of individual teachers and pupils and schools'.[47] The fires had to be stoked but they did not have to be started. Indeed until 1916 the government was able to leave most of the propaganda effort to volunteers; only in the last years of the war did it have to take the initiative.[48] To some extent the Board even operated as a moderating influence— it rejected the demand for compulsory military drill and for lessons in patriotism based on an official manual, pointing out that what was needed was not 'the spur of patriotism, but the curb of discretion'. Frequently it warned against teaching which encouraged 'national animosities'.[49]

Inevitably activities designed to enlist the support of children encouraged national animosities but the excesses of propaganda outside the classroom were avoided by teachers. Yet it is clear that the Board's stand was directed against the excess of zeal (even that took a courage which should not be underestimated) and not against zeal itself. Unmistakably the Board and the local authorities gave enthusiastic support to the war effort. They were ready to co-operate with other governmental agencies; their encouragement and support gave the teachers' spontaneous concerns the atmosphere in which to develop; and where a lead was needed they gave it. Though it was hardly necessary for them to state their support for the national cause, they did. But more impressive than formal statements and more indicative of their attitude was the tone of their reports: it was one of restrained but profound pride in the contribution of the schools, a consciousness of duty nobly done.

Had the Board and educationists generally shared the doubts of the small band of 'cranks or professional jesters' they would have been less willing to work nobly for the cause and quicker to realize the radical educational change they had brought about. The national educational system was being deliberately used to mould children's beliefs and to guide their activities along lines which assisted government policy. And not only children were involved: 'through the children, their parents', the phrase recurs whether the context is war savings, the economizing of food, public health, military secrets or patriotism generally.[50] The public education system was to promote allegiance to a government policy. Probably it was not since the Tudors that government and schools had been so closely linked.

Of course, there had always been some link. From the time

that the state began to finance church schools, and especially when it established its own, the government was forced to concern itself with what went on in the classroom. It had at least to ascertain that public money was properly spent (and particularly that not too much money was spent, whether properly or not) and therefore had to assess the value of school activities. The Revised Code of 1862 made such a judgment, and there is no doubt that this Code, which lasted some forty years, provided a convenient method for distributing the government grant and influenced the curriculum offered to children. By accepting the Code the government approved a system of public education which aimed at producing a decent, law-abiding population, literate enough to appreciate the value of the social order but not uppity enough to want to alter it. The schools were used for political, social and, some would argue, class purposes.

A commitment of this general kind is inevitable because governments are forced to ascertain whether money is being properly spent and, to do that, must make some judgments about the work of the schools. But, for most of the nineteenth century though governments were not neutral, they were passive. They kept the wheels of the educational machine oiled so that it went in the direction that society wished, but they did not actively seek to determine that direction.

However, by the end of the nineteenth century, governments began to use the public schools not just for general social ends but for specific purposes which were not envisaged by those who set them up. Thus the elementary schools were asked to assist the nation in the struggle for industrial and commercial superiority, and subjects such as manual training were introduced for this purpose.[51] More conspicuously, perhaps, was the use made of schools to improve public health. Robert Morant saw the medical inspection of school children as a 'means of extending public action generally in regard to the medical and sanitary conditions of the families whose children attend the elementary schools' and he emphasized that the 'condition' he wanted improved included the home as well as the school.[52]

The war accelerated this trend. In a time of crisis government used the public education system to rally general support for the war effort, to contribute in specific ways to resolving particular problems and, above all, to propagate the opinions it wished its citizens to hold. In the past governments had, as it were, waited upon public opinion: the nineteenth-century elementary school embodied and helped to spread certain values but they were values governments accepted from society at large or from dominant groups in society. During the war the government took the initiative and used the school to propagate its own opinions. No longer was it content to keep the system running; the school was seen as a weapon which could be used to achieve definite political and social objectives.

'The value of a national system of schools and of authorities for education,' wrote Herbert Ward reflecting in later years on the war, 'was well demonstrated by the ease with which government decisions and appeals were circulated. The schools were used in various ways for purposes of propaganda—economy in food and rationing, war savings, schemes for national service.'[53] The Board made a similar point during the war—sometimes vaguely when discussing 'the advantages which can be derived from enlisting the co-operation of the educational institutions of the country in the promotion of various national movements' and sometimes explicitly:[54]

> The War Savings Work has indeed shown what an immense reserve of power the State possesses in a national system like that of education which permeates the remotest parts of the country, reaches every home and yet is directed from a centre.

The importance of this change in attitude is not diminished by arguing that the government had overwhelming popular support for its action. Undoubtedly it had; but it remains true that the schools were used as weapons in a government policy, the efficient waging of a war, to an extent they had never been before. Nor does the legality of the war itself have any bearing on the matter: whether the war was, as most Englishmen believed, a just war in defence of freedom, or just a trade war, the schools were used to enable it to be won.

When peace came many of the schools' war-time activities were stopped but the realization that the education system was a powerful tool for the accomplishment of non-educational ends was not forgotten. Indeed some of the most important reforms of the 1918 Education Act were due, in part, to the desire to make the contributions of the education system more effective by making the system more efficient. Even before the war, for example, the importance of giving the talented few an adequate secondary education was urged as a national necessity. The war further emphasized the importance of the trained man, especially in the scientific, technical or administrative fields. Thus there grew more loud that lament over the 'appalling waste of good human material' by which 'thousands of those whom nature intended to be captains of industry are relegated, in consequence of undeveloped or imperfectly trained capacity, to the ranks, or become hewers of wood and drawers of water.'[55] It was necessary, said H. A. L. Fisher, to 'create an aristocracy of ability'. And *The Times* said:[56]

> The war made it clear, in its demand for efficient man-power and woman-power, that the children of a nation are its real reserve capital, and that physical neglect and imperfect education were waste of capital on a prodigious scale.

The extension of secondary education was the most obvious need if human material was not to be squandered. But it was seen as only one, though the most important, step in a programme aimed to create a comprehensive system of state education. The creaking structure in existence had served the nation during the war but its limitations were clear—and even the success it had achieved made more obvious the potential of a properly integrated system. Time and time again, especially as the end of the war came nearer, the demand for a proper system (which involved, of course, a great extension of secondary education) was voiced. It was met, at least partially, by the Fisher Act of 1918, for as Lewis Amherst Selby-Bigge, Permanent Secretary to the Board of Education from 1911 to 1925, clearly stated,[57]

> the leading note of the Act of 1918 was undoubtedly that of 'systematisation'—the *'adequate'* contribution in every area by every Local Education Authority to a *national system* of education accessible on a basis of equal opportunity to every person capable of profiting by it.

Whatever the limitations of this Act, it made a serious attempt to develop a full system of state schools. Grants were re-organized so that progressive authorities could push ahead with improvements; all authorities were required to submit schemes to show how they were providing for the 'progressive development and comprehensive organisation of education' in their area; the leaving age was fixed at fourteen and the half-time system abolished; medical inspection was extended to secondary schools; and local authorities were empowered to open nursery schools. The most important of all was the provision made for continuation schools: these were designed to take children until they were sixteen (eventually until they were eighteen) for 320 hours in the year and were to be day schools, so that though those attending them were at work they were not to be studying at night. Attendance was to be compulsory.[58] 'Jordan is passed,' cried *The Times Educational Supplement*, 'and men are preparing to lead the seven million children of England into the promised land.'[59]

Even if the Act had been fully implemented the promised land would have been far enough away, but in the early twenties the 'Geddes Axe' fell and the seven million children remained still longer in the wilderness. The caution of some of the Act's proposals (continuation schools, after all, were substitutes for a thorough-going secondary school system) and the failure to implement the Act fully have contributed to an underestimation of its principles. It asserted the state's intention to broaden its educational warrant, downwards into the nursery school and upwards into secondary and continuation schools, until all children between the ages of three and eighteen were, for part of the time at least, under its control. Certainly the machinery it proposed was inadequate but its claim was brave, very radical in 1918, and still radical today, for, even now, eighteen-year-olds have no compulsory link with the educational system.

Thus the war brought home to governments the possibility not only for organizing the social change that lay in the public education system but also, for this reason (but not for this reason only), the importance of having a 'system', a coherent and organized set of schools which would 'trap' the able and give the nation the chance of profiting from their skills. Throughout the twenties and the thirties this realization was acted upon and by 1939 the changes in post-primary education had ensured that the English had a public educational system, by no means perfect but better developed and integrated than it had been in 1914.

The demand for a system of schools was to have important effects on the primary school, but so was another desire which the war fostered in the hearts of Englishmen. 'They expected from an Education Bill,' Fisher wrote of his 1918 Act, 'what no bill on education or on anything else can give, a new Heaven and a new Earth.'[60] What must next be studied is their efforts to make that expectation a reality.

2

The founding of a faith, 1914-1925

In 1911 Edmond Holmes published *What Is and What Might Be*. The first part of the book attacked the elementary schools for which, earlier that year, as the Board's Chief Inspector, he had been responsible. 'Blind, passive, literal, unintelligent obedience is the basis on which the whole system of Western education has been reared', he declared.[1] The second part, 'What Might Be', described a school run by Miss Harriet Finlay-Johnson at Sompting in Sussex—though Holmes called the school 'Utopia' and its teacher 'Egeria'. He had discovered this school while an inspector, and drew hope from it: there children, whose spontaneity and initiative were crushed by the traditional education, were offered that free and joyful schooling which he believed was their due.

At the time Holmes's book appeared the elementary school was in a state of tension. Its methods and curriculum, which had been stable (perhaps ossified) after 'payment by results' was introduced in 1862, were strongly challenged after 1890. The reformers, advocates of the 'New Education', were united more by their opposition to the old ways than by any common creed of their own; indeed they were often as eager to criticize each other as to condemn the traditional educationists. The followers of Herbart and Froebel, for example, disapproved of much of what happened in the elementary schools but differed vehemently about the methods of improving them. And both groups differed with another set of reformers, the practical educationists, who advocated the teaching of manual training, nature study and science. They in their turn looked suspiciously at the Herbartians, regarding them as defenders of the literary education which they wished to reform. Another group, the social reformers, worked for ends similar to those of the practical educationists (for improved physical education, for example), hoping to produce through education a new and better society—whereas the practical educationists wanted to do nothing more than set the old society back on its feet.

These many other differences between the reformers did not prevent important changes and it was clear in 1914 that the task of destruction was substantially completed: the narrow curriculum and rigid methodology of the early payment by results period was widely discredited. Schooling had come to mean more than the three Rs, rote learning was not enough. But, many educationists asked, how much more than the three Rs should be taught? What emphasis should be placed on 'play' or 'interest' or 'correlation' (favourite concepts of the New Education)? How much reliance could be put on the five (or four?) Herbartian steps? The old education had been undermined but it had no clear successor.

Those who expected education to bring a better world closer could not agree on what that world should be like. Some who were convinced of the importance of moral education, for example, wanted the old virtues and beliefs to be restored, all the brighter for their temporary oblivion; others expected to clear away the superstitions that had blinded man to the light of reason. But whatever their differences, pre-World War I educationists were optimistic: the old had been discredited and something good, even if it were not possible to say what, would replace it. They were exciting, fruitful, anxious times.[2]

And they were times which assured for *What Is and What Might Be* an astonishing impact. Of course, his job as Chief Inspector had made Holmes well known and the book had the interest of a Pauline conversion. 'During the first eighteen or twenty years [of his life as an inspector],' Holmes said, 'I did as much mischief in the field of education as I possibly could.'[3] Moreover it presented the spectacle of a man severely criticizing a system of schools which he had recently controlled. As one of Holmes's critics remarked, 'The book will testify to the fact that the authority responsible for the condition of our elementary schools over a period of years was (1) fully conscious that they were gravely defective; (2) unable to discover the true cause of their defectiveness; or (3) to remedy it.'[4] The book certainly caught on. It was published in May 1911 and by November had gone through four impressions; by September 1917 it had gone through eight. It was widely reviewed and immediately involved Holmes in controversy; successful attempts were made to discover who Egeria was and where her school was situated; whispers went around that it was not the utopia Holmes had claimed and Holmes indignantly answered them.[5]

Those who knew Holmes thought him as much a poet as an inspector and probably he was as much philosopher as poet. From the time he left Oxford in 1874 he set about building a better cradle for his beliefs than he had brought to Oxford from his comfortable Irish home and English public school. The rest of his life was devoted to 'thinking out and, if possible ... solving, the supreme problem of existence'. He moved steadily towards an acceptance of 'the Oriental wisdom' and in 1908, while still chief inspector, he published anonymously *The Creed of Buddha*. Poet, philosopher, mystic and school inspector came together in *What Is and Might Be* and, though the synthesis might not have been intellectually satisfying, it was exciting. The importance of freedom was announced, and the child was said to be 'by nature a "child of God" rather than a "child of wrath"', who should be put on 'the path of self-realisation' which in its higher stages is the 'life of love'.[6]

Holmes was to become an important reformer in his own right, but had he done no more than describe Harriet Finlay-Johnson's school he would have left his mark. He was, as Michael Sadler saw as early as 1916, 'the Rousseau before the Revolution'.[7] A great many of the reformers whose names will become more familiar as this book proceeds were first inspired by Holmes. 'Like many other teachers,' said J. H. Simpson, 'I looked back to the appearance of Edmond Holmes' *What Is and What Might Be* in 1911 as to a turning point in my own education.'[8] 'I know that, when I read it in 1913,' E. Sharwood Smith wrote, 'it was like the discovery of a new world.'[9] To young Edward O'Neill, then at Crewe Training College but already wondering about the traditional school routine, it came as a shock and an inspiration.[10] It also seems to have inspired Beatrice Ensor (then De Normann) who, after reading it and something of Homer Lane's, started the Theosophical Fraternity which eventually contributed to the formation of the New Education Fellowship.[11] Others such as A. S. Neill, Caldwell Cook, Norman MacMunn, A. J. Lynch or Belle Rennie paid tribute to the book and supported its criticisms of the elementary school.[12]

More important events were to follow the publication of *What Is and What Might Be* and, out of the confusing mixture of theories and beliefs and practices which was the 'New Education', there evolved a view of education which can be labelled 'progressive'. But, as will later be clear, if a time has to be set for the beginning of progressivism in England, May 1911 when the ex-chief inspector published his attack on the conventional school is probably the best date. Reformers who had been on the defensive gained un-expected support and defenders of the *status quo* were shaken when so eminent an educationist joined the ranks of their attackers.

The next step came two years later, in the autumn of 1913, when Homer Lane began work at the Little Commonwealth. Born in Hudson (New Hampshire) in 1875, Lane was the ebullient though unlikely offspring of seven generations of New England Puritan stock. Determined to excel (he believed, his biographer tells us, that he was 'the only man who really understood the message of Jesus Christ'), unpredictable and restless, he went through a variety of occupations, including those of railroad worker, delivery man, 'sodajerk', upholsterer, sloyd teacher (the form of manual training based on the work of Swedish educationists) and director of the Ford Republic, an institution catering for wayward boys which Lane ran with unorthodox methods and considerable flair. His work came to the notice of George Montagu, later the Earl of Sandwich, who had visited similar 'republics', run by W. R. George, in 1912. The following year Lane was invited to England and became director of the Little Commonwealth, a co-educational community started in Dorset on land offered by Montagu's uncle. Lane believed that the difficult, often delinquent, children of the Common-wealth would reform themselves and, after a period of confusion and chaos, come to realize the value of order and authority—provided they were granted freedom and properly trusted. The thoroughness with which he put this belief into practice, and the degree of self-government attained by the children of the Little Commonwealth astonished and shocked many of his con-temporaries. And not even the tragic and sudden closure of the Commonwealth, or the rumours which followed, could diminish the impact or importance of Homer Lane.[13]

However extreme his views and however vehemently the Little Commonwealth was attacked, Lane fascinated almost all who came to know him. E. T. Bazeley, who worked with him for two years, remarked:[14]

There must be very few of Homer Lane's students who ever

felt for long that they wholly understood him; there must be still fewer who did not feel from the first that he was wholly and completely to be trusted.

And J. H. Simpson, sympathetic but not uncritical, said:[15]

> When I have put together all that I can find to say against Lane ... [he puts together some six lines of criticism] it remains still true that I think of Lane as the man who, more than anyone else whom I have known among educators, loved those among whom he worked with absolute unselfishness, without favour or sentimentality, and made them feel that, whatever they might do, he would still understand their actions and motives, and continue to love them nevertheless.

Scoffers often stayed to pray and sometimes went away to imitate; though, even among the convinced, there were those who insisted that his methods could be used by Lane only, and were therefore no guide to other teachers.[16] On the whole, however, Lane stimulated. The Little Commonwealth was so extreme, the freedom it allowed was so much more than the others had permitted, Lane's trust so complete and the logic with which he followed his beliefs unrelenting and confident—and despite the unconventional behaviour, despite the unpromising material with which Lane had to deal, he seemed, for a time at least, to have made things work. Holmes's Egeria might be ignored (after all, she had married and left the school and the new head was reported to be unimpressed) but the Little Commonwealth could be visited. Lane never watered down his beliefs or diminished his claims and few who visited him denied that he was impressive, and some went off to do likewise—though usually more timorously.[17]

First, there was Holmes to rock the boat, to condemn the public elementary school and to suggest that there might be something in this talk of 'freedom', 'interest', 'play' and 'growth' that kindergarteners had been indulging in for years. Then Lane, to carry everything to an extreme, to invoke the support of the dangerous Freud, and, above all, to carry it off—or at least to have sufficient success to make easy dismissal impossible. 'It [the Little Commonwealth] not only gave us hope,' said Elsie Bazeley, 'it gave us courage, the courage that comes from seeing our convictions realized.'[18] 'There is, perhaps, no experience in life more stirring', wrote the Earl of Lytton,[19] than the discovery for the first time that something hitherto believed to be an unattainable ideal has proved to be a practical reality. This was the experience of those who visited the little colony which lived so short a life, yet revealed so great a truth, among the hills of Dorsetshire.

After Holmes and Lane there was Maria Montessori, intelligent, respectable, religious (though somewhat unfortunate in her choice of sect), a mother and a doctor: a formidable set of qualifications for any educational reformer. Lane had taken the case to extremes, turned the school on its head and left everyone to gape at the spectacle. But he was too extravagant a person and his approach too extreme to act as a model—except for the more radical such as A. S. Neill who, partly because of what he shares with Lane, remains a fascinating and courageous maverick. (Summerhill is a more interesting school than most, and possibly much better; but it has few successors and, when Neill dies, perhaps no future.) The future, even in the years of World War I, lay with Montessori.

Her interest in education began in Rome when she was asked to assist children who lived in a tenement area which was being reclaimed. Her ideas and the apparatus she developed to put her ideas into practice rapidly became known. By 1912 an English translation of her most important book, *The Montessori Method*, was available and so was an enthusiastic account of her work, written by Edmond Holmes who had visited her the previous year. Several schools using the Montessori methods were started; during the war years interest steadily increased and when in 1919 she visited England for the first time, she received an astonishing welcome— H. A. L. Fisher, then President of the Board, took the chair at a banquet held in her honour at the Savoy Hotel. There were a thousand enquiries for the training course she ran that year, more than three times the number she could accommodate, and though as time progressed it became easier to get into her classes, she returned to England every alternate year until the outbreak of World War II to induct neophytes into the mysteries of her method.[20]

To the ground prepared by Holmes and Lane she brought a carefully constructed system based on experiment (or if that is too pretentious a claim, on trial and error), equipment which she said embodied her principles, and a powerful personality. Where Lane was unconventional and shocked, perhaps even enjoyed shocking, Montessori had the respectability of the scientist and doctor. One of her disciples remarked that 'people are apt to forget that she is a doctor, one of that hierarchy to whom we take our children in the last resort, trusting blindly that somehow they will put things right'.[21] Less contented educationists stated, 'Education authorities are willing to listen to a fully qualified medical woman, while they often turn a deaf ear to their own staff, who are only fully qualified *teachers*.'[22]

Thus while her ideas were, by contemporary standards, radical and held with unswerving sincerity, she could take dangerous terms such as 'freedom', 'individuality' and 'independence' and make them acceptable. She was no less committed than Lane or Neill but she was more respectable; she did not dilute her views in order to make them popular; she arrived for herself at a position which was less radical than Lane's or Neill's but pressed it with as much conviction as they pressed theirs. And, perhaps because she had developed her techniques in large classes of poor children, she produced a 'method' and an apparatus which gave a practical expression to her ideas. This is the way C. A. Claremont, one of her English interpreters, describes how Dr Montessori would have 'presented' an object of educational value (in this case a cylinder) to the child:[23]

> in placing these cylinders before the child, the ordinary teacher would probably say: 'Now, Tommy, come and look at this lovely game! You take out all these little men ... etc.' Not so, Dr. Montessori. She places the object before the child without a word; she sits at his side so as not to catch his eye or introduce any element of personal influence; she merely takes out the cylinders, mixes them, and begins to replace them. If the child replies by seizing upon the game and repeating it with avidity, this is a case of pure self-expression; the child has revealed himself as in need of that particular exercise.

A goal of a new kind, self-expression, is put forward but it is not left an abstraction: what it amounts to in the classroom (the child's decision to play the game) is shown and the teacher is given a clear understanding of the part he is to play. The apparatus might eventually be abandoned but had it served no other purpose than that of making clear to teachers what Montessori required of them, it would have justified its existence.

So P. B. Ballard praised Montessori for 'the miracle of making it possible for private study to take place in the infant school' and for devising a means by which little children were able 'to work independently in the same room at the same time'; while Herbert

Ward, though aware that her methods were not adopted in their 'somewhat stereotyped entirety', noted that she 'gave a focus to the prevailing ideas and fortified them by a rationale, easily understood and applied.'[24] She had her critics, of course; some such as Neill within the ranks of the reformers and others less clearly aligned—the *Journal of Education*, for example, which noted that 'She knows everything about savage religions, Greek art, Italian architecture, modern science, and English kindergartens, but of children she knows little.'[25] She could afford to shrug such criticism off for some of the leading reformers explicitly acknowledged her influence, and teachers less committed to reform saw in her work an attainable goal.[26]

Thus, in the years immediately before World War I, when the challenge of the New Education was undermining the certainties of the older ways, there came, first, Holmes to shock those who were still complacent by damning the schools he had lately administered; then Lane to add Freud and a personal twist, and carry everything to an extreme, successfully; and finally Montessori, to bring things back into the realm of the possible and nearly normal, to show that what wilder spirits had preached could be practised, even in the large classes of the elementary school.

The ideas which Holmes, Lane and Montessori helped to spread found many striking manifestations during the war, and for four or five years after 1918: strange new schools sprang up, old schools broke with convention and adopted new procedures, new methods of teaching or of school organization were bruited abroad, new educational societies were formed. It was a period of intense and feverish activity. 'We are all coming to feel,' Michael Sadler said in 1916, 'that we are at the beginning of a new era. There is a change in many of our fundamental ideas.' He continued:[27]

> Now if we look back on the last few years, we see that a number of things have happened in preparation for this great change—a kind of *praeparatio evangelica*—many signs and experiences, heralding the coming of a new time, and it is as though many great educational forces were now being gathered to a focus, without anybody in particular being responsible for it. We see all sorts of people, hitherto obscure, suddenly emerging in different parts of the country, who have found a bit of the secret, and who, acting together, can give the nation what it needs.

The war not only brought a realization of the power of the public education system and a determination to harness it to the war effort; it also acted as a catalyst and sped up astonishingly the pace of educational change.

The new schools

Who were these hitherto obscure people who suddenly emerged claiming to have part of the secret? The best known, of course, are the 'progressives', the starters of 'pioneer' (or, to use the nastier name) 'crank' or 'freak' schools: for example, Neill at Summerhill, J. H. Simpson at Rendcomb, Norman MacMunn at Tiptree Hall, the Russells at Beacon Hill and, in later times, Curry at Dartington Hall and Coade at Bryanston—advertisers in the New Era who taught the arts and crafts, abhorred corporal punishment, liked Freud and 'freedom' and gathered together in 1965 when someone asked 'who are the progressives now?' to say that they were.[28]

Studies of the progressives have concentrated on these people, viewing them primarily as reformers of English secondary education, and particularly of the Public Schools, in the tradition begun at Abbotsholme by Cecil Reddie in 1889 and at Bedales, opened by J. H. Badley in 1893. Such a view is legitimate, though if maintained too rigorously it leads to a narrow view of the progressive movement. It makes the progressives appear exclusively English—yet J. H. Badley, successful product of Rugby and Cambridge, and deeply influenced by the Public School system, acknowledged his debt to Pestalozzi, Froebel and Montessori.[29] Furthermore, though many of the progressives founded schools which could be considered 'secondary' (even if of a strange kind) others founded institutions which were unique or at least very difficult to classify. The Little Commonwealth was created without reference to Public Schools about which Lane knew little when he arrived in England and probably not much more when he left. Other progressive institutions were a boarding school for working-class children (the Caldecott Community), a community of war orphans (Tiptree Hall), a romantic, nature-centred establishment (the Forest School), a research institute for child studies (the Malting House School) and plain elementary schools such as those conducted by E. F. O'Neill or John Arrowsmith. Then there were educationists such as Edmond Holmes, Caldwell Cook, E. A. Craddock, Helen Parkhurst, Robin Tanner, Marion Richardson and Percy Nunn who made important contributions without starting any sort of school.

To identify 'progressive education' with a series of schools starting with Reddie's and Badley's, progressing through Neill's and Simpson's and finding later illustration in Dartington Hall, Bryanston or Wennington is to narrow its outlook and reduce its importance. However excellent these schools were, they are relatively few and, though they may last, they are clearly not rapidly increasing. Progressive education, if limited to them, would be an interesting but peripheral feature of the English educational scene. In fact it is of central importance—the modern primary school, this book will argue, has been made in the progressive image.

But though it was in the primary school that the progressives most notably triumphed, the pioneer schools were their most obvious manifestation and offer a convenient introduction to their ideas. Some were founded before the outbreak of war, others began in the late twenties and thirties; but it was from 1914 until the mid-twenties that the 'hitherto obscure' most frequently came to light and were most confident in proclaiming that they had discovered the secrets of education and life—and it is upon this period from 1914 to 1926 that this chapter will concentrate. The new schools founded after 1926 were not necessarily of less interest or importance than those which had been founded before, but they were fewer and the atmosphere generally was less hopeful. It would be unwise, however, to exaggerate this change in atmosphere, and certainly unwise to take the date at which this chapter ends, 1926, as marking a definite turning point. It is not haphazardly chosen, for it was the year in which the Hadow Report, *The Education of the Adolescent*, appeared—and that report, it is later argued, made recommendations which limited the progressives' effect on primary schools. But the year is best interpreted as a shorthand way of saying 'mid-twenties' rather than as marking a specific and easily identifiable event. It was in the mid-twenties that the momentum of the progressive advance began to slow and the first enthusiasms and hopes to be darkened. The present concern, however, is with the period of optimism before 1926.

It is worth looking first at some of the new schools founded in this period. For example, in October 1911 two experienced teachers, Miss P. M. Potter and Miss L. M. Rendel, started a nursery school in Cartwright Gardens, near St Pancras Station in London. Before long, and almost without planning, it became something else, a school in which community life was stressed and, at the same time, each child given individual attention. In 1917, after the London County Council had condemned the premises, the school was moved to the

country, to East Sutton near Maidstone in Kent. There the Caldecott Community, as it was now called, became a new phenomenon,
a boarding school for working-class children. The pupils, at that
time about forty between the ages of three and twelve, were kept
and instructed at a cost of five shillings per week to the parents;
the rest of the expenses were met by donations and subscriptions.
The community life which the title of the school stressed received
more emphasis than was usual; rural occupations were woven into
a curriculum made steadily less formal; discipline, always mild,
became even more relaxed and 'freedom' for the child was made
a mark of the school. So too was 'individual teaching' in that, for
at least seven hours a week, children were instructed alone or with
one or two others and, even in the general lessons, efforts were
made to cater for the child's 'interests'. A modified form of 'self-
government' was permitted and the school was co-educational.
These characteristics were shared by most of the new schools;
and so was another—the Caldecott Community was in perpetual
financial difficulty.[30]

In January 1919 Norman MacMunn started Tiptree Hall, 'a Community of war orphans and others', in the country not far from
Kelvedon in Essex. He had made a minor reputation for himself
by his work at the King Edward VI School, Stratford-upon-Avon,
but Tiptree Hall was a more radical venture. It began with twenty
boys and girls but by the end of the first year the girls had gone
and MacMunn was left with 'seven small boys of the poorest class,
and of an average age of ten years and one month'. These, and the
very few who joined them in the school's short life, MacMunn
hoped to put on 'the path to freedom'. He called himself the children's 'chief adviser' and insisted that they had 'no masters and
mistresses, no adult imposed laws, no rigid professions or prescrip-
tions'. Only the first occupation of the morning, number, was fixed
—and then by the agreement of the pupils; for the rest of the day
the children constructed their own timetables and the traditional
curriculum was dissolved into less formal activities. A system of
self-government which, like much in the school, owed something
to Homer Lane, was evolved. MacMunn and his wife, who helped
him with the school, were disappointed in their hope that the
country would support a venture which wanted to help the children of 'the fallen' it had promised not to forget. Very soon after
it opened fee-paying pupils had to be taken and trouble arose over
the methods of the school. In January 1924 MacMunn moved with

a few pupils to Italy. He died there suddenly in 1925 but not before some children had been given the benefit of his remarkable personality and some teachers had been spurred to emulate him.[31]

One such was J. H. Simpson who, like MacMunn, drew inspiration from Homer Lane. After teaching in several schools including Rugby, where he tried a cautious experiment in self-government, and serving for two years as a junior inspector of the Board he enlisted in 1917. In 1919, shortly after his demobilization, he was appointed headmaster of Rendcomb, near Cirencester in Gloucestershire, a school which, at the time, existed only in the mind of F. Noel Hamilton Wills (of the tobacco family). Wills, who desired to contribute to post-war reconstruction, planned to choose fifty boys, by examination, from the county's public elementary schools and educate them so that they might win scholarships to Public Schools. Thus a boarding-school education would be made possible for children who might not otherwise have had the opportunity. The school was opened in June 1920 and Simpson soon persuaded Wills and the governing body to drop the principle of sending the pupils to Public Schools (which would have made Rendcomb a preparatory school) and to admit fee-paying students. He instituted a form of self-government which gave the pupils real power—less than Homer Lane gave at the Little Commonwealth but enough to make Rendcomb an object of suspicion. Simpson described himself as being 'like a good many other schoolmasters in the years following the first world war who were temporarily obsessed by the "New Psychology", and groping their way towards a satisfying conception of Freedom in education'. Though less radical than Lane or MacMunn, Simpson's willingness to experiment and his commitment to self-government made Rendcomb a distinctive school.[32]

In 1915 theosophists, who had been active in England for some time, particularly within the Fellowship of the New Life and the Garden City movement, started at Letchworth the Garden City Theosophical School. The following year a Theosophical Educational Trust, directed by Beatrice de Normann (after her marriage, Beatrice Ensor), was established and quickly took control of the new school which was named Arundale after one of the most prominent English theosophists. In 1918 the Trust took over the only other secondary school in Letchworth, a small establishment for girls called the Modern School. They extended it until it accommodated one hundred boys and girls, converted Arundale into a boarding house to serve it and changed its name to St Christopher. The first headmaster, Dr Armstrong Smith, who resigned while it was still Arundale School, stated that he aimed, first, 'to study the children individually in order to allow them to develop along their own particular lines'; second, to provide a spiritual background to education which was, of course, coloured by theosophical beliefs; and third, to introduce co-education. Despite troubles which seem to have reflected problems both of policy and personality within theosophy as a whole, the school prospered. A large degree of self-government was introduced, art, music and eurhythmics given places of honour in the curriculum, Montessorian methods used in the junior classes, social service stressed and corporal punishment abolished. Pupils were attracted from a number of countries but while proud of its 'internationalism' the school denied being cosmopolitan and considered itself a thoroughly English institution.[33]

From the order and quiet prosperity of a Garden City we move to Lancashire and an elementary school in a mill town, 'a good school building placed in a dreary village beside a hideous and gigantic mill'. To this school in 1918 came Edward O'Neill, a young teacher who had served a stern apprenticeship in schools of the more rigorous and traditional kind where he had learned to be proficient and to doubt the value of what he was skilled at doing. He created a school organized on 'a broad and liberal basis of self-activity, self-government, and co-operation'; the traditional curriculum was abandoned in favour of less formal activities (handwork of ingenious devising, music and dancing were prominent); the discipline was made freer and the dismal surroundings improved—even if it meant pulling up asphalt to plant gardens or, when this proved too slow, piling dirt on the asphalt to get a swifter result. 'It little profits that you have taught a child to write,' O'Neill warned, 'if he uses his power to scribble filth on walls'. Others, unimpressed with the furniture the children had built or the books they had written for themselves, worried because O'Neill permitted too much freedom. The mill-owners resented his efforts to have the part-time system abolished and the local education authorities found so dedicated and impatient a man difficult to handle. But gradually he won them over and Prestolee became that rare phenomenon, a public elementary school which was unmistakably progressive.[34]

What Edward O'Neill did in Lancashire John Arrowsmith did in

Yorkshire, and he began much earlier. In 1916, when he discussed his ideas at the Conference on New Ideals in Education, he had already been six years at work in Mixenden (near Halifax), another locality centred on a woollen mill which claimed most children at thirteen and many at twelve—on the half-time system then permitted. Arrowsmith's first act was to cut the cumbersome, old-fashioned desks down to sizes which suited the children thus giving them a physical freedom which, in his view, contributed to mental and emotional freedom. He also dissolved the traditional curriculum and emphasized gardening, art, drama and handwork with blocks or raffia. He stressed the training of the senses, in his own words, 'physiological education'. Books were thought 'a source of second-hand knowledge', competition was abolished—there were 'no honour boards, mark lists, or class places or prizes'. The scholarship and examination systems were considered 'a species of trade rivalry brought into the school from the commercial world'. Stories, dancing, the making of useful objects, acting, play—these were the jobs of the school and they were to be done in small groups; large classes, 'mob classes' were 'an abomination' and could not be defended. Despite opposition, some on the official level, Arrowsmith carried out his ideas and when in 1922 he moved into Cambridgeshire, A. W. M. Bryant had this to say of his work:[35]

> In one village in Cambridgeshire, there is a man who to my mind is a great village teacher, by far and away the greatest village teacher I have met ... John Arrowsmith. He has only been six months in a great straggling Fen village in an isolated province of the county. When he arrived, there were three schools filled with heavy-footed, discontented and bored children. Filled with enthusiasm, he organised evening clubs, instituted games, folk-dancing, music and drama and soon had the village by the heels, all agog with interest in what he was doing. Every child in the village returns of his own free will, one evening each week, to take part in the clubs which John Arrowsmith has founded, and perhaps it will surprise you to hear that every teacher does the same.

Probably the most famous of all schools founded at this time was A. S. Neill's Summerhill. A poor student as a child and an indifferent one as an adolescent (he did not win entry to a training college) Neill developed an interest in intellectual matters later in life and graduated from Edinburgh with a second-class degree at the age of twenty-nine. After a stint as a journalist he returned to teaching as headmaster of Gretna Green village school in 1914. His first attempt to enlist failed but Neill was later called up and served as an artillery instructor at Trowbridge. While there he discovered Homer Lane and through Lane, Freud. After the war he went back to teaching but found even the relatively progressive school at which he worked too stifling and once more fell back on journalism, this time as co-editor of the *New Era* with Beatrice Ensor. He was soon back teaching at an international school under the aegis of the New Education Fellowship at Hellerau in Austria. Political and other troubles brought him back to England and Lyme Regis with five Austrian pupils. In 1927, three years after his return, Neill and his wife moved their school (which had been named Summerhill after his wife's family house in Australia) to Leiston in Suffolk. This school made Neill widely known but his writings, his friendship with Homer Lane and his work for the New Education Fellowship had already made him a leader in 'progressive' educational circles. Dogmatic defender of freedom, provocative and sentimental, a prolific writer of books condemning excessive reliance on book learning, gentle anarchist and brilliant publicist, he has become a symbol of English progressivism and Summerhill, once an experimental school, has become (as he has himself observed) a demonstration school. 'I am convinced,' he has written, 'that if a new generation of parents and teachers will give children freedom from outside fears, hate will gradually disappear from the world.'[36]

On 1 March 1924 Geoffrey Nathaniel Pyke, highly intelligent eccentric, journalist, prisoner of war who made a spectacular escape and, for a time, extraordinarily successful speculator, placed in the *New Statesman* an advertisement which began: 'Wanted. An Educated Young Woman, 18-27, to conduct the education of a small group of children, aged 2½-7, as a piece of scientific work and research.' Susan Isaacs was then thirty-eight, considerably older than the woman Pyke required, but in most other ways was ideally suited. She had brilliant courses at Manchester and Cambridge, been a practising analyst, taught and even been trained to teach; and to everything she brought an enthusiasm and flair which made her strikingly successful. She accepted the job after extracting a promise, which Pyke later broke, that she was to be in complete control and on 7 October the Malting House Garden School in Cambridge was opened with Pyke financing the venture from the proceeds of his speculations in tin and copper. Susan Isaacs remained at the school for four years then, after a series of disagreements with Pyke and financial difficulties (it is not clear which were the more important), she left. But Pyke had a return on his money—the 'piece of scientific work and research' done at the Malting House School provided material for two books, *Intellectual Growth in Young Children* (1930) and *Social Development of Young Children* (1933) and the school itself became well known, in some quarters notorious, during its short life.

The practices and principles which the pioneer schools favoured were given another trial by Susan Isaacs. 'Self-expression', art, handicraft and music; 'the great importance of the creative imagination', the need for 'finding out' rather than being 'taught', catering for the 'needs' and 'interests' of children, a 'freedom' many thought excessive—the Malting House School stood for these things and more. Its work has been well described and will not be further discussed; for many people it was the epitome of the progressive school. When, in 1933, Susan Isaacs was made head of the newly formed Department of Child Development at the University of London Institute of Education, she was placed in a position in which the ideas developed at the Malting House School could be widely disseminated.[37]

Where the Malting House School issued, in part, from the desire for the scientific study of children, Beacon Hill grew out of a very personal motive, parental discontent with the educational system. Bertrand Russell wrote that 'Dora [his wife] and I came to a decision, for which we were equally responsible, to found a school of our own in order that our children might be educated as we thought best.' They rented Russell's brother's old home, Telegraph House, near Petersfield on the South Downs and opened the school on 21 September 1927. It lasted until 1943 though after their separation Dora ran it by herself and from 1934 it was not situated at Telegraph House. Like many new schools Beacon Hill provided for self-government and made considerable use of experimental methods. The freedom it was said to permit (some thought this amounted to licence if not anarchy), was exaggerated; and the Russells, though always ready to experiment, retained a firm belief in traditional intellectual concerns. Yet Beacon Hill was undeniably progressive. Later in life Russell seemed to think it a failure but this feeling might have been coloured by the failure of his marriage to Dora; others criticized Beacon Hill while it was in its prime, but though it could be criticized and condemned it was hard to ignore.[38]

His studies and the horrors of the war led Ernest Westlake, self-taught palaeontologist, to the conclusion that man had moved too far from his primitive state: modern man, if he were not to be corrupted by the deceits of civilization and technology, should return to the simple life. Impressed by the race recapitulation theory which Granville Stanley Hall had popularized and by Patrick Geddes's warning that the old trades and crafts were being abandoned in favour of a narrow literary education, he started in 1916 the Order of Woodcraft Chivalry. The Order, one of several variants of the scouting movement which developed about this time, divided its members into troops of elves (children from four to eight), packs of woodlings (eight to twelve), tribes of trackers (twelve to fifteen), companies of pathfinders (fifteen to eighteen) and fellowships of wayfarers (adults). Each group had its own uniform, badges, rituals and laws in rich, almost obsessional, profusion. For Westlake the Order was an 'amalgam of religion, ritual, tradition, discipline and mystical expression, all coming together in a radical movement opposed to the given social structure.'

The Order, itself an interesting educational experiment, inspired some teachers to apply its principles to schooling. One such was T. J. Faithfull at Priory Gate School in Norfolk but, more immediately important was Westlake's own effort to start a school which would spread his ideas and ensure that they were properly understood. He acquired land in the Hampshire New Forest, but before he could launch his school he was killed in a car accident. It was not until 1928, six years after his death, that his son and three friends floated a company which was to control the new school. The Forest School had many of the progressive school's features—it was co-educational, without formal classes, governed by a council of children; there were no prizes or academic competition, the curriculum was less formal, arts and crafts were emphasized, discipline was gentle. It had, of course, its Order of Woodcraft features: it began in an army hut and remained somewhat spartan, the children were divided into groups of elves, woodlings and such, and the teachers, overly conscious of the Red Indian influence on their movement, gave themselves names such as Great Bear, Rising Sun and Laughing Water. The school survived such enthusiasm but could not survive the war; it was closed in 1940.[39]

More schools were started in this period, for example, J. H. Whitehouse's Bembridge in 1919; one of the most important and successful, Dartington Hall, in 1926; the first of the Steiner schools, at Streatham in London, in 1925. Other well-established and cautious schools took a sudden turn towards radicalism—as Dauntsey's School did when G. W. Olive became headmaster in 1919. If they, and the many like them, are not discussed in detail, it is because sufficient has already been said to indicate the diverse background from which the new schools sprang and the type of work they were attempting.[40]

New methods

The starting of new or the rejuvenation of old schools was not the only manifestation of the desire for reform. Less sweeping experiments, a few destined to be of greater importance than some of the new schools, were started. In 1918, for example, E. A. Craddock, senior French master at the Northern Polytechnic Day Secondary School at Holloway in North London, tentatively began to experiment with a limited form of self-government. He gained confidence swiftly and soon was proclaiming the virtues of the 'class-room republic' and the work of Simpson and MacMunn whose inspiration he acknowledged with gratitude. He was less radical than he thought himself to be—often he seems surprised to find himself taking a position he considered extreme and he was studiously careful to stress the risks he ran. Not for him the confidence of Homer Lane or the aggression of Neill. He did not interfere with the curriculum but gave disciplinary powers to the class which, through an elected committee, organized and supervised punishments, attended to homework and helped in other minor ways. This, Craddock argued, freed the teacher from some of his less pleasant tasks and enabled him to be (the phrase reveals the gap between him and the more daring spirits) 'a fount of pure knowledge to which every thirsty young soul can apply'. But, within the limits he had set, his republic was genuine—and it worked. Teachers who wanted to try the new methods but were afraid of extremes found his approach attractive.[41]

More radical was Caldwell Cook who while working at the Perse School, Cambridge, developed his unfortunately named 'Play Way method'. Before the war he had thought of writing at length of his ideas and contributed a series of articles to the *New Age* in 1914. The war, in which he served (he wrote in January 1919 that he had just finished three years 'in a somewhat uncongenial employment'), made him hurry his writing—'for fear lest the book should never be written at all'. *The Play Way* was finished in November 1915 but not published until September 1917. It argued that play was 'the natural means of study in youth' and terms other reformers had made familiar were called on parade again : interest, activity, joy, learning—not teaching, self-government. The parade was not an empty ceremonial for Caldwell Cook's conviction was infectious and his work in the classroom had shown (and after the war was to show again) that he could put his ideas into practice. Teachers were tempted to imitate him, and the many suggestions he had made in the course of his writings provided guidance for them. The 'good old grinders', as Sir John Adams called them, lamented this further stroll down 'the primrose path' and the book which its author feared might never be written had an important influence on English education between the wars.[42]

When in 1914 Montessori visited America for the first time she was welcomed enthusiastically. A Montessori Society was set up with Alexander Graham Bell as chairman and Margaret Wilson, the President's daughter, as secretary. She lectured at Carnegie Hall (five thousand tried to gain admittance) and took advantage of the San Francisco World Exhibition to publicize her ideas. Helen Parkhurst, a young teacher who had studied under Montessori in Rome, demonstrated her methods and later looked after her interests in America. She served Montessori faithfully until 1918 when she broke her formal links with the Dottoressa in order to work out her own ideas. By 1920 Helen Parkhurst and a colleague had organized an experiment at Dalton High School in Massachusetts where, not long after she had started, she was visited by Miss Belle Rennie, a prominent figure in English progressive circles. Greatly impressed, Miss Rennie wrote of her experiences for *The Times Educational Supplement*. Within a week she had four hundred enquiries from interested teachers and after Miss Parkhurst visited England in 1921 P. B. Ballard claimed that 'Daltonism in some form or other broke out in school after school'. By 1926 two thousand schools were said to be using the Dalton Plan and, though the enthusiast who produced this figure probably accepted tinkerings with the Plan as evidence of its complete adoption, it was sufficiently prominent for Michael Sadler to call it 'one of the chief threads round which have crystallized the hopes for a new kind of responsible freedom in English Schools and Colleges.'

The basis of the Dalton Plan was the assignment system. Work in the 'major subjects' (mathematics, history, science, English, geography and, where appropriate, languages) was divided into 'contract jobs', that is, subdivisions which a pupil was expected to complete in a month. The contract job was broken down into smaller sections each of which was to be done by the pupil working at his own pace. Thus a class (sometimes arranged according to age, sometimes on ability) could be given a month's work and each child left to complete it in the order, at the speed and in the way he desired. The traditional timetable and school organization were to be abolished; for every major subject there was a separate classroom or 'laboratory' staffed by specialists who helped the pupils through their assignments. Provided the month's work in each subject was completed, the child could organize his work in a way which suited him best. The subjects not classified as 'major' were usually taught in a traditional way. These arrangements were varied. Frequently, for example, the form (and not the school as Helen Parkhurst intended) was made the organizational unit: the pupils were asked to complete assignments in their own way, but no 'laboratories' or specialist teachers were supplied. Those who called themselves Daltonians often varied the basic plan greatly but, whatever their variation, the effect was to call traditional school organization into question.[43]

Other plans similar to Parkhurst's had a vogue at the time. The 'project method', linked with Dewey because its originator, William Heard Kilpatrick, was his chief interpreter, was more radical than the Dalton Plan and less popular in England. But it was prominent in discussions through the twenties and thirties and after it had been introduced in the United States in 1918 Kilpatrick found that he had supplied himself with a life-time job explaining it to the world.[44] An earlier system, sometimes named after Gary, the city in Indiana in which it was developed, and sometimes called the platoon system, had its defenders but never caused in England the controversies it stirred up in its own country.[45] Slightly later than the Dalton Plan came Carleton Washburne's proposals which were put into practice in Winnetka, a suburb of Chicago, where he was a school superintendent. They also found their way across the Atlantic but had to be content with less attention than the Dalton Plan.[46] Less attention still was given to the Decroly Method named after its deviser, Dr Ovide Decroly, and best exemplified at *l'École de l'Ermitage* in Brussels; but earnest seekers after the true methodology had heard of it and it figured from time to time in English discussions. Dr M. O'Brien Harris had more success. She produced the Howard Plan, which had similarities with the Dalton Plan and which professed to be an adaptation of Montessori's principles for secondary schools. She operated it successfully for a number of years at the County Secondary School, Clapton.[47]

Philip Ballard once joined his fellow London inspector C. W. Kimmins to show Maria Montessori round some London schools which had adopted her methods. When he suggested that they visit the Marlborough Infants' School at Chelsea she 'indignantly refused, saying that she would there see her own ideas plagiarized, and her own apparatus wantonly caricatured.' Jessie Mackinder, headmistress of this L.C.C. school, who started developing her own materials in 1919, admitted her debt to Montessori but claimed to have developed a method which was cheaper and more suitable for the large classes of the English schools. It was certainly simple (for example, children learned the sound of letters from pictures illustrating the sounds), it seems to have been more immediately concerned with the three Rs than was Montessori's, it permitted individual work and, for a time, was quite popular. Probably Jessie Mackinder was the most successful of a number of English school mistresses at this time who developed materials to assist 'auto-education' as Dr Jessie White, one who had tried her hand at the game, described it.[48]

'Might I ask a terribly ignorant question,' said an anonymous speaker at the Conference of Educational Associations in 1925, 'What is Eurhythmics?' Mr Percy Ingham gave a cryptic reply: 'Eurhythmics is an individual experience.' However, he assured the questioner that if she were at 23 Store Street, London, at ten o'clock the next morning she would be given this 'individual experience'. If she had attended she would have seen a form of musical callis-thenics or dancing in which great emphasis was placed on rhythmic and graceful movement. Its originator, E. Jacques-Dalcroze, was appointed Professor of Harmony in the Geneva Conservatoire in 1892 and, while seeking to improve music teaching, hit upon a method which he believed attuned the nervous system to every rhythmic impulse. He developed three sets of activities: the exercises or eurhythmics which came to be the best known (though advocates of the method were annoyed to hear their work described as 'dancing' or 'callisthenics'); a system for the training of the ear; and, reserved for the teacher of eurhythmics, improvisations to accompany pupils' free rhythmic expression. His school at Hellerau in Austria (where for a time Neill taught) became the centre of the movement. His name was known in England in 1912 —but not much more was known than his name and the fact that it was connected with something called eurhythmics. Then after Ingham, a public-school master, invited him to visit London, a Dalcroze Society was started and centres established to train teachers. In 1919 a new *Syllabus of Physical Training for Schools* was published and its provisions, especially those for children under seven, showed evidence of the Dalcroze influence. Throughout the inter-war period it continued to arouse interest and its followers explained that it was more than a form of physical education: 'All the life of man needs is rhythm and orderly adaptation. By bringing our whole organism under the educative influence of harmony we become ourselves finished products of harmony.'[49]

Thus the war years and those immediately following not only saw new schools established but also a remarkable flowering of new methods. No doubt the majority of teachers managed well enough with what they knew; indeed the frequent opposition met by the pioneer schools and advocates of the new methods makes this clear. At the same time the signs of experiment and search for new ways were striking. It is not often that an article such as Miss Rennie's elicits four hundred enquiries or that voluntary courses, such as Montessori's, have a thousand applicants for three hundred places. The last few years, said Percy Nunn, writing in 1923, were 'one of the most important germinal periods in the history of education in this country.'[50]

New societies

Indirectly Maria Montessori helped another vital development which began during the war. In 1914 the Montessori Society held a successful conference at East Runton which, the following year, became something more ambitious, the Conference on New Ideals in Education. A gathering of the more radical educationists, the Conference proclaimed 'reverence for the pupil's individuality and a belief that individuality grows best in an atmosphere of freedom.' Its purpose was not to assist any particular group but to provide a meeting place for all who shared this belief, to offer them a platform for the discussion of difficulties and the communication of the results of experience or reflection, to bring isolated experimenters into touch with one another, and to give to pioneering work the encouragement of criticism and recognition.

For the next five years the Conference did this admirably. Under the guidance of Holmes it attracted to its platform Homer Lane, the Earl of Lytton, MacMunn, C. W. Kimmins, Belle Rennie, Edward O'Neill, Beatrice Ensor, Percy Nunn, Michael Sadler, Cyril Burt, Ernest Young, John Arrowsmith, Margaret McMillan—in fact almost all the leaders of the movement for educational reform. There was an enthusiasm and vitality about its meetings, its numbers increased, its reports sold well; it was possible to believe that the conference was keeping the light burning in the home country 'while those who had gone out from amongst us were doing their best to defend it in the trenches'.[51] John Adams regarded the Conference as 'a sort of clearing-house for the exchange of the various new ideas that are being worked out in different parts of the country'; and J. J. Findlay indicated that he had a similar view and commented on the very valuable work the conference had done.[52]

A group who met under the auspices of the Conference were the Theosophical Fraternity in Education whose existence has already been mentioned (p. 34). By 1920 the Fraternity was sufficiently large to hold a separate conference at Letchworth. In January of that year Beatrice Ensor, the theosophists' secretary, started a magazine, *Education for the New Era*, which had as one of its aims the furthering of international co-operation. The magazine became important when the Letchworth meeting of theosophists decided to call a conference of 'New Educationists' to meet in France in the summer of 1921. Believing that invitations issued by the Fraternity might inhibit attendance, they issued them in the name of the magazine, by then called *The New Era in Home and School*, and soon (to convey something of their intentions and yet avoid a link with theosophy) they decided to call the conference the New Education Fellowship. When the 1921 conference accepted without serious modification Beatrice Ensor's plans for an international educational body the name was easily transferred.[53]

After the Fellowship had started the Theosophical Fraternity seems to have withered but the Conference on New Ideals continued to meet annually until the eve of World War II. However leadership passed to the N.E.F. and the *New Era*, now its official English publication, grew in influence. N.E.F. conferences, at Montreux (1923), Heidelberg (1925), Locarno (1927), Elsinore (1929), Nice (1932) and Cheltenham (1936) became important means for the interchange of ideas and gave prestige and solidity to the progressive cause. The vague principles to which those joining the Fellowship gave assent were published in the report of the 1921 conference (*The Creative Self-Expression of the Child*). Because its founders wanted the Fellowship to be an international body no rules were made for members and it was unnecessary to apply for membership—that came automatically by subscribing to the *New Era* in England or to its equivalents in the other countries. The links were loose but they held together throughout the inter-war years and gave educational reformers a forum, a clearing house for new ideas, a permanent symbol and sometimes even money.

The new book

Holmes, Lane and Montessori were the heralds of the new ideas and, together with people such as Neill, MacMunn and Caldwell Cook, led the efforts to put them into practice; but it was Nunn who gave them their definitive and most influential expression. Thomas Percy Nunn was born in Bristol in 1870, took London B.Sc. and B.A. degrees, made a name as a mathematics and physics teacher, then moved to the London Day Training College of which he became vice-principal in 1905 and principal, in succession to Sir John Adams, in 1922. In 1909 the College became a School of the University and from 1913 Nunn held the position of professor of education at London. He was a man of diverse talents who earned the admiration of such different personalities as William McDougall and Bertrand Russell. His philosophical writings were few but, according to J. A. Passmore, his work 'had an influence out of all proportion to its modest dimensions'.[54]

However, his educational writings were plentiful, though none were as important as *Education: Its data and first principles*. The product of an optimistic age, as its title indicates, the book has now dated, but whatever its defects it put many of the educational practices and ideas of the reformers in a theoretical framework— a framework derived, in large part, from biology and psychology.

Caldwell Cook and the Caldecott Community, Homer Lane, Holmes, Simpson, Montessori, MacMunn and their like were discussed in a sane and rational manner and Nunn's learning and wide reading were concentrated on making a moderate and sensible case for the new ideas. He was astonishingly successful. *Education* was published in 1920. Before it was revised and expanded in 1930 it had gone through fourteen reprints. It went through nine more by 1941; a new revision was published in 1945. F. A. Cavenagh, writing in 1936 and surveying English education since 1920, remarked that it was undoubtedly 'the outstanding book of the period'. 'The studies of a generation of teachers in training have been based on it,' he claimed, 'and it has profoundly affected their outlook and their subsequent practice.'[55] Almost all his contemporaries agree with this estimate, even those who do not agree with the arguments advanced in the book. It gave the progressives a textbook.

The new beliefs and practices

What Is and What Might Be had a popular success. It startled, stirred controversy, stung the enemy into action—so successfully that, as we have seen, Holmes was forced to publish *In Defence of What Might Be* in 1914. Nunn did not have to write 'In Defence of *Education: Its data and first principles*'. His book received instant acclaim and, even its few critics were respectful, recognizing that they differed from an authority. Holmes wrote an *exposé*, Nunn wrote a textbook.

The textbook expressed in a systematic way much of what the progressives held in common. Norman MacMunn, when addressing the Montessori Conference at East Runton in 1914 had said that he felt 'something like a shipwrecked mariner who has reached land at last', that instead of troubles previously encountered he now felt sure 'that certain postulates have been already conceded to me.'[56] It was because Nunn expressed these postulates that progressives thought so highly of his book—and of him.

What were these postulates? Certainly the principles embodied in the new schools and the experimental methods cannot easily be reduced to a neat pattern. Indeed the Conference on New Ideals and the New Education Fellowship were careful to avoid any suggestion of dogmatism: the Conference declared that it did not exist 'to voice the opinions of any particular pedagogical school or to give exclusive assistance to any sectional propaganda' and

47

the Fellowship that it wanted to 'establish a very elastic association, which can be adapted to the idiosyncrasies and methods of
each individual country' and, as we have seen, it proposed no rules
for membership.[57]

This flexibility and ambiguity were characteristic of the views
of the reformers yet, provided reasonably relaxed criteria are
applied, certain similarities (especially in what they wanted done
in the classroom) emerge. There are similarities, for example, in
their vision of the way a teacher should act. Homer Lane joined
in the activities of the Little Commonwealth's unruly inhabitants,[58]

> became one of the gang, and by so doing speedily spoiled the
> fun. As the recognized authority in the community, my sanction
> and encouragement of midnight pillow-fights, larder raids and
> hooliganism did away with the element of danger involved, and
> it ceased to be fun.

MacMunn labelled himself 'chief adviser' to the Tiptree Community
and hoped that teachers and children could simply interact 'as
natural human units, who had to live together as peaceably and
comfortably as they could.'[59] And Neill's doubtful dominie (who
was never too doubtful about advising adults) urged a reluctant
teacher struggling to introduce self-government to get off his pedes-
tal and 'become one of the gang'. 'Smash a window,' he suggested,
'chuck books about the room ... anything to break this idea that
you are an exalted being whose eye is like God's always ready
to see evil.'[60] And, of course, these men practised what they
preached, thus giving expression to a conception of the teacher's
role which was startlingly different from that which most of their
contemporaries accepted. It was also more extreme than that accepted by most of the other reformers, though they at least were prepared to travel some way along the track blazed by these intrepid
spirits. O'Neill informed teachers that they were not parrots, so—
'let them come off their perches. They should adventure with the
children making things, thinking things out, doing things all round
the school.'[61] Caldwell Cook considered himself a 'playmaster'; the
Montessorian teacher remained present (too conspicuously in Neill's
view) but not as the dominating presence her predecessors had
been; instead she was 'the sensitive observer who follows and
assists the children in their development.'[62] Craddock announced[63]
to the citizens of his republic that

I shall neither punish nor reward. I shall give no orders, and organise nothing that it is in the power of the boys to organise for themselves ... In matters of discipline, I shall accept without cavil the decisions of the class as a whole. The powers I relinquish are now vested in the class.

MacMunn would not have sung such a song about it and he would have given more power to the class, but he would have recognized that he had more in common with Craddock than with the majority of teachers. The theosophists, Simpson and the Caldecott Community were more cautious than MacMunn, yet they encouraged a marked narrowing of the gap between teacher and pupil. Helen Parkhurst saw the Dalton Plan as a means of developing a closer partnership between teacher and children, though the contract which the pupils signed made it clear where she thought the power lay.[64] Holmes's Egeria was closer to the Montessorian ideal for she believed that the teacher must 'as far as possible efface himself, bearing in mind that not he, but the child, is the real actor in the drama of school life.'[65]

Clearly there are marked differences between these educationists; they share not a defined programme but a tendency to move in the same direction, though the speed with which they moved and the distance they went varied considerably. Lane and Neill were prepared to break more clearly with the accepted view of the teacher's authority than was Helen Parkhurst; Craddock followed in MacMunn's footsteps, only more slowly and with many a backward glance. The reformers did not share a party-line unity but the less precise commitment of a common attitude.

But even this was sufficient to distinguish them from their contemporaries. When the progressives were feeling militant and confident (which was most of the time) they contrasted their approach with that of the conservative teacher. He was, they said, an authoritarian concerned to ensure that his word was law; he decided for himself and without reference to his class the activities best suited for it; he assumed that his values were those the children should most respect, he was swift to detect the wrong-doer and swift to punish. It is not necessary to accept this caricature of the existing practices to realize that the progressives had designed for teachers, and had themselves adopted, a different rôle. They tried to reduce the teacher's overt authority at least, though they were often less successful than they thought—for it did not always follow that the removal of the trappings of authority signalled the removal of its substance. Yet, almost anxiously, the progressives protested that they did not want to dominate the child, were not ruling him strictly and preferred not to rule him at all. Children were given some say in what happened in the schoolroom, they were permitted real, if often limited, disciplinary powers, they were trusted to make decisions that once they would not have been consulted upon. Some teachers at least tried to become Montessori's passive observers or to share Homer Lane's masterly inactivity, and a considerable number were to give children that degree of independence which went with signing a Daltonian contract.

These practices, and the attitude to the teacher's authority embodied in them, marked the progressives off (at least in a rough and ready way) from the traditional teachers. Sharp contrasts were possible—if, for example, Homer Lane or Neill were compared with one of the latter-day Gradgrinds whom it was still possible to find. Mostly, the contrasts were less striking and could become blurred—as less enthusiastic Dalton Plan users made clear. But they existed and, as progressive educators who were not even as provocative as Neill discovered to their cost, these differences could lead to a questioning of the teacher's competence and sometimes of his goodwill.

A constant reminder of the teacher's authority, a provider of opportunities to display it, a deadening influence on the intelligent and a depressing revelation to the slow child of his inferiority— so the progressives thought of the class lesson, the staple teaching technique of the time. According to MacMunn the class was 'a wholly mistaken unit for young children, robbing them of most of their natural activities, imposing on them a wrong *"tempo"* of thought, and turning natural questioning beings into answering machines.'[66] Caldwell Cook thought that 'nothing surely could be conceived in educational method so inadequate, so pitiably piecemeal, as *the classroom method of teaching subjects*'.[67] The progressives launched an attack on the class lesson which others gave considerable support.

Even if Lane, Neill and MacMunn had not disliked the class lesson in principle they would soon have dispensed with it or reduced its importance. They could not easily allow children to 'follow their interests' without abandoning the timetabled lesson. And when they increased the time given to art, handwork and drama, even the convenience of the class lesson, a most important source of its appeal, became dubious. Thus O'Neill found that he required fewer formal lessons—he hoped that by 'keeping to no set time-table, working to no progressive scheme, but following the lure of the moment'[68] he would generate an interest that more formal methods had not provided. Montessori specifically rejected the class lesson, though she was prepared to keep the class as an organizational unit, and most reformers (Mackinder, Ballard, Simpson, Arrowsmith, Parkhurst for example) can be found attacking the technique.[69]

Despite the agreement on the need to abolish or to reduce the dominance of the class lesson there was no agreement on a substitute. Neill or O'Neill were not greatly interested in the problem, preferring to leave themselves as free as possible to capitalize on the lure of the moment. Others such as Montessori and the Daltonians had careful plans and may even have envisaged a more organized classroom than had existed with the class lesson. Yet, though there was not agreement on a substitute, there was no doubt that the staple technique of the old education was under strong attack.

Two symbolic gestures by teachers in elementary schools draw attention to another characteristic of the progressive's practices. Edward O'Neill, aware that adherence to a timetable was cramping his efforts, covered the timetable with a colour print of the 'Laughing Cavalier' and proceded to do what he pleased. John Arrowsmith unscrewed the iron legs which fixed the school furniture to the floor and cut the tables to a size which suited the children. Probably each teacher had some intention of defying authority but each also wished to express, through a direct action, their allegiance to a more relaxed and permissive discipline.

The progressives set themselves against what they considered 'unnecessary' (which in the case of Neill and Lane was almost all) drill and direction, against the ' "Sit-up-straight. Now-children-I-want-you" attitude.'[70] In their schools the march did not take place or became a casual walk; timetables disappeared, or lost their rigidity, or were constructed by the children, or, as in the Caldecott Community, became the subject for amiable negotiation between teacher and child;[71] competition for places or prizes was played down (at St Christopher, for example) or abolished altogether, by Neill at Summerhill. As for punishment, Edmond Holmes said of Egeria's school:[72]

That anyone should be punished for failure seemed to the children ... as unreasonable as that anyone should be rewarded for success ... And if punishment as such was unknown, corporal punishment was, I need hardly say, undreamed of.

Some were less confident about abolishing corporal punishment and preferred to retain it in a mild form, though if they did (and were like J. H. Simpson) they insisted that 'the real basis of sane and orderly (though not goody-goody) happiness of the place was that the boys were *trusted*.'[73] Self-government in one form or another was widely practised. Some saw it as a preparation for democracy, as the learning early and by 'doing' of community living; for the more radical such as Neill it grew out of the belief that 'you cannot have progression unless children feel completely free to govern their own social life. When there is a boss, freedom is not there, and this applies more to the benevolent boss than to the disciplinarian.'[74] Most would have agreed with Percy Nunn that 'the power of moral ideas depends, in general, upon their being learnt from first-hand experience, and used as guides to one's own responsible actions.'[75]

The 'slackening' of the traditional expectation for the quiet and docile student, the dissolving of the formal timetable, the lack of emphasis on competition, the mildness of punishment generally, the aversion to corporal punishment and the practice of self-government—all contributed to what many contemporaries regarded as the excessive freedom of the progressive school. They were 'do as you please' schools—Bertrand Russell even found that children came to Beacon Hill expecting more freedom than he and his wife were prepared to allow.[76] Some progressives fed this belief: Neill claimed that the most frequent comment made by visitors to Summerhill was 'that they cannot make out who is staff and who is pupil'.[77] Probably more typical was J. H. Simpson[78] who thought that at Rendcomb

to a greater extent than I had known at any other school, the boys were not hampered and restricted by prohibitions, and for unusually long periods were not tied down to school engagements, but were, to put it bluntly, let alone.

Or Alice Woods, once principal of the Maria Grey Training College and a publicist for progressive education, who claimed[79] that educators wanted to free children from the traditional convention of many of their [the teachers'] own plans and methods; their rigid time tables, clanging bells, silent cloak-rooms, cramping desks, and absurd rules which required a child to ask leave even to borrow a pencil, and refused to allow her to say 'Thank you'.

The reformers also had views on what the school should teach. The three Rs which had dominated the nineteenth-century curriculum were given less emphasis, and art, craft, music, drama, dancing and literature given greater prominence. More radical than the attention given to such neglected subjects was the deliberate dissolution of the subject-curriculum into informal activities, 'learning experiences' of the kind practised by O'Neill, Arrowsmith, the Caldecott Community or Harriet Finlay-Johnson. They built upon the child's interests and avoided the situation which Nunn attacked in 1918:[80]

> From 10.15 to 11 twenty-five souls are simultaneously engrossed in the theory of quadratic equations; at the very stroke of the hour their interest in this subject suddenly expires, and they all demand exercises in French phonetics! Like the agreement of actors on the stage, 'their unanimity is wonderful'—but also, when one comes to think of it, ludicrously artificial. Can we devise no way of conducting our business that would bring it into better accord with the natural ebb and flow of interest and activity?

The reformers believed that the way they ran their schools was the best answer to Nunn's question. But they had other answers and did not rely totally on practical demonstration. To a few ideas in particular they were attracted, almost like children to a Christmas tree, not fully certain what to expect but confident that it would be pleasant.

When Alice Woods had finished visiting experimental schools in 1920 she put some of these ideas into one sentence: 'The cry is almost world-wide for greater freedom in education, and for "the development of individuality".'[81] 'Freedom' and 'individuality', the reformers returned to these ideas constantly to draw sustenance for further efforts. Nunn's *Education: Its data and first principles*, which Ballard called 'the individualist's bible' aimed at reasserting 'the claim of Individuality to be regarded as the supreme educational end'.[82] 'Now,' said Craddock putting his classroom republic to the acid test, 'does the scheme do what I claim for it, that is, develop the individuality?'[83] MacMunn was confident that his approach did meet the test because under his approach 'all the time each boy is unconsciously developing his individuality', while Olive Wheeler, another advocate of progressive ideas, tied the development of the individual in with 'all sound educational practice'.[84] And those who were worried about the direction in which education was heading asked whether the stress on the individual were not to blame.[85]

Defenders and attackers of 'individuality' had at least one thing in common and that was confusion over the meaning of the word. For some the key to its meaning lay in the concept of 'difference': MacMunn, for example, argued that individuality meant a boy 'becoming different from the boys around him'.[86] Or, as another writer said, 'The term "individuality" implies a variation from the average or normal type, and is often used to designate the sums of the qualities which mark off one person as different from another.'[87] The relationship between 'individuality' and 'difference' became more complicated when the concepts were combined to support each other, and the term 'individual differences' and its variations emerged. The result was untidy but generally 'individual differences' was taken to mean that a child could differ from another in a variety of ways: in his 'tastes, aptitudes, and capacity' as MacMunn put it, or according to others in his 'interests', 'character', 'skills', and above all, his intellectual ability.[88]

From this viewpoint certain practical conclusions could be drawn for, it is essential to note, the progressives were always quick to move from theory to practice.[89] In this case it followed or at least it could be said to follow, that the class lesson should be abandoned: how could such a procedure take account of the differences between pupils? how could so inflexible a method allow the bright child, and the slow, to work at the appropriate pace? what contribution did a pre-determined curriculum make to the development of individuals whose interests were different? did not such a curriculum pretend that all were the same and thus ignore their 'individuality'?

To the differences between children or between groups of children some educationists added the differences between the individual and society. They warned against 'a tendency to submerge the individuality of each pupil though enforced conformity to a conventional standard of conduct' and they worried about the attempt to impose on the child the teacher's own 'individuality' or, as Craddock said, some other 'generally accepted type of individuality'.[90] On this view the 'most sterilising influence in education' was that of 'rigorous conformity' while the most productive influence was that which gave 'the greatest possibility for the full development of individual diversity of talent.'[91] Individuality, in this sense, was opposed to, or at least not easily reconciled with, society. The individual represented the free spirit which society might curb or even destroy.

'Individuality' had yet another meaning. 'By the individuality of a man,' said Edmond Holmes, 'I mean the particular lines along which he, being what he is and having the various tendencies and capacities with which nature has endowed him, is predestined to grow.'[92] Individuality was linked with 'growth' and 'development', those naturalistic concepts which the kindergarteners had most prominently represented in English education. Many were prepared to state this simply: 'individuality', in Simpson's words, was 'some kind of completeness of growth'[93] or according to an exponent of child-study, T. C. Tibbey, it connoted 'all the possibilities of development that lie within the organism'.[94] But sometimes matters were pressed much further until they bordered on the mystical. Individuality was not just that which distinguished one person from another, nor was it to be equated with growth or development. 'When we speak of a man as an individual,' said Percy Nunn,[95]

> we do not merely mean that he is an entity distinguished from other human entities by a particular name and address. What we have in view is something that makes him not only different from others, but unique. That something is his life—taking the word to cover all that issues from, or is expressed in, his physical. mental and spiritual nature ... The common sense of mankind holds that different human beings are, through and through, themselves. and themselves only : that each contributes to the music of humanity a part which. however poor it may be. is yet his own and could never issue from another.

This sense of the uniqueness of the individual, of the importance of the 'inner self' constantly recurs in the writings of the progressives. Sometimes, as with Holmes, it is linked with Indian philosophy : [96]

It is for the sake of the ideal self that the child should be helped to realize his individual self. For if he is to outgrow himself, he must do so in his own particular way, the way which Nature seems to have marked out as best for him: in other words, he must at once realize and transform his individuality—and realize it by transforming it, and transform it by realizing it—and so win his way to his own true self.

More typical was Alice Woods, who concluded that the development of individuality 'may be taken to mean the help given to the child to fulfil the unique promise that exists in every human being'.[97] Those who thought of individuality in this way were as quick as the others to apply it to the classroom: repressive discipline, for example, led to a forced conformity, to an imposing on the 'inner self' of views manufactured by others. Let Holmes put the case:[98]

> The adult who exacts from a child blind faith and literal obedience, and, having secured these, proceeds to tell the child in the fullest detail what he is to do, to say, to think (or pretend to think), to feel (or pretend to feel), is devitalizing his whole personality ... Unless the child himself—his soul, his self, his ego, call it what you please,—is behind his own actions, they are not really his.

The detour through Indian philosophy which brought Holmes to this conclusion did not attract many other travellers, but when he reached his destination he would have found a goodly company. Neill, Lane, MacMunn, Dr Montessori, Caldwell Cook, Helen Parkhurst and the directors of the Caldecott Community would have been there to welcome the traveller from the East, though they might have wondered about the necessity to approach from that direction.

They would not have wondered, however, when Holmes announced his belief that the development of individuality implied freedom. Montessori herself had said that 'the *liberty of the pupil*' was essential in order to permit 'a development of individual, spontaneous manifestations of the child's nature'.[99] The importance of freedom was stressed by most reformers. Lane, the Russells, Neill, Susan Isaacs, Beatrice Ensor and MacMunn made constant reference to it, O'Neill claimed that 'the atmosphere of freedom is best for a nation, best for a man, best for a teacher, best for the child',[100] Helen Parkhurst said that 'Freedom is ... the first principle of the Dalton Laboratory Plan',[101] Dr O'Brien Harris called her discussion of the Howard Plan *Towards Freedom*; freedom was prominent in Simpson's idea of 'sane schooling',[102] for Nunn it was 'the condition, if not the source, of all the higher goods'.[103]

But, like the higher goods themselves, freedom was hard to define. For some, some of the time, it meant the abolition or reduction of restraints. MacMunn stated:[104]

> To have arrived in actual practice at the ideal of a school free from rewards and punishment—from compulsion of any sort; to have reduced subjects pursued in common to the small minimum of two; to have eliminated the class and based all on individual taste and choice—this is to imply a new and not yet easily-digested educational creed.

Probably his practice was not based as completely on individual choice as he believed, nor was his creed as new as he thought, but he certainly lifted more restraints than was customary. Similarly a great deal of what Neill did, or of the work of Russell, Susan Isaacs, or the Order of Woodcraft Chivalry, of O'Neill or Lane or Simpson, was intended to remove or to lessen the restraints associated with schooling. The difference between Neill and, for example, Simpson was one of degree: Neill removed more restraints and removed them more thoroughly. Montessori, worrying about the restriction caused by desks, or Helen Parkhurst and Beatrice Ensor, disturbed by the tyranny of the fixed timetable, were in the same tradition.[105] Freedom meant the lessening of restraints and, especially of course, restraints in the classroom.

But for some progressives freedom had a more complicated meaning. 'True liberty is, therefore, not a mere condition of life which can be arbitrarily 'given' or 'taken away' by economic conditions, social conventions, or political institutions,' wrote one of them. 'It is a quality which springs from within and has to be gained by effort and perseverance.'[106] An inner quality ('if your action issued from the depths of your being, it was free', said Olive Wheeler) or 'an inner condition' according to H. Millicent Mackenzie.[107] Of what kind? The answers vary but this note is constantly struck:[108]

> when we postulate 'freedom' as an end in education, what we should mean is, that we aim at setting free in turn all the various elements which constitute that complex creature—man —so that he may become a self-controlled, self-governing agent in life and a free co-operator with the spiritual forces of the

world. Freedom is thus to be regarded as a spiritual value and the necessary basis of other spiritual values.

Montessori understood liberty to involve the demanding of 'those conditions adapted to the most favourable *development* of his [the child's] entire individuality.'[109] For Professor J. Shelley, an ardent advocate of progressive ideas, freedom meant 'power towards self-realisation';[110] for Nunn it involved among other things, an 'expansion of the self';[111] for Holmes it meant enabling the child to 'develop himself, fully and harmoniously, on all planes of his being'.[112]

Thus 'freedom' led, as we have seen 'individuality' could, to the concept of an *inner growth* or *development* or *self-realization*. These terms, often used interchangeably, betray the educational metaphor which pervaded progressive thought. Edmond Holmes expressed it most directly:[113]

> The process by which the 'speck,' which is scarcely distinguishable from 'nothing,' is transformed into the mightiest of all trees, is a process of *growth*. It is in this sense that I use the word, when I say that the function of education is to foster growth. In any process of growth a certain form or type, which exists potentially in the seed or germ, gradually evolves itself; and when (if ever) this form or type has fully evolved itself, maturity has been reached, and the process of growth, or self-realization, is complete.

The process of growing was 'natural' and followed laws of its own. Lillian De Lissa, a prominent kindergartener and principal of the Gipsy Hill Training College, noted:[114]

> Science has discovered that the development of mentality and of spirituality is part of nature's plan for a human being, and, consequently, that they develop as naturally as do bones and muscles. It has discovered further that they are governed by their own natural laws, which, when uninterfered with and unhampered, bring the development to far higher planes than when they are thwarted by human interference.

Many of the reformers had recourse to this conception of the educational process though often the theory of 'growth' was given an idiosyncratic twist: Lane and Susan Isaacs expounded it in Freudian terminology; Neill learned of Freud from Lane and developed his beliefs from there; Montessori drew from Itard and Seguin and her own researches; Holmes was influenced by oriental philosophy; MacMunn drew on Freud and his teaching experience; Simpson seemed to absorb common attitudes and filter them through his schoolmasterly common sense; the theosophists had their religious beliefs to guide them, the Order of Woodcraft Chivalry fell back on scouting and Faithfull, at Priory Gate, learned from the Order and Freud. Thus the 'growth' metaphor took on strange shapes and was expressed in a variety of forms but it lurked under much of the discussion.[115] There were, then, at least these three—'individuality', 'freedom' and 'growth'—inextricably intertwined and sometimes almost indistinguishable, and very important for progressive theory in the ten years after 1914.

'Theory' often refers to an organized set of propositions, one following from and leading to another, all based on evidence of some kind and leading to conclusions which can be tested in various ways. The progressives claimed to have a theory, as the sub-title of Nunn's book, 'its data and first principles' implies. 'Individuality', 'freedom' and 'growth' do not constitute the progressives' full conceptual repertoire but they are typical of it—and obviously difficult to describe as 'theory' in the strict sense: their meanings merge, overlap and sometimes blend, the links between them are blurred, it is hard to see how they could be put to the test.

Of course, it is possible to select from the writings of Nunn, Russell, Neill and their colleagues particular ideas, to prune these of excrescences, to resolve their contradictions and remove their ambiguities—and thus to produce a coherent set of concepts which are as entitled to the description, 'theory' as any group of educational ideas could be. This theory might even be used as a definition of progressive education or as a model against which could be checked the claims of any pretender to the title, 'progressive'. But no matter how successful the policy it is unlikely to result in a completely satisfactory piece of reasoning. Indeed modern educational philosophers, led by R. S. Peters in England and Israel Scheffler in the United States, have spent much time carefully analysing concepts central to progressive educational theory: 'individuality', 'freedom', and 'growth', for example, or other familiar ideas—'interest' 'play', 'activity', 'creativity', 'child-centred', 'need', and the meanings they gave to 'learn' and 'teach'.[116] Their work has made it clear that educational castles built on these concepts rest on uncertain and shifting foundations. To say this is not to say that progressive theory is beyond saving—and it is to say very little about progressive practices. But at least the work of these philosophers makes it evident that we cannot claim for the progressives the unity that comes from acceptance and adherence to a precisely enunciated set of ideas. They shared not a dogma or a doctrine but a tendency of thought: they used that set of ideas and arguments we have discussed (but not always in the same way); they shared a general attitude to children and teaching (but not uniformly), they were preoccupied with a similar set of problems (but not all progressives worried equally about all of them); they reached similar (but not identical) conclusions; they agreed that the old education was bad (but not always for the same reasons).

But not only have the philosophers shown the need to be cautious about the progressives' theories, they have also cast doubt on the manner in which the reformers moved from theory to practice. The progressives were certainly swift to do this. From his interpretation of Freud, Homer Lane drew conclusions about desirable practices in the schoolroom and in the home. Neill's dominie (and Neill himself) was never slow to rebuke the less enlightened teachers who followed practices his theories had shown to be unsatisfactory. Craddock deduced his classroom republic from democratic principles; from similar principles and his belief in individuality and freedom Simpson took guidance for Rendcomb. The directors of the Caldecott Community adopted individual instruction and flexible timetables because they seemed to be required by their broader educational beliefs. Montessori felt that her elaborate apparatus could be deduced from her educational beliefs; less dogmatically, but uncompromisingly nevertheless, the founder of the Dalton Plan based her methods on general principles. So too, if one looks at their writings did Caldwell Cook, Russell, MacMunn and O'Neill. Holmes traced the practices he favoured back to his principle of growth and those he did not approve were identified with a belief in original sin.

Again it can be said that present-day philosophers have shown that the path from theory to practice, though still negotiable, is much more difficult and complex than the progressives allowed.[117] Thus, even if we could show a tighter theoretical consistency than has been evident here, it would not follow that we could get to some unity of practice. And in any case, an examination of their educational practices reveals that these cannot claim a higher degree of cohesion than their principles. The progressives all agreed on the need for 'individual teaching' but when that term is un-packed many different practices emerge. Compare Montessori's with the Dalton Plan, or the Caldecott Community's or E. F. O'Neill's and the diversity is obvious. So too 'self-government' though in general approved, in practice meant many different things—from the extremes of Neill, Lane or MacMunn to the more highly-structured classroom republic of Craddock or the Order of Wood-craft Chivalry. There is not unanimity on practice but, just as there was with the theory, a disposition (which varied from individual to individual) to act in particular ways.

And this disposition was not new in the English educational tradition. For if one accepts the account that has been given of the New Education,[118] the progressives' views can be seen as a continuation of the naturalistic impulse which, before 1914, was most obviously represented by the followers of Pestalozzi and Froe-bel. Of course even so brief an outline of progressive ideas and practices as has been given shows that they learned from many more sources than Pestalozzi or Froebel, yet the stress on 'freedom', 'individuality' and 'growth', the concern with 'interest' and 'learning by doing', the belief in the passivity of the teacher and the sanctity of the child were shared by both groups. The progressives, whether wittingly or not, were to resolve the con-flicts inherent in the New Education, by developing that part of it which can be described as naturalistic and ignoring the works of Herbart and the others.

This chapter began by arbitrarily bestowing the title 'progressive' on a small number of people who worked in England in the ten years following the outbreak of World War I. The establishment and then the patronizing of the Conference on New Ideals and the New Education Fellowship, the sense of community evident in the reports of their meetings, and their broad agreement on ideas and practices is evidence that these people did have something in common—and, therefore, that giving them the same title, 'pro-gressive', was more than an historian's device to make his material manageable. The chapter ends by warning against too neat and rigid a view of their common ideas and practices. The progressives were not a disciplined army marching, united, on a particular town. They were a group of travellers who, finding themselves together on the road, had formed a loosely united band. They did not all intend to finish in the same town and while on the journey some were to leave the band and new travellers were to join it. But, for a while at least, they were all travelling along the same road.

Observers who watched them from a distance sometimes thought they were pilgrims.

3
The faith founded

The logical coherence of progressive thought is probably what most interests a philosopher; the historian may be more concerned with the simple fact of its existence. For him, progressive education is not just a set of arguments and practices to be accepted, modified or rejected. It can also be thought of as an event—at least in the sense that certain people (who came from different backgrounds and had widely different interests, attitudes and beliefs) determined, at approximately the same time, to break with accepted educational practices and to work in ways which had considerable similarities. And the historian asks: why did this happen? why should the ten years after 1914 have seen so much activity? why, if progressive educational theory is now thought deficient, did it satisfy highly intelligent people such as Russell and Nunn? An answer to these questions enables the progressives to be better understood and hence, though it means retracing ground which has already been covered, is worth attempting.

The missionaries

A beginning can be made by drawing attention to a quality most evident in the first progressives, their almost messianic enthusiasm: they were out to win young converts, to show the way to salvation. A. S. Neill's dominie is a self-righteous young man, a dedicated and condescending prophet who busies himself showing others the error of their ways and the rightness of his. Holmes proclaimed Egeria's work as 'the true gospel of education',[1] Montessori had her own gospel and Lane had his. When the advocates of the Dalton Plan or eurhythmics, of the classroom republic or the Caldecott

Community, when headmasters such as Simpson and Neill, T. J.
Faithfull and O'Neill published descriptions of the work, it was in
the hope of persuading others to imitate. 'For myself,' said Norman
MacMunn capturing the mood of the progressives, 'I dare not hold
back for one moment from the work of spreading the new truths
on which Montessorism depends for its existence.'[2]

'Spreading the new truths.' Progressive education was not produced by cool, poised, detached philosophers intent on sifting
ideas until they found the few grains of truth. Its theories did not
result from the careful piecing together of an intricate argument.
They came white-hot, forged on the reformers' anvil, they aimed
at conversion, at changing attitudes and behaviour and did not
allow for doubts and qualifications; they were not attempts to
arrive at truth, they were proclamations of the truth; they did not
define, they demonstrated. 'We have seen a vision of what might
be if we can change the education of the children,' said Beatrice
Ensor at the first N.E.F. Conference in 1921, 'and now we must go
forth and do something to help forward the new era which depends
upon the new education being introduced into all the countries of
the world.'[3]

The progressives were missionaries and like all missionaries had
a strong reverence for the major deities of their cause which
was easily translated into discipleship. Holmes was the focus for
such an attitude and so was Montessori, of whom one admirer
wrote:[4]

> she has disciples, where others have students of their work.
> Dr. Montessori knows so much: knows far more than she can
> tell. She knows so much about children that those who are about
> her are half afraid lest she never succeed in saying it all. That
> is why they hedge her about with care; keep what check they
> can on her reckless energy; shield her from irrelevant criticism,
> and husband her powers.

Neill, who gave his loyalties to few apart from the children
with whom he worked, said that Lane 'convinced me that I knew
nothing about education',[5] while, as we have already noted, Edith
Bazeley, Lane's close associate at the Little Commonwealth remarked: 'One could never find a weak point in the metal of which
he was made.'[6]

Like missionaries, the progressives were ready to confess past
errors. Holmes's *What Is and What Might Be* is a long act of

public repentance for the evils he had done or condoned as an inspector. O'Neill found it necessary to declare 'what I have been and what I have stood for'. He had taught large classes, he had 'flogged all round the class' and 'parsed and analysed the Lord's Prayer and called the Lamb of God a common noun (in a Church school)'; he had 'fought for and had "results"'.[7] Neill made similar confessions.[8] Montessori, it seems, had always been right, but others had to journey for a while before they found the truth. Yet, as their confessions indicate, they did find it and, having found it, could look back upon their earlier wanderings and reflect that they had not always possessed their present certainty— *once* they had been in the wrong.

Now, of course, they were right: a conviction of their own rightness pervades the writings of the progressives. Neill's dominie might have been doubtful in the face of the great mysteries of life but he knew about schooling and insisted upon acquainting others with his views. Holmes's views, once he had seen Utopia, radiated the intense light of certainty. 'What that day did for me,' he said speaking of his visit to Egeria's school, 'was to change it [his educational belief] into *a conviction*, and so give it the driving power which had hitherto lacked.'[9] When O'Neill, MacMunn, West-lake or Dora Russell describe their methods their confidence is unmistakable. So, too, when they are discussing the Howard or Dalton Plans, is the confidence of O'Brien Harris or Helen Parkhurst. Lane's biographer, though sympathetic, is compelled to admit that Lane began 'to see himself as the one true interpreter of God's will on earth, the only man who really understood the message of Jesus Christ.'[10] When Montessori sought for parallels for the discipline in her Children's Houses she found them in 'the pheno-menon of conversion ... the superhuman heightening of the strength of martyrs and apostles ... the constancy of missionaries ... the obedience of monks.'[11]

There is a meeting recorded between Edward O'Neill and A. S. Neill.[12] Neill arrived at the Lancashire village ('one of the ugliest villages in the world'), walked past 'slag-heaps and all the horrors of industrialism', and entered the school. 'I walked into the school,' said Neill, 'and two seconds after entering I said to myself: "E. F. O'Neill, you are a great man!"' After Neill had spent some time looking at what the children were doing 'a young man came forward, a slim youth with twinkling eyes.'

> E. F. O'Neill?
> A. S. Neill?
> We shook hands, and then he began to talk. I wanted to tell him that his school was a pure delight, but I couldn't get a word in edgeways. If anything, he was over-explanatory, but I pardoned him, for I realised that the poor man's life must be spent in explaining himself to unbelievers.

It is a meeting of two missionaries in a heathen land, men struggling in a hostile environment who share the relief of a brief conversation with a kindred spirit.

At least they had one comfort that all missionaries have: not only were they right but they were right about something important. Through all they said and did, there runs the belief that great things were at stake—the salvation of the world, they sometimes say, without any embarrassed sense of disproportion. They were, in their professional capacity at least, intense, single-minded and humourless. They lacked balance, detachment and irony: the cause was too great and their absorption in it too complete to permit the distancing such qualities require. But scorn, sarcasm and the willingness to denounce errors they had in plenty. For many of them (Holmes after his retirement and Lane, T. J. Faithfull, John Arrowsmith and Montessori all their lives) the personal and the professional were almost impossible to separate. They were uncompromisingly dedicated. Here, in typical mood, is Sir William Mather closing the New Ideals Conference in 1915:[13]

> I am prepared to say that all of us, (I have noticed the glow on the faces of these young teachers,) are agreed that this has been a great week. You perhaps have not had quite the time to meditate upon what great things have been done every day, but when you begin to think over this week's work you will feel that we have utilised this time in the highest sense of the word in preparing ourselves for the future, the more strenuous future, a future that will be for a long time full of troubles, difficulties and dangers, but which we shall face with the confidence that nothing can shake. There is a Divinity which shapes our ends if we do our duty. This has been a time of great movement with each one of us towards high ideals, not only in education but in life.

This at the end of an educational conference! Yet it was a common attitude. Caldwell Cook who completed *The Play Way* in 1915 somewhere in France, hurriedly, 'for fear lest the book should never be written at all', wrote:[14]

For the past ten years, all the good I have seen in life or have been able to learn from books ... has been to me stone upon stone in building up that ideal republic in my fancy. Whenever I have seen boys and girls playing happily or working well I have imagined they must be citizens of my Play School. Whenever I have spoken seriously with any man or woman I have told them of my dream. Even the invigoration of a frosty morning, or the enchantment of the moon at night, have always made me think: Here is gone by another morning or another evening which might have made some occasion of good hap in the Play School. The one thing upon which my heart is fixed is to make this dream come true in this our England.

Of course, the progressives did not rely simply on enthusiasm and a conviction of the importance and rightness of their cause. 'I am a member of the Order of Woodcraft Chivalry,' said H. D. Jennings White, 'because I see in it the germs of an organisation for the conscious creation of superhumanity; again translating that into orthodox religious terms—for the creation of heaven or the Kingdom of God upon earth.'[15] As missionaries have always done, they argued their case; and writers such as Nunn, Montessori and Russell brought a formidable range of reading and acute minds to the task. Yet the reader is usually aware that a case is being presented rather than an argument being developed. Nunn admitted in 1918 that 'the counsel's position is one I find it impossible to repudiate. I have become more persuaded of its essential soundness the more I reflect on the problems of education'.[16] The arguments are marshalled, called into line, paraded to convince; they are not the products of men groping towards the solution of subtle and delicate questions; there is little opportunity for the arguments to take on a life of their own and drag their user in directions he had not planned to go. To say this is not to question the progressives' sincerity: they were not intellectual card-sharps who shuffled the facts until they produced the results they required. They were honest men but concerned to present a case, to show how they had reached their conclusions. Not for them the lure of the half-glimpsed possibility, the agonizing choice, the teetering on the brink of a conclusion. They were sure. Their writing may lack the tension that comes from trying to analyse, clarify and define, but it has the excitement of conviction.

And for all their pages of discussion, the progressives sometimes seem to work with beliefs felt to be beyond demonstration or argument, to have reached certainty by following an intuition or a sudden insight. Homer Lane confessed that he began by believing that human nature could develop successfully only if outside influences were at work. Contact with young first offenders caused him to question this belief, and work with delinquents led him to recognize 'a tendency to do right which had been twisted by environment into what had the appearance of wrong.' He had a 'new vision', and the more he lived with child criminals 'the more I felt the mystery of wrongdoing.'[17] Montessori, sternly rational and scientific though she could be, once confessed that it was not her didactic material, 'but my voice which called to them, *awakened* the children.'[18]

MacMunn declared:[19]

There are few people who know as yet whether a child is growing wisely and well. Only two kinds of people perhaps really know it—a good mother and a man or woman with the understanding heart of a child.

Neill sensed that Edward O'Neill worked in this way. 'I don't think he has any theoretical knowledge,' said Neill and added that 'anyone could trip him up over Freud or Jung, Montessori or Froebel, Dewey or Homer Lane. But the man seems to know it all by instinct or intuition.'[20] Nunn, who devoted *Education: Its data and first principles* to providing an intellectually respectable home for his educational practices, fell back upon, or perhaps began with, a vision. 'Upon what basis,' he asked,[21]

does that historic claim to liberty rest if not upon the truth, seen darkly by some, by others clearly envisaged, that freedom for each to conduct life's adventures in his own way and to make the best he can of it is the one universal ideal sanctioned by nature and approved by reason; and that the beckoning gleams of other ideals are but broken lights from this? Such freedom is, in truth, the condition, if not the source of all higher goods.

Edmond Holmes made his act of faith when he defined the aim of life as being self-realization, stated that self-realization was the 'perfection of his nature' and what that may mean, he declared, 'we cannot even imagine'. 'Let the end of the process of growth be what it may. Our business is to grow.'[22] Caldwell Cook, the bluntest educational protestant of them all simply said (he was talking of the views expressed in his book):[23]

to have one's feet thus planted on a rock of certainty ... does not come of having accepted a doctrine after logical consideration, but it comes of innate belief; for the springs of human action lie not in the reasoned intention of the individual, but in the intuition of man's mind, in the gathered energy of inherited tendency and communicated desire. And so this expression of an educational ideal will ultimately appeal only to those who already feel an answer to it within themselves.

Like missionaries again, the progressives had a special view of history. Holmes's 'What Is' (which could also have been called 'What Was', for he described elementary education since the payment by results period) is an elaborate description of the old tradition. It tells of large classes, severely and sometimes cruelly disciplined, of cramming and rote learning, of large helpings of unimportant facts forced upon unwilling children, of rigid teachers concerned with getting results.[24]

> The strength of the child, then, is to sit still, to listen, to say 'Amen' to, or repeat, what he has heard. The strength of the teacher is to bustle about, to give commands, to convey information, to exhort, to expound. The strength of the child is to efface himself in every possible way. The golden rule of education is that the child is to do nothing for himself which his teacher can possibly do, or even pretend to do for him ... His teacher must stand in front of him and give such directions as these: 'Look at me,' 'See what I am doing,' 'Watch my hand,' 'Do the thing this way,' 'Listen to what I say,' 'Repeat it after me,' 'Repeat it altogether,' 'Say it three times'. And the child, growing more and more comatose, must obey these directions and ask no questions; and when he has done what he has been told to do, he must sit still and wait for the next instalment of instruction.

Writer after writer returned to the theme. Bertrand Russell tells how dissatisfaction with the old education led to Beacon Hill, Neill stressed its arrogance in forcing on children the views of adults, Montessori its denial of true freedom, Lane and Susan Isaacs its ignorance of child development, Caldwell Cook its spoon feeding, Lynch and other Dalton Planners its reliance on the class lesson.

This view of history was of practical importance. By identifying an enemy it showed the progressives what they were fighting against and, by showing what they were against, made clearer what they were for: their own ideas and practices stood out more clearly and were therefore more understandable, and more

obviously right, when contrasted with the old system. Once again
Holmes is the representative figure for he set 'What Is' against
'What Might Be'; but so did Neill and Montessori, Jessie Mackinder
and John Arrowsmith and, almost without exception, the remainder
of the progressives. Constantly, consciously and explicitly the new
is balanced against the old. When Montessori wants to clarify what
she means by 'liberty' she contrasts her procedures with those
'where the children are repressed in the spontaneous expression of
their personality till they are almost like dead beings'.[25] MacMunn,
to establish what he means by 'activity', discusses the children of
the past: 'All they asked for was work in activity. The schoolmaster replied, "You must work in passivity or not at all. What
you call work in activity I call play. And as I know everything
it *is* play. And if you play you shall be punished."'[26] Craddock,
trying to show how his classroom republic enabled children to
develop their own values, criticized the teacher who 'devised a code
of laws which shall apply to every member of the class, no matter
what the child's individual character may be' and complains that
children 'who are organisms of the highest degree of individuality,
naturally find it difficult to conform to a rigid standard.'[27] However much they wanted to abolish the old ways, they could not do
without them: the old education helped to tell the progressives
what they were.

Being a missionary or a reformer can be a lonely task. Custom
has been rejected and the received practices, which bring with
them a feeling of purpose and security, are often unacceptable.
And a teacher who is told that what he has done in the past (and
may still be good at doing) is ineffective or inadequate can be hard
to convince. He may point to the many like him who are doing
work which others think satisfactory and may lead the missionary
to think that the powers are arraigned against him. In these circumstances it can be consoling to have history on your side, to
know that the changes you advocate have some basis in experience,
and that a study of history will produce precursors who actually
said what you are saying (or something very like it) or did what
you are saying should be done. The missionary often claims to be
rediscovering or interpreting for his time the ideas and practices
of great men, to be (in Caldwell Cook's words) contributing to 'a
fresh realization of the oldest truths'. So Lynch traced the ancestry
of the Dalton Plan back through the days when mass teaching
techniques were employed to 'those early days when disciples . . .

sat at the feet of their master'[28] and Dorothy Revel, with the Order of Woodcraft Chivalry in mind, claimed that 'Just as all new truths are old truths re-combined, so all new schools are really old schools remade.'[29] Henry Wilson, a leading member of the Conference on New Ideals, could claim that 'creative education' had been the driving force behind many movements for reform because it was 'the method of life itself ... the one law of the arts ... the soul of religion'.[30] It was, furthermore, the method

> adumbrated by the younger Pliny in the school he established at Como; Comenius advocated it; Voltaire in the little industrial Colony he established round his country home, put it into practice.

He added Ruskin and Morris to his list of ancestors, and others, of course, added Froebel and Pestalozzi and Rousseau.

Not only did history show the progressives that they were part of a long and noble tradition but, as it often does for missionaries, it gave guarantees for the future. The old ways were not natural and inevitable; they were not, Nunn pointed out in 1918, 'firmly based in the nature of things as the everlasting hills' but 'only prejudices or, at best, conventions'. When the old was superseded, school society 'instead of dissolving in hideous ruin, may actually become a vastly healthier medium for young people to live and grow in.' The present methods of school organization and discipline belonged to the old tradition and 'as that tradition disappeared those methods must vanish also or become profoundly modified.'[31] Cramming was possible, another said, 'only so long and so far as the teachers believed in it.' Now, she was able to say, 'the ideal has shifted, faith in the old practice is dying, is sustained only as a feeble, though at times virulent, flicker by a small company of lost souls'.[32] MacMunn projected himself into the future and, gazing from that vantage point on the old practices, concluded that 'all this will seem simply incredible'.[33] 'It is,' said Beatrice Ensor, 'this seeming inevitability of certain fundamental ideas which helps us to believe that we are on the track of something real, something that is in line with the progress of evolution.'[34]

The historian will probably be as mistrustful of progressive history as the philosopher has been of its general theorizing. Its account of the earlier practices does not emerge from a detached analysis, from a patient searching of the documents, from a careful weighing and sifting of evidence. There is little to show that the progressives made an effort to comprehend imaginatively the world of the nineteenth-century teacher. When Montessori said, 'In such a school the children, like butterflies mounted on pins, are fastened each to his place, the desk, spreading the useless wings of barren and useless knowledge which they have acquired',[35] she was not interested in describing the past; she wanted her readers to react to it, unfavourably.

When description was attempted it was with a few and bold strokes so that the resulting picture was simple and dramatic and therefore memorable, but ultimately a caricature. It seized upon obvious features of the nineteenth-century elementary school, looked at them out of context and left them so engrained on the mind that all else was inconspicuous. Thus cramming, rote learning, discipline, drill and the determination to fit the child into a mould of the teacher's contriving pre-occupied the progressive. The motives of the teachers of the past were over-simplified and cheapened. Ballard, describing 'the old regime of school discipline', stated that the pupil 'can only do what he likes when what he likes is precisely what the teacher likes.' The most frequently heard word, Ballard continues, is 'don't' : 'Don't talk, don't fidget, don't shout, don't whisper, don't sprawl, don't cough ... He would like to say "Don't breathe", if there were any chance of his being obeyed.'[36] Where Ballard saw the teachers as martinets Holmes saw them as fools, 'To leave the child to find out anything for himself, to think out anything for himself, would have been regarded as a proof of incapacity, not to say insanity, on the part of the teacher.'[37] Neill saw them as trapped beyond rescue within their own inhibitions. 'I have had to give up lecturing [to] Mac,' his dominie says of a teacher friend, 'for he always takes me as a huge joke. He is a good fellow, but he has the wonderful gift of being blind to anything that might make him reconsider his values.'[38] Missionaries find it easy to believe that people who do not share their views are martinets, fools or beyond the reach of reason.

It is not difficult to show that neither the theories nor the practices of nineteenth-century education were as uniform or depressing as the progressives claim; in fact, many of the suggestions they offered were first made during the last years of the century. Furthermore he would be a brave man who would claim that the opinions of Joshua Fitch, Joseph Payne or Simon Somerville Laurie were so obviously foolish as to merit instant condemnation.

But from the progressives they got condemnation because they studied the past not in order to understand it but to judge it and justify themselves. They ignored its true shape in much the same way, and for similar reasons, as a cartoonist ignores the shape of a politician's face to concentrate on his prominent nose or protruding jaw.

People possessed by a vision, guided by an intuition which convinced them that they had the key to salvation, intensely aware of the importance of their cause and firmly believing in its rightness, determined to win others to new ways of thought and action, confident that history justified them and that the future was theirs, enthusiasts who had not come to enquire but to announce the truth and demonstrate its workings—the progressives have the hallmarks of the missionary. And, some might say, of the ideologist.

Considering the progressives not just as educational theorists but as missionaries enables a more sympathetic appreciation of their ideas than the modern philosopher is likely to allow—though, of course, it does not improve the quality of their reasoning. But to label them as ideologists is immediately to risk any sympathy that has been gained. Ideologists, it is usually implied, are nasty people. Nazis, Stalinists, supporters of black power or white supremacy are often used as examples of the ideologist. Moreover, most accounts of ideology credit them with a basic dishonesty, for there is an implicit contrast between the ideology (frequently taken to be a surface phenomenon) and the baser realities lurking underneath. Thus a person may justify putting a rival out of business by appeal to the principles of private enterprise when, or so it is claimed, he is *really* motivated by spite or by a desire for personal aggrandisement.[39] The ideology he vehemently defends simply makes reputable a bitter clash of interests and in arguing as he does the ideologist is guilty either of self-deception or a cynical public relations trick.

If 'ideology' has this meaning only, it is impossible to apply it to the progressives without appearing to condemn them. After all have not such people reduced reason itself to a weapon—a sword to force others into submission, or perhaps a flute to beguile them into surrender? Are not these ideologists anti-rational beings who reduce reason to the level of force or money or influence, regard it as a means for the triumph of their ideologies and nothing more? And, if they are, can a group be labelled ideologists and discussed with any fairness? Almost certainly not, if there is no more to ideology than this. But well established though this meaning is, it does not exhaust ideology's possibilities. A look at the manner in which the progressives' theories were related to their missionary intentions may help to clarify the issue.

It should be clear, first, that reformers are driven to theory in a way that conservatives are not. A teacher content to accept the *status quo* has many of his decisions made for him. Of course, he need not be an unthinking drudge; he may, in fact, have thought deeply before accepting the *status quo*, but if he wishes to avoid justifying his actions he is in a good position to do so. A person is not asked to defend what he is doing if he is doing what is expected, he does not have to justify being obedient and co-operative. However, the reformer or missionary asks for change and change has to be justified. If he tells a teacher that his methods are inadequate, the teacher will ask 'why?' and the more frequently and vigorously he criticizes the more he will be asked for reasons. To supply those reasons the reformer must go beyond his programme for action so that, even if he began with no more than a series of *ad hoc* suggestions, he is forced to construct an intellectual framework for them. He has to show not only that his suggestions will work but, since often the *status quo* is working tolerably well, that they are preferable, either because they achieve present aims more satisfactorily or assist in the achievement of new aims.

With proposals as radical as Lane's this is obvious. A teacher is unlikely to make so daring a change lightly and may not even tolerate it in others unless it is very ably defended. Even less radical proposals, such as those of the Dalton Plan or Montessori's apparatus, cannot simply be set in opposition to the established practices and left to fend for themselves. Their existence implies criticism and criticism requires justification. Sometimes the criticism can be disposed of pragmatically: by saying, for example, that the reforms would involve a doubling (or halving—which can be quite as disastrous) of the number of teachers and leaving the question to statisticians. But this escape is not always available and deeper issues have to be faced. Questions might be asked about children's rights, about whether the school was attempting what it should, or whether its attempts were properly organized. And the missionary must have answers to these questions or he cannot hope to convert. His desire to change behaviour forces him to theory.

Reformers are the more likely to need theory because they are usually outside, or at least on the periphery of the institutionalized agencies. They may acquire influence or earn status but in a great many cases they begin without formal authority. Holmes will serve as a symbol of the progressives for he was an *ex*-chief-inspector when he wrote *What Is and What Might Be*. Neill first tried his ideas at Gretna Green but after the war had disturbed his efforts and he had discovered Lane and Freud he turned from the established schools to begin the search which has kept him ever since a lonely and independent figure. Beatrice Ensor and J. H. Simpson both had experience as inspectors before they began to work at their private schemes. MacMunn and Lane acquired reputations as cranks as they developed their ideas. The New Education Fellowship was created by individuals working outside the formal educational structure; though willing to work with educational officials (some of whom were, in their private capacity, members of it) they followed an independent line. Montessori tried to win converts in the public schools but the centre from which her influence radiated was the society she and her followers started. The few progressives who worked within the public system, Edward O'Neill, Jessie Mackinder and John Arrowsmith for example, did so of their own choice and not because they had been asked by the authorities; indeed their paths were often rough—O'Neill, when asked how he had obtained permission to carry out his work in a public elementary school, replied that he 'had never asked permission'.[40]

During the ten years after 1914 the progressives were a small and loosely-knit group of outsiders, sometimes ignored by the authorities, sometimes obstructed and occasionally helped, but never part of the public system. They were independent of the Board and the local authorities and frequently opposed to their policies, they did not follow a lead given by the authorities but themselves had the initiative, they did not work from within the system for reform but stood outside and went their own way. They had, therefore, little authority in their own right, little power conferred on them by position; they were challenging custom and consequently had none of the support which adherence to custom can bring. Like missionaries everywhere they had to seek attention, engage in debate, criticize, discuss. Unless they were to remain as eccentrics on the edge of the educational world (and like most missionaries they wanted the centre of the stage) they had to convince others that their practices were of value for all schools.

Here, for example, is a typical reformer's tactic: he first makes a dramatic gesture which focuses attention on his position and stresses its difference from the conventional, then he explains the gesture until, from seeming radical or even senseless, it appears reasonable. Fifty years of permissiveness have not fully dulled the daring of Homer Lane who gave a child a poker and informed him that, if smashing dishes made him happy, he should set the poker to work immediately—then allowed him to smash the dishes. Nor has it made fully acceptable Edward O'Neill's decision to pull up the asphalt and plant flowers, or Arrowsmith's work on the school desks. And Neill's words can still shock: 'Let us think of a bad school. I mean a school where children sit at desks and speak when they are spoken to'.[41] Even if such gestures now seem tame they were at the time astonishing and utterly at variance with received opinion. Convinced of easy victory (for how could such actions be defended?) the defenders of the traditional ways rush to the attack. They are confronted by Lane who produces his version of Freudian theory, explains why he allowed the crockery to be smashed, argues that this apparent connivance at vandalism is reasonable and may in the long run obtain a cure—by it the child's 'unconscious and irrational desire to smash authority by smashing property is dissolved'.[24] Many, especially at first, see the reasoning as no less extravagant than the action; some find it simply unconvincing; but a few, a very few, who remember that the Little Commonwealth was said to *work*, find that their whole educational orientation is disrupted, that what they had believed unshakeable is no longer secure and that what had at first seemed ridiculous may have something to be said for it.

To say this is not to claim that people accept a reformer's suggestions because they are convinced by his reasoning. Of course some do, but others act for reasons different from, perhaps conflicting with, those of the reformer: as a means of making a protest (any kind of protest) against the establishment, because they see a personal advantage, or because they have succumbed to the charisma of a leader. What can be said, however, is that whether a missionary's ideas convince or become irrelevant, *some* ideas are essential at the beginning, just to get him a hearing. If, to charges that he is disturbing the educational peace with ridiculous schemes which offend all principle, his only reply is 'No comment', he will have no chance of convincing others. He must persuade people that he has something of value; he must, as it were, get his product on the market; and to do this he requires theories—that is arguments which justify his practices. Of course it sometimes happens that his product is bought for reasons of which he does not approve. But the clear-sighted reformer will recognize that, whatever the eventual fate of the theories he produced, unless he had been able to produce some theoretical justification for his proposals they would have been ignored. At the very least, irrespective of how incoherent they may be, theories are essential at the start of a reform movement—they make possible communication between the missionary and his potential converts.

Once this is granted it is easier to understand the ideological nature of a reformer's commitment. No matter how seriously the theories are challenged, the prior commitment—to the practical suggestions—may survive. Thus Neill ended *A Dominie in Doubt* wondering whether the 'more or less complete Freudian' who began writing still saw eye to eye with Freud. Yet he had not altered his belief that what he wanted to do in schools was right; and today Neill will justify some of what he does by referring to William Reich whose influence on him was unimportant before 1937.[43] Similarly Montessori first put the ideas of Itard and Seguin successfully into practice, and only then copied out their works by hand 'in order that I might have time to weigh the sense of each word'.[44]

The movement of the reasoning in these cases seems to be from practice to theory and may even be considered to have a temporal sequence—first the practice, then the theory at a later date. That is, the theory looks suspiciously like a rationalization; the arguments seem to have been produced to bolster or make respectable conclusions reached on other grounds. However valuable its function in getting the debate started, the logical link between theory and practice is even looser than usual. One can easily imagine that the justifications produced by Neill or any of the progressives might have been different had he lived in a different country or at a different time, met different people, gone to a different university or got on better with his mother.

The suspicion that the theories can be reduced to rationalizations is increased when the reformers expound their ideas formally. In

this case the direction of the reasoning is often reversed: first
the theory is outlined, then the practice follows. Thus impression
is created, by the design of the exposition, that practices not only
follow (in time) but follow from (logically) the theory: in discovery the reformer argues one way, in exposition the other; and
the change in direction of the argument gives it increased plausibility. And plausibility gained in this way creates suspicion.

Yet the suspicion should not be exaggerated, for ultimately the
coherence of the progressives' views depends on neither the order
in which they were discovered nor their order of exposition, but
upon their logical order, the relation of premise to conclusion. It
is just possible that a prejudiced person, one determined to justify
his position at all costs, who constructs an argument to lead to
the conclusion he wants (this is, of course, to put the progressives'
case at its very worst) may present a logically coherent case. To
deny this possibility is to judge the validity of an argument by
the motives of its propounder. Once it is admitted that a 'rationalization' could be reasonable there has to be some hesitation before
dismissing the progressives' theories as special pleading.

And once this hesitation has occurred it is possible to look more
sympathetically at the fact that, even if the progressives accepted
particular theories because they permitted the justification of certain practices, they also thought the theories were right. Whatever
the psychological mechanism which produced assent to their theories, however much it was influenced by desire to give their
practical programme an intellectual justification, once the assent
was given it was complete and completely honest. Nowhere in the
writings of Neill, Montessori, Holmes, Lane or the others is there
a trace of that detachment or cynicism which enables the deliberate
manufacture of theories which will bolster practice. Like all good
missionaries they believed in what they believed: simply, they
thought it right.

The honesty of the progressives' convictions does not improve
their logic one whit. The merest beginner of philosophical analysis
may be able to demonstrate that a theory is self-contradictory or
confused or that a particular practice does not follow from a theory
upon which it is said to depend. But if people believe that it does follow, then in an important sense, it does: not logically, but as a
matter of fact. The movement of the stars does *in fact* influence
those who accept the tenets of astrology, they will not travel if the
signs are inauspicious; if the signs change, so does their behaviour—

—they travel. Whatever the reason for their first acceptance, once theories come to mean as much as they did to the progressives they cannot easily be set aside. Ideas matter to a missionary and because they matter they may lead him to alter his behaviour. More than most, he tries to practise what he preaches.

So, while much of Lane's work can be attributed to his intuitive grasp of the way children think and act, it still cannot be doubted that some of what happened in the Little Commonwealth was influenced by its founder's version of Freud's theory: however primitive his psychoanalytic techniques, they were an important part of the Commonwealth's routine. 'So far as I am aware,' Lane said in 1918, 'no other teacher has attempted to employ the Freudian methods systematically in any school.'[45] MacMunn was worried about the effect of the class lesson on children and sought in 'freedom' a justification for his procedures. But when Montessori and Homer Lane taught him to take his theories seriously, he was driven to take more radical steps until he finished in Tiptree Hall. He was not going to be guilty of the error of educationists who asserted that 'a good theory is not good enough to try in practice.'[46] Perhaps he began by believing so that he could feel secure in action, but in the end he was acting as he did partly because of what he believed.

A similar development is evident in Montessori. After putting the methods of Itard and Seguin into practice she examined their theories and realized that Seguin's approach, because it was formed 'upon the analysis of physiological and psychological phenomena, must come also to be applied to normal children'. Seguin became 'the voice of the forerunner crying in the wilderness' and she set about a new series of experiments 'filled with the immensity and importance of a work which should be able to reform the school and education'.[47] Holmes will serve as the final illustration: Egeria's school so shocked him that he attempted to get to 'the bed-rock of her philosophy of education'.[48] When he had finished this task he found that the obscure Sussex school had led him not just to an attack on the methods of elementary education but to a criticism of the entire educational system and, indeed, of Western civilization.

Ideas mattered to this group of reformers for they sometimes led to the adoption of new practices. To dismiss their theories as rationalizations will mislead if it obscures the fact that they influenced conduct. Whatever their logical status may be, progressive theories not only made it possible to start a discussion, they also played a part in determining where the discussion went.

They had a third value. Consider, for example, this statement of Holmes: [94]

> the normal child, if allowed to make natural growth under reasonably favourable conditions, will grow happily and well. It is taken for granted that the potencies of his nature are well worth realising; that the end of his being—the ideal type towards which the natural course of his development tends to take him—is intrinsically good; in fine, that he is by *nature* a 'child of God' rather than a 'child of wrath'. It is therefore taken for granted that growth is in itself a good thing, a move in the right direction ...
>
> Above all, it is taken for granted that the growth which the child makes must come from within himself; ... that the teacher must therefore content himself with giving the child's expansive instincts fair play and free play; and that for the rest, he must as far as possible efface himself ...

So wrote the Oxford-educated inspector, poet, amateur theologian and, in his later days, admirer of Buddha. Beside it put the words of Edward O'Neill, elementary schoolteacher and product of an elementary school who worked in the Lancashire mill town: [50]

> there is no choice, no scope for initiative or responsibility, no power *not* to do the practical work, no *self*-activity—only activity. Activity is preferable to paralysis; but self-activity is life. In self-activity, as in real life, practical and theoretical work themselves out, and assume the right proportions for each individual case. Not until the whole school is on a self-active or real life basis will there be an end to the long antagonism between interesting and uninteresting, though necessary work.

And beside these put the words of Homer Lane, the American railroad worker and delivery man who married his 'deceased wife's sister' and came to believe in Freud: [51]

> Human nature is innately good; the unconscious processes are in no way immoral. Faults are not corrected by, but brought about by, suppression in childhood ... The freer a child is, the more it will be considerate and social, the more its chief interests will be progressive and the more its fundamental instinct, always to find new difficulties to conquer, will have valuable outlets. It is the attempt to create a conscience in children which leads in adults to unconscious conflict and to neurotic inefficiency. A 'conscience' cannot be imposed.

Or consider Montessori, stern Catholic and dauntingly efficient doctor whose work began in an Italian slum:[52]

> The fundamental principle of scientific pedagogy must be, indeed, the *liberty of the pupil*;—such liberty as shall permit a development of individual, spontaneous manifestations of the child's nature. If a new and scientific pedagogy is to arise from the *study of the individual*, such study must occupy itself with the observation of *free* children.

And, finally, J. H. Simpson who came through Rugby and Cambridge to the inspectorate and then to Rendcomb. He thought of education increasingly as providing the right conditions for growth, and decreasingly as bringing up, or moulding character, or training the mind. 'I believed, too, that it must be growth of the individual and of individuality, though not in the least individualistically in the political sense.'[53]

Different individuals with some differences in what they recommended, but the same ideas recur: growth, nature, instinct, freedom, play, activity, self-activity, innate goodness, development, individuality, spontaneity, interest. These words had specific (and sometimes different) connotations for each speaker—Holmes bowed to Buddha while he used them, Lane thought of Freud, Montessori remembered all the pages of Itard and Seguin she had transcribed, and many of the other progressives thought of Holmes, Lane and Montessori. Yet all the progressives used these ideas so that they bound together diverse and individualistic people who shared a dissatisfaction with the existing order.

Their attitude to play gives an indication of the way in which their ideas united them. For Lane play was a means of getting rid of excessive self-assertion in a socially acceptable way; for Harriet Weller (née Finlay-Johnson, Holmes's Egeria) it was a romantic reversion to a golden age when 'the little children lived the free and happy lives of kittens and puppies' and by watching their elders at work learned the tasks society required of them: 'they played themselves into knowledge.' For Holmes, influenced by Egeria, play was 'play-acting', drama: for Jessie Mackinder the 'spirit of play' was most in evidence when 'tasks imposed by the teacher and ... done simply because they are so imposed' were replaced by 'activities into which one throws oneself with energy and diligence because one feels they are intrinsically worth doing.' For MacMunn it was simply work done at a faster pace—to a child 'work and play are the same thing in essence'; for Caldwell Cook play was sometimes the truest expression of a child's nature, sometimes enthusiasm ('by play I mean the doing anything with one's heart in it'), sometimes an expression of the child's interests, and sometimes an indefinable absolute: 'Play is one of the fundamentals of life, capable of anything but a further explanation.' For Nunn also play had many meanings: a device of nature to use the child's spontaneous energy in order to prepare him for the business of life; the prime manifestation of youth's creative energies; the activity which could be taken up or dropped as the child pleased, and thus distinct from work which was done under compulsion or from a sense of duty; under some circumstances it was 'make-believe' or, as in Caldwell Cook's Play Way, a method of teaching.[54]

From educationist to educationist the meaning shifts and within the work of one man many variations can be noted. But the vagueness of the term is, from the reformer's point of view, its strength. Whether 'play' is an idea, an attitude to children, a fundamental process of nature, or anything else it was said to be, it is something the reformers agree about, something to which they can give allegiance. Similarly 'growth', 'nature', 'interest', 'freedom' or 'individuality' are scattered throughout their writings, single words which contain a diversity of meanings and, because they are single words, at least give the impression of binding things together. Their function is not unlike that of musical themes, which through constant variation and re-occurrence, impose a pattern on a succession of sounds and bind them into a unified movement—though considered separately the themes might have little in common with each other. It was the very looseness of their theories which helped to bind the progressives together, helped to make them feel that they were not isolated individuals crying in the wilderness but a small group with something in common. As we have seen they could not claim the unity which follows from the acceptance of an argument where neatly stated conclusions follow from neatly stated premises and one can be led, step by logical step, to agreement. The progressives' premises were often different (compare the Orientalist Holmes with the Catholic Montessori), their methods of reasoning very different (Neill's Freudianism is almost instinctive, while Nunn is elaborately rational); yet their conclusions, provided they are expressed very generally (and because they are expressed very generally) bind them together. And, however vague they may

82

be, they are not so ambiguous as to include everything. We would be jolted if we found the progressives supporting propositions such as 'the state has the duty to compel all children to hold definite religious beliefs', 'frequent corporal punishment is desirable', 'the teacher is a sculptor who should leave his own impress on the mind of each child in his class', 'the repetition of unpleasant tasks is good for the child', or 'strict and severe discipline will produce the best citizen'. The walls of his theories might be easily broached by a predatory philosopher, but to the progressive they marked an area within which he could operate safely.

Thus, whatever their weaknesses, progressive theories had important functions, functions so important that, had they not been discharged, progressive education might never have gathered impetus. First, by providing at least the appearance of a rational justification for his practices they enabled the progressive to get the debate started. Second, they had some influence on what he did. Third, they gave to the movement a sense of unity in shared ideals. And they made these contributions irrespective of their logical defects.

In fact it can almost be said that they made them because of their logical weaknesses—or at least that the discharging of these functions requires attributes which are difficult to reconcile with the demands of the philosopher. He wishes, rightly, to clarify, define and limit. Play, the philosopher will assert, cannot be used simultaneously with all those meanings. If we wish to use it as part of a rigorous argument we cannot slip, especially in unobtrusive, undeclared and unpredictable ways, from one meaning to another. We must specify and define—and to define is to exclude. And exclusion means the end of agreement and unity. The movement is divided. To retain unity and confidence a reform movement may require that looseness of meaning which 'play', for example, had. To some extent the movement must accommodate differences, not exacerbate them, and thus, provided ambiguity is not too extreme, reformers will gain from it.

It is not too whimsical to say that reformers or missionaries cannot afford to have an analytical philosopher in their midst. His cool and detached scrutiny may reveal differences in ideals, potential conflict, confusion. Philosophers question, expose undeclared and perhaps unsuspected assumptions, raise doubts, erode confidence. The missionary's enthusiasm, his certainty that he is right, his belief that he has history (and the future) on his side—qualities which are essential if he is to be a successful evangelist—are put at jeopardy. Doubters are not won to causes which are doubtfully pursued, neither are they persuaded to change by reformers whose confidence has been pricked by the philosopher's needle of anxiety. The looseness of their theories is a source of strength which intellectual rigour might remove.

In another way also, the philosopher is dangerous. It is essential for the reformer to be able to move swiftly and easily from theory to practice if he is successfully to defend his suggestions. The philosopher will not do this. Conscious that the move from theory to practice is long and difficult, aware that between a theory and its embodiment in practice there may be a multiplicity of assumptions not contained in the theory, he moves cautiously. If he gets to practice at all (and sometimes he refuses to dirty his hands) it is only after painstaking thought. The missionary cannot wait for him. And were he to wait, the urgency, enthusiasm and confidence would probably have cooled.

It should be clear, therefore, that if the progressives are considered not just as theorists but as missionaries, as people determined to convert others to a new educational life, some of the defects in their ideas (which have, correctly, disturbed educational philosophers) become advantages. They required not a defensible set of philosophical propositions but an ideology, a series of beliefs which resisted challenge, justified certain practices and were held with unswerving dedication. For about ten years after 1914 they had what they wanted.

The romantics

Viewing the first English progressives as missionaries or dedicated reformers helps to explain their anxiety to have theoretical justification for their practices. It also makes more understandable, though not more logically satisfactory, certain peculiarities in the theories they adopted—their tolerance of vagueness and ambiguity, for example, or their confident march from theory to practice. What it does not explain is why the progressives settled for the particular group of theories they did.

Theory may be essential to any group advocating changes in behaviour so that, if asked 'why this particular change?', they will not be speechless. But, provided their answer is not so ludicrously wide of the mark as to leave the proposed change without defence, a wide range of answers will do. From this point of view any answer which makes the proposal appear reasonable can serve as a theoretical justification for specific changes. Yet the progressives agreed upon a limited, if loosely linked, set of ideas. What attracted them?

Part of the answer can be gained by reflecting upon the times in which the early progressives worked. An anonymous clergyman provides the first reflection. 'I am changed by the war,' he is alleged to have said in 1918; 'I will sell three-fourths of my theological books, and cast into the waste-paper basket every sermon I preached before the war.'[55] Others went much further than this troubled gentleman, sold all their theological books and never gave or listened to a sermon again. Some few found that the horrors of war drove them back to orthodoxies previously abandoned or rejected. And for some there was just despair:[56]

> The word 'education' dies upon our lips, for are we not engaged in wrestling with a foe, whose methods and conceptions of education have repeatedly been held up to us in this country as something to which we should strive to attain. And then we remember Belgium; Liège, Louvain, Rheims echo in our hearts and we are baffled. In our despair it is not surprising if we exclaim, 'Human nature is incorrigibly bad; this time there is no excuse.'

Not only despair but a desperate hope was common: in those, for example, who seemed to be 'almost rejoicing in disaster' because it would now be possible to 'build from its foundations a world far better than the old.'[57] So the Labour Party, when it saw (or thought it saw) war consuming the existing social order, prepared its plan to bury the old political system 'with the millions it has done to death'.[58]

These millions could never be fully ignored; they remained in monuments, memorials and lists to cast shadows in the world they had left. They remained in entries such as this (from the London County Council's record of the war):

> *Watkins, Frederick* (1914–18); Private, 20th Hussars; France 4 yrs 2 months; Killed in action, 7th November, 1918.

Four more days and he might have lived. But the record does not pause to reflect, there are too many entries to be made; page after page, name after name, the lost generation is recorded. The size of the loss precluded too extravagant a display of public grief, though outlets were found elsewhere: in the desire to add one more death, the Kaiser's, to the list and in the determination, which even persisted for a few years after the war, to remake England so that it would be worthy of those who had made the 'great sacrifice'. For, as W. H. Dawson said,[59]

> they died for two Englands—the England which we know, with all its social evils, that shame our culture, baffle our morality, and make our national greatness seem a cruel mockery; yet perhaps more truly, if not more consciously, for another England altogether, an England that lives as a 'vision splendid' in the imagination of all true hearted youth ...

Visions are notoriously insubstantial fare but many people were sustained throughout the war and the early post-war years by hopes of what might be built on the ruins the war had made. The vision was partly an acknowledgment of a debt owed to the dead, partly an attempt to assuage guilt, especially the guilt of being prepared to pay so high a price for victory, and partly an effort to bestow meaning on the war—if, after all the agony, the world (but particularly England) were no better, the exercise had been futile. In the long run the debt was forgotten, the guilt deadened by time and the search for meaning uneasily abandoned; but for a short time it was believed that 'We have to perfect the civilisation for which our men have shed their blood and our women their tears'.[60] Reconstruction became a national preoccupation: 'the city which we saw beyond the rim of the shell-pocked battleground,' said Professor James Shelley, 'was that magic city whose name was *reconstruction*.'[61]

In this, of course, education shared. Schemes for a better system or better schools multiplied and the Fisher Act of 1918 which grew out of this hope (as well as out of the more pragmatic motives already discussed) was passed on a wave of enthusiasm. 'The war', said Fisher later, 'was my opportunity. I was sensible from the first that while the war lasted reforms could be obtained and advances could be made which would be impossible to realize in the critical atmosphere of peace.'[62] The past had been judged and found wanting; the future, if it were to justify the agonized present, had to be made to lead to good. The country, according to the Workers' Educational Association,[63] could

> if it pleases, so organise its education that twenty years hence it may find itself strengthened, not exhausted, by its agony, because

it has discovered some compensation for the lives which have been sacrificed and the hopes which have been shattered, in the development of the inexhaustible potentialities of a new generation of its children.

Such an atmosphere increased the appeal of progressive ideas. The horrors of the war made their policies and practices seem doubly attractive partly because the war had, in Caldwell Cook's words, brought a 'spiritual freshening'[64] to education and partly because what the progressives had to offer contrasted strikingly with the futility of the trenches and the grimness of the home front. At a time of mass slaughter, and rationing, the progressives promised a new world in which the individual mattered; they spoke of freedom, growth, play, the creative arts, self-government. 'Drill' and 'discipline' were anathema to them; they stressed differences, not uniformity; they wanted co-operation, not competition; they were eager, confident, optimistic, dedicated.

It is not difficult to understand the appeal of a word such as 'freedom' at that time. *The Times Educational Supplement* claimed that the Germans were the first to realize 'the possibilities of large-scale organization, penetrating into every corner of life, securing ready submission from the individual to the orders of the expert controller.' And why this ready submission? Partly because their system of education, 'created by Germans of an earlier day for loftier ends, has served as a willing tool in the monstrous achievement.'[65] According to MacMunn, the older school discipline 'has found its *reductio ad absurdum* in the grotesque tragedy of German subserviency'.[66] Against this could be put what he and the progressives offered. Nunn, the apostle of individualism, thought that the German belief in the State could be attributed partly to the education system which had been used 'as an instrument to engrain these notions into the soul of a whole people.'[67] The war-time enemy was the enemy of freedom; thus Edward O'Neill could show the errors of the old educational ways, with a telling comparison: they represented 'the real militarism of education'.[68] 'It is for freedom that we are fighting in the war,' said William Temple in 1916 making the point explicit; 'it is for freedom that those who care for education are struggling at home ... In the name of those who have died for the freedom of Europe, let us go forward to claim for this land of ours that spread of true education which shall be the chief guarantee of freedom for our children forever.'[69]

Consider also the emotional appropriateness of 'individuality'.

With 19,000 dead and 57,000 casualties in one day on the Somme, talk of 'individuality' might have seemed a bitter mockery, but it was also a hope. And contrasts could again be made with the enemy. The difference between Germany and England was the difference between a 'dull flockishness drilled and a lively individuality developed'.[70] Germany has taught us, said the inspector Cloudesley Brereton, 'that the steam-roller form of civilization, that crushes out every type except its own, is not only inimical to the world's growth but destructive of individuality within its own sphere of action.'[71] When A. J. Lynch wanted to categorize the old ways ('sitting on rigid desks, marching to and fro to commands shouted in approved military fashion') he could find no more appropriate term than 'Prussianization'.[72] When the teachers who had been at the fighting line returned, Foster Watson believed that they would indicate a strong preference for developing 'the highest individuality among our children'.[73]

The appeal of progressive thought, however, was to deeper feelings than could be captured by terms such as 'individuality' and 'freedom'. This description of MacMunn's Tiptree Hall gives some indication.[74]

> Tiptree Hall is away in the country towards the coast of Essex. From Kelvedon, a light railway jolts one in a friendly fashion to Inworth, whence one can either walk the mile and a half to Tiptree Hall, or be bundled along in the blacksmith's high cart ... Driving down a long avenue of flowering chestnuts and other trees, one emerges in front of Tiptree Hall. Before the doors stand two statues of women, quaintly out of keeping with the whole effect; across the drive, masses of violet-coloured rhododendron bushes give an exquisite touch to the scene.

Where did Holmes find his Egeria? In a small village which 'nestles at the foot of a long range of hills; and if you will climb the slope that rises at the back of the village, and look over the level country that you have left behind, you will see in the distance the gleaming waters of one of the many seas that wash our shores.'[75] Then there were the Caldecott Community in their Jacobean house on the side of the Kentish hills 'with the wonderful sweeps of the Weald rolling away into the blue distance',[76] the theosophists' schools at Brackenhill and Letchworth, Westlake and the Order of Woodcraft Chivalry in the New Forest, the Little Commonwealth in the hills of Dorsetshire, Simpson at Rendcomb in the Cotswolds, Neill at Summerhill, the Dartington Hall complex, T. J. Faithfull at Priory Gate, the Russells on the deeply-loved family property at Beacon Hill. Where they were free to choose, the progressives turned their back on urban life. When they were not free they made symbolic gestures: as we have seen, O'Neill pulled up asphalt and when that proved too slow spread soil on top and planted flowers in that. Montessori in a Roman slum set up[77]

> a vast courtyard, cultivated as a garden, where the children are free to run in the open air—and, besides, a long stretch of ground, which is planted on one side with trees, has a branching path in the middle, and on the opposite side, has broken ground for the cultivation of plants.

'And what does the town offer [the child]?' asked Professor James Shelley. It offers him 'unyielding and non-mysterious pavements and asphalted playgrounds', stones which he is not allowed to throw, grass he cannot walk on, lamp-posts instead of trees, and policemen to spy on him.[78] 'Man,' said Homer Lane, 'is more capable of appreciating the beauties of nature in the open air than any other animal, yet he alone lives in stuffy buildings and crowded areas.'[79] The city had been the original habitat of most of the progressives yet when they could they left it, thinking it dirty, noisy and evil. 'Standing on the high roads of Scotch Lancashire,' said E. F. O'Neill, 'you can look down on the towns in the hollows, which look like black swabs of smoke.' He wanted to convince all to come down from the mountain tops and examine the conditions in 'the hideous depths of the Lancashire valleys, and their mills and mill life.'[80] He could not move his school but Beatrice Ensor envisaged a day when, she hoped,[81]

> No schools ... will be in the town. That is one of the biggest reforms that we have to achieve. I have a horror of schools shut up in a town, the children kept within four walls and occasionally let loose in a gravelled courtyard.

Dorothy Revel, who taught at Priory Gate and at the Forest School, also believed that 'the town schools must be moved to the country', and envisaged a system by which the buses which took 'the suburban population into the town each morning could be used on their return journeys to bring the town children out to the country, and *vice versâ* at the end of the day.'[82]

Neill knew that such dreams were not for the masses; for them life meant 'dirt and disease, ugly factories, sordid homes, mean streets'.[83] Henry Wilson was more emphatic:[84]

Down a long slope stretched rows of low grimy cottages, with grimy gardens, stunted trees, consumptive flowers struggling for existence in the poisoned soil. Grog shops and chapels, mission rooms and gasometers, sweet shops and fly papers, butcher's shops and blue-bottles, horrible enamelled signs, squabbling children, mangy dogs yawning on dirty doorsteps, sardine tins and frightened cats, crawling babies grubbing in the gutters . . .

And then their voices, the waste paper, the garbage, the unseemly patched and pitiful washing.

The world they were complaining about was the world of 'broken blinds and chimney pots' which T. S. Eliot was describing as they wrote. Part of every progressive was a decent middle-class romantic disturbed by the evil and ugliness of the city and harbouring atavistic longings for the green and pleasant land. So, if they could, they built their schools in the country or, if they could not, they broke up the asphalt and stressed the 'primitive occupations and simple crafts' that flourished in the country. Robin Tanner who, with Marion Richardson, led the remarkable resurgence in the teaching of primary-school art in the years between the wars, turned in revulsion from the ugliness of London. 'I never knew ugliness until I came to south-east London : then I saw enough to fill my life many times over.'[85] He saw in art a means of removing the ugliness. J. J. Findlay, writing from Manchester,[86] spoke of the 'reaction' which

takes us back from the noise, the competition, the crowd, and the glare of the city to the wholesome fresh air and labour of the country; it finds little use for scholarship apart from the employment of learning in the achievement of designs. Hence it insists that craftsmanship, whether in literature and language, or with tools and materials, must be exalted in the school above the credit assigned to book learning. In the hands of reformers like Mr Caldwell Cook and Professor Shelley, it insists that fine art, music, and drama (to which many in this distracted world, overturned by the war, are looking for salvation) shall take pride of place among the leisure pursuits of the school.

At best, however, the recreated environment and the arts and crafts could only check the canker eating at the heart of English civilization. For it was not just the city that disturbed the progressives. Like a greater romantic before them they were haunted by the dark Satanic mills; and even when they had fled into the country they could not escape their influence. Industrialism had brought ugliness, physical deformity, spiritual impoverishment and, of course, a war more terrible than any which had preceded it. It had reduced the individual to 'a cog in the industrial machine';[87] produced a state of affairs where, Holmes claimed, the highest praise which could be given a workman was to say 'that he does his work with the sureness and accuracy of a machine'. Even the schools had been corrupted: 'salvation by machinery has found its most exact counterpart in education by machinery'.[88] So James Shelley could say in 1919:[89]

> The terrible negation, and even destruction, of millions of potential human beings by employing them as mechanical cogs in the industrial machine, is the most inhuman form of tyranny I can imagine, and there seems to be no escape from it except by adopting a life of crime.

And Findlay drew the educational moral.[90] The new movement meant that

> men and women everywhere are concerned to find a new basis for society, a new conception of industry, a better way of living than was contained in the legacy bequeathed by the industrial revolution to our fathers of the last century. Educational reform, in a word, is bound up with social reform; and the pioneer schools are plainly seeking, by experiments in self-government and communal life, to allow to children some scope for learning how to behave as friends and brothers, in contrast to a world which has exhausted itself by fratricide.

Among many of the progressives can be detected the feeling that modern Western civilization, and especially that part of it which was industrial and urban, had become corrupt. 'The world today,' wrote Neill in 1921, 'is a moralist-made world ... It has just killed a few million men and in the coming second world war, heaven knows how many men will be killed.' Moreover, he continued, 'it possesses a "moral" and criminal code that enforces barbarities.'[91] Montessori, working in the slums of San Lorenzo, was shocked by 'the evils of crowded living, promiscuousness, immorality, crime';[92] O'Neill, when he walked through the streets of Lancashire, saw similar sights:[93]

> The pale empty faces of the unhealthy looking mill-women, the crowds of loungers at the street corners, smoking, playing pitch and toss, shouting their filthy remarks at passers-by, scrawling

them on public lavatories—a nasty thing for me to mention in public. Yes, so nasty that teachers pass it by on the other side lest they should be defiled by it. It doesn't touch them.

Craddock saw civilized man 'threatened with a complete atrophy of the spiritual, mental, and bodily powers. He does not develop; he vegetates.'[94] Henry Wilson saw 'the whole social and industrial system in Europe and America ... dissolving into its elements before our eyes, preparing perhaps for universal indiscriminate war.'[95] Holmes considered that 'The war has revealed to us the hollowness of the materialistic civilisation on which we had prided ourselves.'[96] The war led Bertrand Russell to a similar conclusion:[97]

> I had supposed until that time that it was quite common for parents to love their children, but the War persuaded me that it is a rare exception. I had supposed that most people liked money better than almost anything else, but I discovered that they liked destruction even better. I had supposed that intellectuals frequently loved truth, but I found here again that not ten per cent of them prefer truth to popularity.

MacMunn claimed of his work at Tiptree: 'Our action is flat rebellion against the traditions of civilised man since he first began to educate.'[98] Caldwell Cook feared that, after the war,[99]

> we shall find ... that we are in for another stretch of years under the domination of the money-god, that king who sits all day in his counting-house counting in his money. Our people will continue to live as a race of petty and exploited town-dwellers; having their homes in tenements, slums, and villas, seeking their amusement in the music hall, the cinema palace, and the gramophone, their sport in the vicarious football of hirelings, their food in tins and packets, and their literature and politics in halfpenny newspapers bribed by the advertising manufacturers of soap, drink, tobacco, underwear, and patent medicines.

'We stand at an hour,' said Percy Nunn more succinctly, 'when the civilization that bred us is sick—some fear even to death.'[100]

And a little child shall lead them

Against this corrupt industrial civilization which war was destroying the progressives placed a fresh new world,[101]

> the little child's world of wonder and curiosity, with the glory and the freshness of a dream; a world where he should be as

happy, not as an earthly monarch, but as a king in fairyland. Whether of royal blood or not, he looks for beauty and adventure, and for love; he hopes to marry a princess and live happily ever after.

And so, in a way, did the progressives hope: to live happily ever after by returning to what they had left behind, the world of the child. They understood that earlier romantic, William Blake,

> Piping down the valleys wild,
> Piping songs of pleasant glee
> On a cloud I saw a child ...

They saw a child and made him 'the centre of the problem of education, its alpha and omega ... the one and only indispensable factor'.[102] Their efforts to make education 'child-centred' became perhaps the known feature of their work.[103]

And between the child and the adult, it is essential to note, they envisaged at least tension and often direct opposition. The teacher, said Caldwell Cook, might have a 'beautiful system, a course of work schemed, graded, and ordered in admirable shape, and thoroughly approved by his or her chief, and by his Majesty's inspector to boot.' But, he asks, 'what if the child's mind does not work orderly?—which happens to be the case. What will his Majesty do then, poor thing?'[104] John Arrowsmith was prepared to answer.[105] The teacher settled for providing

> desiccated, minced and peptonised pieces of adult knowledge, put in by the spoonful and the dose repeated *ad nauseam* until mental indigestion ensues and the soured mass is ready to be expelled at the bidding of an examiner ...

In fact (and the image crops up constantly in progressive literature even today) the child became '*the chattel of its parents*'[106] and subject to 'one of the worst of tyrannies—the tyranny of adulthood'.[107] Teachers insisted (in Homer Lane's words) upon the child becoming 'a duplicate of ourselves';[108] they considered themselves (this time the words are O'Neill's) 'the master-hand playing on the instrument'.[109] Hence they refused 'to wait for nature' and endeavoured to 'hurry the child on for the convenience of their own schemes' or for other 'ignoble motives'.[110] The child was just treated as 'a toy', claimed Dora Russell, 'and afterwards ... it becomes a horrid little nuisance.'[111] The 'heavy deterrent force of adult interference'[112] constantly weighed the child down, preventing the development of individuality and making his relationship with adults stiff and formal at best.

So the argument went until familiarity began to lead to contempt, especially to the contempt with which clichés are dismissed. Yet when Ballard wrote of the teacher under the old dispensation that 'he becomes in his small way a sort of Caesar who prints his image and superscription not merely upon the coinage of thought, but upon the very minds and souls of his pupils',[113] he was voicing one of the progressives' most important objections. Distressed and alienated by contemporary values, convinced that the holocaust of war at the one time symbolized contemporary life and destroyed it, they shied away from imprinting the future generation with the marks of the present. The teacher assumes, wrote Holmes,[114]

> that the child ought to desire and aim at the ends which he— the adult—desires and aims at, and that the child's failure to do this is proof of some defect in his nature (due no doubt to his immaturity) which education must correct. But all the while the child's outlook on life, before it has been perverted by education, is fundamentally right, while the adult's is fundamentally wrong.

Or putting it positively, here is Neill: [115]

> I want education to produce the best that is in a child. That is the only way to improve the world. The naked truth is that we grown-ups have failed to make the world better than the gigantic slum it is, and when we pretend to know how a child should be brought up we are being merely fatuous.

Making the child the alpha and omega of the educational process perfectly fitted the mood of a group who were at odds with their own society. To reject 'adult values' was to reject contemporary values; tyrannical adults forcing children to conform were compromising the future. Yet, if the child was allowed to develop without adult interference, if he were not corrupted by adult values, mankind might retrieve its position. 'Child-centredness' was of profound psychological importance for it enabled the progressives to be disgusted with their own civilization and, simultaneously, to believe that a better world might be built.

Thus Edmond Holmes could lament that 'we grown-ups' had 'grown hard in the moulds in which, first, a dogmatic and dictatorial education and then the prejudices which are engendered by environment ... have imprisoned us.' But his view of childhood enabled him to say that 'Our hope lies in the young.'[116] Or a teacher could report : 'I remember Professor Shelley turning to an audience of teachers and saying—"Yes, we and the parents educate the children to make them like *us, us.*" I think we all flinched under the lash of his contempt for such unworthy models.'[117] If one retained the progressives' view of the child it was possible to shrink with this teacher in horror, embarrassment or shame from the adult world and, at the same time, believe with MacMunn : 'There is *one possible remedy*—and a slow and difficult one at that. Reform can only come through the children themselves.' Tiptree Hall and the other progressive schools were 'schools of the positive and hopeful', places in which 'children can really live and let live', perhaps 'the only hope of ever saving the world.'[118] J. J. Findlay may be permitted the final statement.[119] 'For us,' he said,

little remains : our own generation, if not we ourselves, have somehow missed the goal : and our faith does not enable us to forecast the course of progress : nay, we may be so far disillusioned as to doubt whether any principle of progress can be asserted. Nevertheless our devotion to the young is not quenched : whatever fate offers, in morals, in politics, in science is for *them* : they at least remain, courageous, hopeful, plastic in our hands : what has survived to us from the waste of war shall be dedicated to their service.

Not only 'child-centredness' but that important metaphor, the metaphor of growth, to whose inadequacy so many critics have since drawn attention,[120] had psychological importance for the progressives. The 'growth' analogy once more takes control from the adult; the child will develop 'from within', what the adult has to do is to avoid interfering and thus bringing all his false values and corrupt practices to bear on the child. Craddock's advice made the metaphor clear :[121]

people have not realised that development can only go on from within and cannot come from without. The living plant must develop its own cells; the most skilful gardener is incapable of producing in the plant even the most imperfect and rudimentary growth of cells. The best he can do is provide conditions which will favour development—nourishment, air, space.

Whatever its philosophical limitations, the metaphor enabled people to continue hoping though they lived in a corrupted world. 'Every baby born into the world is a self-activist,' declared O'Neill, and the teacher's job was 'to see that this tremendous life-force is

not crushed out'.[122] The living organism 'with potentialities waiting to unfold themselves' (as Holmes put it[123]) offered hope. 'We
cannot know the consequences of suffocating a *spontaneous action*
at the time when the child is just beginning to be active: perhaps
we suffocate *life itself*', Montessori argued.[124]

One of the central ironies of the progressive position was that
the concept of growth (which might have brought adult and child
closer together—by stressing that the one developed from the
other) in fact divided them. Childhood was the period of hope, of
goodness unspoilt by adult contamination; nature would ensure
that good came provided the child were left free to grow. 'Think of
the little child,' said Harriet Finlay-Johnson,[125]

> with all its innate potentialities, of budding, unfolding and
> blossoming into manhood and womanhood! And then turn and
> survey the unwieldly, costly, gigantic machine [the educational
> system] which we have built up and in which we have tried to
> change the very nature of children.

Or, as Alice Woods put it, searching for a rebuke the child might
address to the adult who had ruined his world: 'Unhand me, grey-
beard loon!'[126]

The grey-beard loon had once been confident of his position.
Here, for example, is Sir Joshua Fitch, a sensible and reasonably
enlightened member of the old school speaking of the teacher's
attitude to children:[127]

> Every good ruler economizes power, and never puts it all forth
> at once. Children should feel, when they see us exercising
> authority, that there is a great reserve of unused strength and
> resolution behind, which they can neither see nor measure. It is
> not the visible exercise of power which impresses children most,
> but the unseen, which affects their imagination, and to which
> they can assign no limit.

The concept of adult 'interference' with child growth is, of course,
totally alien to Fitch. A little ponderous, but very confident, he
gives his instructions. The progressives, sickened by contemporary
society and especially by the war, no longer had faith in the
civilization which had produced them. They could not continue to
hope and believe unless the future (the child) could be detached as
far as possible from the present (the adult) and the theories of
'child-centredness' and 'growth' enabled them to make the separation. 'Truly,' said Montessori, 'our social life is too often only the

96

darkening and the death of the natural life that is in us.' Her
methods, she believed, would keep the child's 'real nature un-
spoiled and ... set it free from the oppressive and degrading yoke
of society.'[128] Bertrand Russell, different from Montessori in so
many ways, also thought that a generation which had been educated in 'fearless freedom' might avoid being 'twisted and stunted
and terrified in youth, to be killed afterwards in futile wars which
their intelligence was too cowed to prevent.'[129]

In one other way 'growth' and 'child-centredness' had an important emotional appeal. The progressives were heirs to that gradual
destruction of certainties that had been a part of nineteenth-century
England. The German biblical scholars, Oscar Wilde, the Pank-
hursts, Carson in Ulster, Lloyd George's budget (and, for some,
Lloyd George himself), G. E. Moore constantly showing people
that they did not understand what they were saying—or could
not mean it if they did understand, Frazer and *The Golden Bough*,
Havelock Ellis, Freud, and the most brutal, costly and frustrating of
wars—all conspired to continue into the twentieth century the
erosion of the old certainties. Just as the progressives were on the
fringe of the educational world so most of them were on the
fringe of the world that accepted the older religious, moral and
political values. There were exceptions,—Montessori, perhaps; but
Nunn, O'Neill, Holmes, Lane, Caldwell Cook, the Russells, Westlake,
Neill had, to a greater or lesser extent, tried to forge individual
value systems. And as Nunn, by no means the most radical, noted
in 1920, they came speedily to the conclusion that 'there can be
no universal aim of education if that aim is to include the assertion
of any particular ideal of life; for there are as many ideals as there
are persons.[130] Because agreement was not possible, the lure of the
child left free to 'grow', to 'develop his individuality', increased.
Provided the child was without interference from the dangerous
adult there at least appeared to be no need for final decisions or
ultimate values. 'Finality,' said O'Neill, 'is a false lure, it is death
in education. Ceaseless change, growth, is the one thing constant.
Aim has taken the place of system and method. "Where are we
going?" must be our cry.'[131] We must become conscious, said
Josephine Ransom, who carefully studied 'the schools of to-morrow', of that spirit 'which is eternally engaged in the discovery of
vaster horizons, and can therefore brook no particular and limited
view for very long.'[132] 'We could tell you what our theories were
three years ago,' said Miss Potter of the Caldecott Community, 'but

we cannot say what they will be to-morrow, nor dogmatise on our methods of to-day.'[133] The 'present cataclysm' had been powerful enough, Caldwell Cook thought, to 'break the old habits of thought, to clear away the obscuring mists of prejudice, self-sufficiency, and hypocrisy' but the same process of scarifying would again be needed unless a solution to the world's ills could be found. He decided: 'I can neither make clear to myself what I believe, nor teach another what he shall believe. All I can hope to do by my art is to get others to bring their imaginative powers into play, to make them gods of their own.'[134] 'It is ... taken for granted,' said Holmes, 'that growth is in itself a good thing, a move in the right direction; and that to foster growth, to make its conditions as favourable as possible, to give it the food, the guidance, and the stimulus that it needs, is the best thing that education can do for the child.'[135]

Montessori, despite her firm religious convictions, thought along similar lines for she believed that the remedy for the 'scholastic slavery' and mismanagement of education was 'to enfranchise human development'.[136] Neill disliked Montessori but believed, of course, that the child should be left alone partly, it seems, because Neill himself did not know what he wanted to pass on to the child:[137]

> We must hand on what we have learned to the children, but we must do it without comment. We must not say: "This is right", because we don't know what is right: we must not say: "This is wrong", because we don't know what is wrong. The most we should do is to tell a child our experience.

Unlike Neill, Sheila Radice was fond of Montessori and confident that she had produced the solution to most educational problems but, like Neill, she was convinced that too much adult direction only produced trouble. The teacher should stand aside and 'not confuse them with dark counsels'.[138]

'Dark counsels', the 'tyranny of adulthood', 'adult interference', knowledge that was 'desiccated, minced and peptonised', adults who were 'unworthy models' or 'grey-beard loons' responsible for the sorry state of Western civilization—so the progressives wrote, and betrayed their own uncertainties, and disenchantment with the world they and their fathers had made.

Progressive thought, however unsatisfactory for a philosopher, held distinct advantages for missionaries—it provided an ideology, a set of ideas, so firmly held as to defy doubt, which led to and justified a programme of action. If it had this value only it would have been powerful—but it had a deeper appeal. The progressives were not only missionaries but latter-day romantics who escaped with their small schools into the English countryside where, sometimes, it is still possible to believe that the industrial revolution has not happened. Like William Blake and his successors they were anguished by the machine's despoiling of society and by humanity's inhumanity. Their belief in the child, in freedom, individuality and growth was at once a rejection of their own civilization and an expression of hope for the future. A cold theory cannot carry so deeply emotional a weight and for the ten years after 1914 this small group of educators were the captives, and the purveyors, of a myth.

Georges Sorel had more important people in mind when he wrote of myths but his words apply to the progressives. Speaking of those 'anticipations of the future' which 'take the form of ... myths' he remarked that a myth could enclose 'all the strongest inclinations of a people, of a party or of a class, inclinations which recur to the mind with the insistence of instincts'. These myths, he believed, 'give an aspect of complete reality to the hopes of immediate action by which, more easily than by any other method, men can reform their desires, passions and mental activity.'[139] Upon such a reforming the progressives were set. Like many who have come to believe, they would not rest until they had acquainted others with the good news.

4

Spreading the good news, 1926-1939

L. P. Jack tells[1] of how, at an education conference in the 1920s when the eminent chairman had finished summing up, one of the audience,

> a hard-bitten schoolmaster by the look of him, sprang to his feet in the middle of the hall, and informed the assembled pundits, in a rather truculent tone, that the main cause of our failures had been overlooked by every one of the speakers. The main cause of failure in our educational system, he said—or rather shouted, for he seemed very angry—was
> 'THE STUPIDITY OF THE PUPIL'.
> and with that he sat down.

And no doubt he sat down satisfied, for conferences in the years between the wars constantly reminded the schoolmaster that schools existed for the child's sake not his, insisted that 'repression' of the natural instincts of the child was to be avoided, and urged him, when a child was troublesome and slow to learn, to examine his own techniques before deciding that the child was to blame. The blunt assertion of a fact which most teachers believe to be true—that some children will defeat the best efforts of the best teachers—seemed an essential corrective to the optimism of the progressives.

The necessity to emphasize so well known a fact at a teachers' conference is an indication that progressive thought had begun to infiltrate the ranks of the less radical teachers. There were other signs which suggested that the cause was flourishing. New schools continued to be established in the second half of the 1920s and in the 1930s—the Russells, as has already been noted, started Beacon Hill in 1927, Dartington began the previous year, and the first

Steiner school the year before that. The *New Era* was always able to report new schools and new experiments. Books continued to discuss their activities. Dorothy Revel's *Cheiron's Cave* appeared in 1928 and *Tented Schools* in 1934. In that year also L. B. Pekin published *Progressive Schools* and Trevor Blewitt, *The Modern Schools Handbook*. When Dover Wilson, in educational matters a conservative, produced *The Schools of England* in 1928 and confined himself to the established order, he was taken to task by F. A. Cavenagh:[2]

> there is a sufficient number of little schools run on 'progressive' or 'modern' lines—'freak schools', as many people would call them—to warrant inclusion, whilst the experiments carried out in many of them are of real value to the national system.

The New Education Fellowship expanded and grew in influence in England and abroad, new Neill books appeared regularly and even government reports showed signs of being affected. The new ideals, according to E. Salter Davies in 1932,[3]

> are, for the first time, beginning to permeate the great body of teachers, and to find realisation not only in what are called 'pioneer schools' but in varying forms and in varying degrees in the schools of the people.

There were many who agreed with Salter Davies: 'a complete revolution in many infant departments', 'elementary education is not only a pleasanter and more humane, but a far more effective process', 'new era in education opening out before us', 'the many minor changes that have ... taken place have but served to swell the common current that has been heading steadily towards freedom and individualism.' So wrote informed educationists such as Lillian de Lissa, F. H. Spencer, C. W. Bailey and P. B. Ballard, and clearly very many of their contemporaries agreed with them.[4]

Historians have echoed their views. The testimony of some, Herbert Ward, Charles Birchenough, W. O. Lester Smith and H. C. Dent, is of double interest—not only do they write on the history of this period, they also played a part in making it.[5] Other historians less immediately involved have agreed that the period was one of reform, of remaking and transformation.[6]

The forces of change

Missionaries are inclined to be optimistic about the number of their converts and the extent of their influence. The progressives were no exception—for, as has already been pointed out, the period from the mid-twenties to the outbreak of World War II probably saw the progressives' enthusiasm dampened and their momentum decreased. Yet it is true that, despite the obstacles (which will be examined in the next chapter), the progressives did make some progress. They succeeded in having important changes made and they gained considerable support. It is worth examining the nature of the support and the advances it enabled the progressives to make.

First, support came from a number of thinkers whose work was not in origin educational. There was, for example, William Mc-Dougall. This exceptionally talented psychologist was born in Lancashire in 1871, graduated from Manchester in science and from Cambridge after studying physiology, anatomy and anthropology, and in 1894 qualified in medicine at St Thomas's Hospital, London. His work as a psychologist in London and Oxford was carried out under conditions he found unsatisfactory and often in the face of criticism. He left for America in 1920 where he spent the rest of his teaching life. He published prolifically, though his most important book (for present purposes at any rate) *An Introduction to Social Psychology*, appeared in 1908, relatively early in his career; it was reprinted at the rate of an edition a year for twenty years and was still popular in the 1930s.

McDougall claimed that the department of psychology of most importance for the social sciences was that 'which deals with the springs of human action, the impulses and motives that sustain mental and bodily activity and regulate conduct'.[7] He was himself quite clear about 'the springs of human action':

> directly or indirectly the instincts are the prime movers of all human activity; by the conative or impulsive force of some instinct (or of some habit derived from an instinct), every train of thought, however cold and passionless it may seem, is borne along towards its end, and every bodily activity is initiated and sustained.

Without instincts the human organism 'would lie inert and motionless like a wonderful clockwork whose mainspring had been removed or a steam-engine whose fires had been drawn.'[8] Reason could aid in 'determining what is good, and in deducing from our knowledge of the good conclusions as to what actions are right'; but it did not initiate action. McDougall argued that 'unless a

man already hungers for righteousness, already desires to do whatever is right, to be whatever is virtuous, unless, that is, he possesses
the moral sentiments and moral character, reason cannot impel
him to do right or to desire it.'[9]

What were these instincts upon which human activity was
based? McDougall complained that contemporaries used terms
such as 'instinct' or 'instinctive' 'so loosely that they have almost
spoilt them for scientific purposes',[10] though his own usage was
by no means beyond criticism.[11] His best known, and most formal
definition,[12] described an instinct as

> an inherited or innate psycho-analytical disposition which deter-
> mines its possessor to perceive, and to pay attention to, objects
> of a certain class, to experience an emotional excitement of a
> particular quality upon perceiving such an object, and to act in
> regard to it in a particular manner, or, at least, to experience an
> impulse to such action.

McDougall viewed each instinct as being tied to a corresponding
emotion—for example, with the instinct of curiosity went the
emotion of wonder, and with pugnacity the emotion of anger. He
produced a classification of instincts and emotions which was
widely studied and often severely criticized. The many efforts made
to clarify McDougall's theories or modify or refute them need not
concern us. His importance for education lay in his insistence that
the behaviour of human beings was, without exception, determined
by instinctive impulses; 'all the complex intellectual apparatus of
the most highly developed mind is but ... the instrument by which
these impulses seek their satisfactions.'[13]

Although *An Introduction to Social Psychology* was published in
1908, was an immediate success and known to educationists before
1914, it was most popular in educational circles during the 1920s
and 30s. It is clear that McDougall's views, especially those of the
Social Psychology, were accepted by most educational psychologists
and theoreticians in this period. Nunn, speaking of McDougall and
A. F. Shand (another who stressed the role of instinct), claimed that
they had thrown 'a flood of new light upon the genesis and laws
of development of human behaviour'; thus, though they had said
little about education directly, they were 'among the main pillars
of modern pedagogy'.[14] In 1936 C. W. Valentine, then professor of
education at Birmingham and an important educational psychologist in his own right, stated that McDougall's view on instinct and

emotion was 'widely accepted by educational writers' and reflected in 'much of the post-war literature on education'.[15] Speaking more generally, James Drever, whose work at Edinburgh gained him a wide reputation, reported that the McDougall concept of instinct 'has been hailed with something akin to enthusiasm by the great majority of those who are practically concerned with human psychology, doctors, teachers, and preachers more particularly, as not merely helpful, but illuminating'.[16] Certainly most of the respectable and influential educational psychologists and theorists of this period (people such as Cyril Burt, Godfrey Thomson, R. B. Cattell, Olive Wheeler and R. R. Rusk) accepted McDougall's view that behaviour was derived from the instincts.[17] Not only psychologists but the writers of the most influential textbooks accepted this view. Nunn's, the most important of them, was avowedly based on McDougall's theories—though, of course, not on them alone. In fact the intellectual relationship between the two men was close. Nunn chose the term 'hormic' to describe instinct psychology because it captured the purposive quality of the theory and McDougall accepted it saying that he was 'following the suggestion of Professor T. P. Nunn in his very excellent little book, "Education, Its Data and First Principles"'.[18] Other books widely read among teachers, especially the important ones by Sturt and Oakden and Hughes and Hughes, also found a use for his ideas. And that most respectable of documents, the 1931 Hadow Report (The Primary School) fell back on McDougall.[19] Fred Clarke, who succeeded Nunn as Director of the London Institute in 1936 and consistently opposed his stress on 'individuality', recognized the enemy in McDougall and set about attacking his views on instinct.[20] There was, therefore, every reason to conclude, as E. G. S. Evans did when he studied the development of educational psychology in the twenties and thirties, that 'the theory which ... exercised the greatest influence on British educationists was that of William McDougall'.[21]

Yet though most of the textbook writers discussed this theory and some even tried to draw up their own list of instincts, McDougall's importance did not lie in inspiring teachers to put his theories into practice. More typical was the reaction of Ward and Roscoe who wrote in 1928 that the teacher 'need not be greatly concerned with theories of instinct, or attempt deliberately to encourage some instincts as such and to control others. It is enough for him to know that in fact children are curious and inquisitive.

that they show fear and timidity'.[22] Of course, not all took the stuffing out of the doctrine so completely but few attempted to use it to give specific direction to their classroom activities.

Probably McDougall's contribution was to support the theories and practices of the progressives rather than form them in any direct way. When he said that 'mankind is only a little bit reasonable and to a great extent very unintelligently moved in quite unreasonable ways',[23] he was expressing a view which met a ready acceptance from people shocked by the ultimate irrationality of war and disgusted with the values of their own civilization. McDougall helped to explain their plight and even to suggest possibilities for improvement. For, so the progressives argued and McDougall was taken as reinforcing their views, education by too exclusive a concentration on the intellect had neglected the emotions from which behaviour sprang. The 'book' had ruled. 'We have made a fetish of knowledge in the past,' said Alice Woods, 'and it will be very hard to replace it'.[24] She placed some hope in the arts and crafts—as did many others who allowed themselves to slip perilously close to anti-intellectualism as they exalted 'hearts not heads in the school'.[25]

'Why this everlasting slavery to books?' asked Caldwell Cook. 'It is not knowledge we store in books, it is ourselves we bury; for we do not use our book as an encouragement, a test, or a diversion; we make it the very prop and mainstay of our lives.'[26] Neill was still more direct:[27]

> During the last few decades education has been almost wholly intellectual and material; intellectual education gave us the don, and material education gave us the cotton-spinner. The emotional and the spiritual in mankind had no outlet. In the unconscious of man there is a God and a Devil, and intellectual activities afford no means of expression to either. And when any godlike or devilish libido can find no outlet it regresses to infantile primitive forms; thus, while the brain of man was concerned with mathematics and logic, the heart of man was seeking primitive things —cruelty, hate, and blood.

It was by justifying this sort of attitude, by providing support for the progressives' efforts to break with the old mechanical ways that McDougall made his most important contribution. Even if they could not agree on the list of instincts, even if they did not care at all what the list was, even if they did not bother to deduce precise educational consequences from McDougall's theories, the progressives could claim that their general position was supported by the best known English psychologist of the period. As Nunn concluded:[28]

> the comparative fruitlessness of so much educational effort is mainly due to neglect of the feelings which are the proximate sources of human energy, the real springs of educational progress whether in learning or in conduct ...

Because they were trying to atone for this neglect by allowing the child 'freedom to develop', by removing adult constraints which restricted his growth, by stressing art, drama and literature, the progressives felt that they qualified for McDougall's blessing.

An even better known psychologist, who suffered from the twin disabilities of being foreign and of advancing views which 'collide rather violently with certain English prejudices',[29] had a similar value. As the formation of the London Society of Psychoanalysis by Ernest Jones in 1913 showed, Freudian ideas were making ground in England before the war; after the war writers such as Wilfred Trotter, W. H. R. Rivers, William Brown, J. C. Flugel, J. A. Hadfield, C. W. Valentine, Crichton Miller and A. G. Tansley helped to make him better known. None of these was a strict Freudian and some English analysts, Melanie Klein is a conspicuous example, were considered by the devout Freudians to be decidedly unorthodox. Yet there is little doubt that in the twenties and thirties Freud's ideas were making a considerable impact. Certainly Freud encountered in England the problems he met in other countries: disbelief at the outlandishness of interpreting dreams, distress at his gloomy view of humanity, concern at the fanatical zeal of his disciples, the worry that he based too much on pathological cases, his preoccupation with sex, his 'gruesome theory of the "Oedipus-complex"' (to use Nunn's words).[30] But as Adams remarked, 'psycho-analysis has been the subject of endless lectures up and down the country and a subject of debate at all manner of conferences of teachers.' The 'intelligent practical teacher,' he thought, 'who keeps abreast of educational literature, cannot but be affected by the prevailing discussion of ... psychology.'[31]

At any time the number of teachers who are fully abreast of the literature is probably small, though at this time there were some who had taken notice of Freud. Lane, Susan Isaacs and Neill are examples, even if they interpreted him in odd ways. And even if they were not well acquainted with the literature teachers were ready enough to discuss Freud. Inevitably most of the discussion centred around psychoanalysis itself—what was its value to the teacher? Should he undergo analysis himself? What was the value of self-analysis? What did psychoanalysis reveal about the child?[32] Usually it was decided that teachers should understand the principles of psychoanalysis but not practise it—that was 'entirely beyond the province of the teacher and ... a task for the specialist.'[33] Perhaps they might study children's dreams, which C. W. Kimmins, the London County Council inspector, considered 'throw much light on the special interests and desires of the child';[34] they might even attempt the popular task of self-analysis. Certainly the self-respecting teacher would have had that acquaintance with Freudian terminology which was essential for anyone with intellectual pretensions and which could be acquired without going to the trouble of reading the original. But few combined, as Susan Isaacs did, a thorough grasp of Freudian theory and practice and a determination to put it to work in the classroom. Teachers were no better versed in Freudian lore than other Englishmen of the period for whom the master's teachings could be summarized in Oscar Wilde's words: 'Never resist temptation.'

> Such was the Freudian gospel as it filtered down into people's minds, through translations, interpretations, glosses, popularizations, and general loose discussion. 'Intriguing' new technicalities were bandied across the tea-cups or the Mah-Jong table: 'inferiority complex', 'sadism', 'masochism', 'agoraphobia', 'sublimination' (which got mixed up with 'sublimation'), 'id', 'ego', 'libido' ... the *Daily News* commented ... 'We are all psychoanalysts now, and know that apparently innocent dreams are the infallible signs of the most horrible neuroses ...'[35]

Teachers were not so flippant and certainly their textbooks were more solemn, but superficiality in their understanding of Freud was evident. Nevertheless, especially by the outbreak of World War II when the initial shock caused by Freud's ideas had been reduced, his work was seen as confirming, in the same general way as McDougall's, the educational practices of the progressives.

A protest of Ernest Jones's gives an indication of the manner in which the Freudian influence worked. It was, he said, in 1935, 'sheer nonsense to say that psycho-analysis says "a child should not be repressed" '[36] but there were many who were ready to say it—and to give to technical terms such as 'repressed' simple and popular meanings which reinforced the progressives' call for a freer discipline and a more permissive attitude to children. Thus:[37]

> parents and teachers should realise the grave dangers of repression. The attempt to force all children into a mould, without regard to the individuality of each, is foredoomed to failure. And not only will such attempts fail: in some cases they will cause serious harm.

The belief in 'enforced control' was, according to Crichton Miller, 'largely the projection of the distrust of our own unconscious energies'.[38] The *New Era* was still more positive: 'suppression of any kind', it announced, 'is dangerous.'[39]

The progressives and their followers were quick to draw the pedagogical consequences of such beliefs. Some, Lane, Neill, Susan Isaacs, T. J. Faithfull at Priory Gate and Dorothy Revel, for example, often drew from Freud's theories specific and elaborate methodological conclusions. But though this direct influence should not be ignored, his most valuable contribution was the support he gave (or at least appeared to give) to the movement as a whole. Thus Norman MacMunn concluded, 'The believers in a great extension of freedom for the child owe much gratitude to the new study of psychoanalysis',[40] and Nunn wrote:[41]

> It is, in fact, unquestionable that the records of psycho-analysis greatly strengthen the argument for making the autonomous development of the individual the central aim of education. They reveal in what dim depths the foundations of individuality are laid, how endlessly varied are its natural forms, and how disastrous it may sometimes be to force upon the growing character a form discordant with its principle of unity.

Others were more specific. C. W. Kimmins praised Montessori for an approach in accordance with the new principles, Drever wanted to review 'the whole question of punishment' in the light of the new psychological knowledge, Olive Wheeler thought that the need for a more sympathetic discipline was 'deducible from the new views of personality'.[42] Psychologists with no close connection with education, J. C. Flugel for example, argued (in 1935) that the findings of the psychoanalysts afforded 'welcome support to the general position' which the reformers had adopted.[43] This support for the 'general position' was of great value to the progressive for it enabled them to benefit from the intellectual initiative which Freud had seized.

They also benefited from the work of another group—that group which aimed to make the study and practice of education more 'scientific'. Quantification, research, experiment, laboratory hypothesis, proof—the almost magical words rang out, promising firmness and certainty, the standard that is 'independent of private opinion'.[44]

Nunn warned against the 'disposition to suppose that laboratory experiments and the measurement of correlations can and should supply the whole basis of educational procedure', but he admitted that education must 'accept increasingly scientific regulation'.[45] Others were less cautious. 'It is the experimental approach', said Cyril Burt, one of its most prominent practitioners, 'which, more than any other, has turned psychology into a reliable branch of science.'[46] R. R. Rusk, another prominent in this field, believed that when the teacher's technique 'is based on research, teaching will no longer be regarded as one of the black arts, but will assume the status not of a dismal science, but of a progressive and enlightened procedure.'[47] Education, like any self-respecting but not highly respected field of study, was aspiring to that certainty and solidity of result which other areas of human endeavour appeared to have.

The aspiration was not new, even in England. As early as 1875 a society to study the 'Science of Education' had been established, by 1901 the British Association for the Advancement of Science had admitted education to its ranks, and ten years later J. A. Green founded the *Journal of Experimental Pedagogy*. Child-study societies were active, though not numerous, before the outbreak of World War I and certain English workers—for example, Galton, Burt, Karl Pearson and Spearman—made important contributions. After the war the work continued.[48] A committee for research in education was founded by the British Psychological Society in 1922 with Susan Isaacs (then Mrs Brierley) as secretary. Its function was advisory as it did not wish or could not afford to employ research workers. Despite some important contributions in the inter-war years, there is little doubt that the original English research work was less than the American. Susan Isaacs reported in 1925 that the enquiries of her committee had shown that 'the amount of research being done is small'.[49] A year earlier Percy Nunn had reached a similar conclusion and seven years later R. R. Rusk, then director of the Scottish Council for Research in Education, indicated that the situation had not improved.[50] Yet though the English did not lead the field, the new 'research work' (to use a phrase which the search for a scientific approach brought into the educationist's vocabulary) had an important impact. Its range was wide: for example, fatigue, memorization, tests of intelligence and attainment, methods of teaching, examinations, learning theory, child development and, of course (and wearisomely), transfer of training.[51] As happens in any new field of study premature claims were made and solutions confidently advanced which later had to be withdrawn. But despite its difficulties and embarrassment the work continued and became another source of support for the progressives. Unmistakably the educational textbooks of the period—those of Nunn, the Hughes combination, C. W. Valentine, Ballard, T. A. Raymont, Olive Wheeler or Godfrey Thomson for example—saw the scientific approach as confirming the views of the progressives, not necessarily in detail but certainly in general terms.

This confirmation was useful because the scientific approach brought to education the appearance (and sometimes the substance) of a professionalism and objectivity which had previously been lacking. The new psychology was more than the guesswork of gifted and prejudiced amateurs; it produced 'findings', confirmed or disproved 'hypotheses', gathered 'data', 'quantified'. To the enthusiastic idealist pushing his nostrum with zeal and persistence there could now be opposed the cold, organized scientist—perhaps a dreary and pedestrian man, even self-righteous, but because he was detached, more likely to be right. 'Research has shown', 'the findings of this experiment', 'an intelligence quotient of'—so the stern words went, distancing the opinions of the progressives from the strange group of missionaries who had begun to preach them. 'A scientist who is concerned to discover permanent elements in human conduct', wrote T. A. Raymont in 1930 with the work of the educationist firmly in mind, 'is not concerned to judge the actions which spring from these elements in terms of the morality current at his own day.'[52] Or, as James Drever put it:[53]

> To the chemist, so far as he is a chemist, lead is as interesting as gold. Similarly to the psychologist a bad act is on precisely the same footing as a good act, as regards its value ... psychology knows only cause and effect; it has nothing to do with ideals, values, purposes, and ends, except as mere facts of the mental life.

Thus when the textbooks said, as they frequently did, that one or another progressive practice was in accord with the findings of the psychologist or the educational research worker, they said something important—the enthusiastic missionary could claim the support of the detached scientist.

Of course the relationship between the research worker and progressive ideas or practice was more ambiguous, as can be seen by looking at the work of one of the most distinguished and influential of the scientific educationists, Susan Isaacs. Two of her most important works, *Intellectual Growth in Young Children* (1930) and *Social Development of Young Children* (1933), drew on the observations she had made at the Malting House School and she claimed that these were 'direct and dispassionate observations, recorded as fully as possible under the conditions; and as free as possible from evaluations and interpretations.' However, she realized that the detachment implied by this statement was not possible of achievement and she stated why: 'the material was gathered in a school, not in a laboratory'.[54] Even as an observer, neutrality would not have been possible, for despite all her care, she recorded only a very small number of the events that happened in the school during the four years she was there; and the choosing of certain facts rather than others presupposes decisions as to what was worth recording. And even if neutrality as an observer could have been guaranteed, it was impossible for a teacher. As a teacher Susan Isaacs had to make the day-to-day decisions involved in running a school and, in making them, she did what she thought best for the children. For example, she began her work believing that non-interference was the best policy when stronger boys tyrannized smaller ones. But 'a very short experience with a group of aggressive boys of uneven powers of self-defence made the issues perfectly clear': 'firm interference' was necessary.[55] As teacher she had acted sensibly: faced with a problem she weighed the arguments, came to a decision and took the action she thought best for the children. However, by doing so, her work as observer was seriously disturbed. The observer tried to avoid interpretation and 'evaluatory or summarising phrases, such as "the children were very interested—polite—quarrelsome"'; to an observer in search of 'full objective records'[56] children do not 'bully' or 'tyrannize'—they simply act in certain ways which one tries to describe accurately. But to a teacher they fight, and have to be stopped; a teacher is forced to be a judge. As teacher, therefore, Susan Isaacs influenced what she observed; she could see only what she permitted herself to see—that is, Susan Isaacs, the detached scientist, could observe only what Susan Isaacs, the dedicated teacher, thought should happen.

And Susan Isaacs, the teacher, had a definite set of values. She had decided that the usual curriculum should be abandoned in favour of informal activities, that the teacher should keep in the background, that children should work in ways which expressed their interests, that certain behaviour was unacceptable. She ran a particular school that had opted for a particular set of values, a 'progressive' school.

The work done at the Malting House School had many values. It deepened Susan Isaacs's insight into the behaviour of young children, it enabled her to develop her theories of child growth and to show that, at least under the circumstances her school provided, children did not always fit the pattern of development suggested by Piaget. But to view the Malting House endeavour as a cold and detached investigation which resulted in the confirmation of certain hypotheses is clearly to oversimplify. She was not concerned simply to put particular ideas and practices to the test, she also wanted to put them into action; she had first to believe in them enough to make them work before she could justify a detached examination of the effects of their working. She had to do the impossible. Being Susan Isaacs she did it very well, but even her best could not convince. She might say that 'if we watch him when he is free to play as he will, the child shows us all that he is wishing and fearing, all that he is pondering over and aiming to do', and claim that this opinion was derived from 'the knowledge and judgement of a great many observers ... pooled in scientific study'. But the opinion was not only a conclusion reached as the result of 'the scientific study of the behaviour of young children', it was also a belief which preceded the study and, indeed, partly motivated it.[57]

With the possible exception of the work on 'mental testing' there were few more influential manifestations of the desire to make education scientific than the studies of child development—of which (in the 1920s and 30s at any rate) Susan Isaacs provided the best, and the best known, English example. All the workers in this field faced her problem of trying to be detached, objective and 'scientific' in a study where value-judgments are impossible to avoid. Probably few of them were as aware as she of the difficulties they faced. But whether they were aware of them or not, and however inadequately they faced them if they were aware, many concluded that the new 'scientific' approach to education supported the progressives' ideas. It was valuable support, for it enabled the progressives to share vicariously in the prestige of science. When to this there was added the support of Freud and McDougall, the atmosphere among psychologists and especially among educational psychologists was favourable.

The educational philosophers

What Freud and McDougall were to the educational psychologists, John Dewey was to the philosophers. In the United States he played a dominant part in the progressive movement, though he could not prevent it from developing habits of which he disapproved.[58] In England, too, he was important. The educational theorists of the twenties and thirties, writers such as Nunn, Findlay, Olive Wheeler, Godfrey Thomson, R. R. Rusk and T. A. Raymont all knew of Dewey, all referred to him respectfully even if they disagreed with him, all invoked his support for their ideas. There is no doubt that Dewey mattered and that being able to link his name with their educational practices was of assistance to the 'progressives', whose very name was probably borrowed from their American counterparts.

Dewey's fame, his undoubted influence in the United States and the respect he was accorded by English theorists may, however, have led to exaggerated estimates of his influence on English education at this time. In fact, Dewey does not seem to have greatly influenced the reformers who were at work in the ten years after 1914. Susan Isaacs was, of course, an exception and so was Helen Parkhurst, but Holmes, Neill, O'Neill, Lane, Montessori, Caldwell Cook, Beatrice Ensor, Ernest Westlake and their like relied very little on him for inspiration. Furthermore the textbooks of the period, while respectful, show no signs that Dewey's ideas had deeply penetrated the minds of their writers. Exceptions can again be found—in the work of Findlay for example; but in that most important of textbooks, *Education: Its data and first principles*, Dewey is almost completely ignored—while McDougall's presence is quite unmistakable. Nunn does say that Dewey's *School and Society* 'is a powerful plea for basing the education even of young children upon the study of the essential arts and occupations',[59] but he says it in a footnote. There are only two other references to Dewey in the book, both in bibliographical notes. Other theorists such as T. A. Raymont, Olive Wheeler and Godfrey Thomson made more use of Dewey than Nunn did, but he is rarely accorded the attention he received in the United States. The books on educational method (for example, those by W. G. Sleight, M. Sturt and E. C. Oakden, H. Ward and F. Roscoe, H. C. Barnard and A. G. and E. H. Hughes) are respectful, prepared to quote Dewey if it suits their purpose, but not markedly influenced by him. There is evidence that Dewey had some influence on the writers of the Consultative Committee's report, *The Primary School*, but it is inconclusive.[60] Godfrey Thomson in 1929 stated:[61]

> In Great Britain, except in Scotland ... I have been repeatedly struck by the absence of references to Dewey's ideas and sometimes by evidence of complete ignorance of them, although the same views in other dress are often mentioned in their practical aspect.

Probably Thomson overstated the case but at least his remark should prevent too swift an acceptance of the claims made for Dewey's influence. Surprisingly few of the theorists or textbook writers were closely acquainted with his work and, when references are made to him, they are to the earlier books, *School and Society* and *The Child and the Curriculum*, not to *Democracy and Education* (1918). The former are closer to the practical problems of the classroom and more accessible than the difficult, sometimes convoluted, reasoning of Dewey's most famous book. On the whole, the English were too pragmatic to be pragmatists.

Those who wrote on the philosophy of education did not allow their comparative coolness towards Dewey to turn them against progressive education as the English understood it. However, they approached it in a different way, most of them beginning from an assumption which Bertrand Russell made explicit: 'The education we desire for our children must depend on our ideals of human character, and our hopes as to the part they are to play in the community.'[62] More formally, R. R. Rusk said in 1928:[63]

> The answer to every educational question is ultimately influenced by our philosophy of life. Although few formulate it, every system of education must have an aim, and the aim of education is relative to the aim of life. Philosophy formulates what it conceives to be the end of life; education offers suggestions how this end is to be achieved.

This conception of the relationship between education and philosophy would, these days, be seriously challenged, but in the late 1920s and 30s it was accepted by almost all who wrote on education.[64] Its very commonness led to a widespread difficulty: linking education closely to philosophy meant importing all the disagreements about what men conceived 'the end of life' to be.

H. G. Stead wrote in 1936 that, since the war, 'there has been a bewildering loss of faith in nearly every sphere of thought.' He believed that 'a spiritual hunger and a home-sickness of soul beset to-day the whole human race' and he argued that what was needed 'amid the chaos of a stunned and bewildered world' was 'the *force of an ideal*'.[65] The trouble was that nobody could agree as to what this ideal should be. Findlay thought that 'there will be as many aims for education, as many ideals for the development of the young, as there are teachers to foster the ideals.'[66] Or as Nunn had said,

> any educational aims which are concrete enough to give definite guidance are correlative to ideals of life—and, as ideals of life are eternally at variance, their conflict will be reflected in educational theories.

According to Nunn there were some who thought that the resulting differences 'were too radical to be harmonized and too serious to be exposed to the public view.'[67]

Of course they were exposed. The educational philosophers were involved in an intellectual dilemma of the most critical kind—for what was at stake was the credibility of reason itself. The generation which fought World War I had, as E. L. Woodward pointed out, been faced with challenges to its most firmly held beliefs. The horrors of war intensified these challenges and even, as we saw with the progressives, led to doubts about the rationality of man. But at least the challenge was made against remembered certainties. 'We carried with us,' Woodward said, 'through doubts and enquiries a conviction that human society could be established on a rational basis; we could not accept a defeatism of the intellect turned against itself.' Thus they could continue to observe conventions 'which meant nothing to us save that it had been our habit to observe them.' The generation that had come to maturity in the 1920s and 30s was totally alien to Woodward. 'To them the changes and confusion did not mark the shifting of boundaries on an old map. There were no boundaries, no maps.' And what was worse the chance of creating maps was being lessened, for 'the most ingenious and subtle developments in philosophy and psychology were attacking the very citadel of man's confidence in himself.'[68] Reason itself was being brought into discredit.

This seemed evident to many of Woodward's contemporaries as they watched countries abandon their efforts to walk the tightrope of political democracy which called for restraint, tolerance and respect for reason and march down the broader roads of totalitarianism—whether of the right as in Germany, Italy and Spain or of the left as in Russia. In June 1919 Rutherford published his account of 'the first artificial transformation of matter' and as his work became more popularly known its impact began to shake severely the old views of causation. In May of the same year Einstein's predictions were verified and, as A. N. Whitehead related, the Astronomer Royal announced the result of the fateful observations while 'in the background the picture of Newton [was there] to remind us that the greatest of scientific generalisations was now, after more than two centuries, to receive its first modification.'[69] The upset to the Newtonian world view was significant in itself but as 'relativity' passed into the popular vocabulary its meaning was extended and coarsened. 'Everything was relative'; values, opinions, beliefs were shaken still further. 'Applied to morals,' Beatrice Ensor said, 'this Law [of relativity] will revolutionize our ideas'.[70] Nothing was to remain firm or fixed. Thus when an educationist struggled in 1927 to decide what was best for children—and gave up, the chairman commented, 'I noticed, although he did not mention the word, that the doctrine of relativity ran through the whole thing.'[71]

Philosophers generally (but not, at this time, educational philosophers) retreated from their ambitious hope 'to unify completely, bring into clear coherence, all departments of rational thought' (in Henry Sidgwick's words) to the more limited function of 'under-labourers in the garden of knowledge' concerned to clean up, set boundaries, and clarify, but not to build systems.[72] The higher hopes had not been fulfilled. Sociologists and anthropologists (in England, especially Malinowski) struck further blows: the proper study of mankind might have been man but the more he was studied, and especially in the differing circumstances in which the anthropologists found him, the more he seemed the captive of his own conventions. Natural law or even universally applicable laws appeared more and more dubious. Ruth Benedict, whose *Patterns of Culture* summarized for many the new views, warned against too simple a belief in 'the uniformity of human behaviour' and asked her readers to take into account 'cultural relativity'. They should not impose a super-cultural or super-human set of standards; instead men should accept 'the co-existing and *equally valid pat-*

terns of life which mankind has created for itself from the raw materials of existence.'[73] Reason, it seemed, was not a cool calculating machine which produced the same answer to the same question anywhere and at any time. How one acted depended in part on geography: what was abhorred in Manchester was approved and put into practice in Melanesia. More profoundly Karl Mannheim, struggling to advance the sociology of knowledge, argued that there were 'modes of thought' which could not be understood 'as long as their social origins are obscured' for, though only individual men could think, no man was truly an individual: 'He speaks the language of his group; he thinks in the manner in which his group thinks. He finds at his disposal only certain words and their meanings.'[74] Yet, if this were true (as indeed it appeared to be) how could one be sure that any piece of reasoning was truly objective? Was it not conditioned, and therefore limited and perhaps warped, by the social experiences of its propounder? Might not an apparently sound and objective judgment, if seen from another social perspective, be simply a piece of culture-bound special pleading?

While some were worrying at the limitations on human reasoning which followed from man being a social animal, Freud, his fellow analysts and their popularizers, seemed to undermine reason's citadel from within. When Crichton Miller wrote that 'The tendency to externalize and objectify a problem is a characteristic of primitive thinking, and it is an anachronism to which there is a constant temptation to return,'[75] he was, whether he meant to or not (and whether Freud meant him to or not), causing many to doubt the very possibility of the old concept of a rational man. A. G. Tansley's study of psychoanalysis, which Ernest Jones praised highly, pointed out that

> When we give a wrong account of the causes which have led to an action it is generally the case that we have unconsciously 'faked' a set of 'reasons' on grounds that appeal to us as 'rational', and put them in the place of the real causes, of which we are unconscious. This process of 'rationalization' is so exceedingly common as to be practically universal.

But it was not only when man was giving the causes of an action that he was unreliable—the place of reason in life generally had been 'absurdly overestimated'.[76] The underworld that psychoanalysis claimed to reveal shook the confidence of many thinkers. Once when a man gave reasons to justify taking a particular decision, he could be argued with—one could say that the reasons were wrong or, if the worst came to the worst, that the man was lying. Now he could be, by all previous standards, honest and yet produce a set of reasons which were not the *real* reasons; for, Ernest Jones had warned, 'we are allowed to know only a part of ourselves that has been carefully selected for the purpose.'[77] Thus, for example, religion, which some had thought a divine revelation and others the opium of the people, was accounted for by 'the mechanism of compensation'.[78] In the years before the outbreak of World War II the questioning of established views came to a climax. What was at stake was not the validity of particular pieces of reasoning, but the possibility of being rational—at least in the old sense of being detached and objective.[79]

Faced by this dilemma some educationists became possessed by a feeling of futility. Education, like life, C. R. Fletcher reflected in 1929, 'is full of uncertainties—at least I have found it so—of doubts as to what we ought to attempt, doubts as to how we ought to try to do what we are doing, and, not least of all, doubts as to whether we are effecting anything that is worth effecting.'[80] Bertrand Russell expressed this mood most poignantly in 1931:[81]

When I survey my life, it seems to me to be a useless one, devoted to impossible ideals. I have not found in the post-war world any attainable ideals to replace those which I have come to think unattainable. So far as the things I have cared for are concerned, the world seems to me to be entering upon a period of darkness ... For my part, I find in the most modern thought a corrosive solvent of the great systems of even the recent past, and I do not believe that the constructive efforts of present-day philosophers and men of science have anything approaching the validity that attaches to their destructive criticism.

My activities continue from force of habit, and in the company of others I forget the despair which underlies my daily pursuits and pleasures. But when I am alone and idle, I cannot conceal from myself that my life had no purpose, and that I know of no new purpose to which to devote my remaining years. I find myself involved in a vast mist of solitude both emotional and metaphysical, from which I can find no issue.

Less sensitive souls reacted similarly. J. H. Nicholson, then professor of education at Newcastle-on-Tyne, lamented that 'we are an uneasy generation, most of us to some extent ill-adjusted to present conditions' and should therefore, he concluded, 'beware of passing on our own prejudices and maladjustments to those we educate.' Furthermore

> We cannot forsee the conditions for which we are educating. We do not know what the society of 1950 will be like. We can only be sure that it will be so different from the society in which we grew up that the traditional wisdom and the traditional attitudes will be a completely inadequate preparation for it.

What should be done? Nicholson suggested an answer: 'We should leave the younger generation free. It will have to make its own decisions in any case and can learn little from our experience.'[82] The answer was similar to one the first progressives had given when, in the years following World War I, they had faced a similar question. Nicholson was not fully satisfied with this answer though others were. Thus Ballard argued, 'we do not know what the future will be. We do not therefore know how to mould these children's minds; and the best thing we can do is not to interfere with them at all. They are simply experiments, and therefore let us merely watch them.'[83]

'Merely watching' is not as simple as it sounds and, if the efforts made by the Malting House School are any indication, may not even be possible. But the policy of non-interference was attractive to the theorists of the 1920s and 30s who had tried and failed to find an accepted set of philosophical truths upon which to base their educational practice. Concepts such as 'growth', 'natural development', 'individuality' and 'freedom' offered these theorists what they had promised the first progressives during and immediately after World War I: the possibility of consensus without the need to specify the final end of the educational process. The result of that specification, they seem to have sensed, would have been another object for the sceptics to attack, and another piece of the intellectual débris which the twentieth century had discarded.

The good news received

The fifteen years before the outbreak of World War II thus brought some consolation to the progressives. Not only did the number of their schools slowly grow, the N.E.F. expand and methods such as the Dalton Plan become more popular, but they gained support from educational theorists and psychologists. Others were working to prepare the ground for the seed the progressives wished to scatter. What were the results of their activities? What gains did the progressives make?

Some progressives ask us to imagine classrooms up and down the country being transformed like those at the Seaside School, Bexhill. When taken over in 1923 by an enthusiast for the Dalton Plan the school was in 'a moribund condition ... it was run on such excessively old-fashioned lines, almost like a museum! The atmosphere seemed absolutely dead, so devoid were the children of life or ideas of their own.' Three years later: 'Well, we have changed all that. Our children are now overflowing with keen enthusiasm about everything.'[84] Such changes did occur, and some of them even survived the first fine careless rapture to become part of the everyday educational world. But the evidence does not suggest that a wholesale conversion of the English primary school to the progressives' ideas took place. There was, however, one significant change: progressive practices might not have been widely adopted in primary-school classrooms but progressive ideas became the established educational theory. By 1939 a substantial majority of opinion leaders worked within the progressives' intellectual orbit. Most of those who wrote books on education, spoke at conferences, produced official reports or sat on important committees, trained teachers, or contributed to the educational journals came to accept progressive views as a basis for their own thinking. Of course all discussion was not controlled by the progressives: many who said things the progressives might have said lacked the fervour of the truly converted; and some attacked the new ideas. But as the twenties and thirties progressed it became clear that the progressives were dictating the terms of the debate: their problems were being discussed, the questions they asked were being answered, the solutions they offered were being accepted or rejected.

Thus the Conference of Educational Associations, a widely representative body on which progressive groups were in a minority, discussed (at its 1927 meeting) 'the teaching of the arts and crafts', 'the new duty of art lovers to the countryside', 'the child in the changing home', 'the evolutionary value of co-education', 'creative education', 'the human aspect of the Dalton Plan', 'woodcraft as an essential in education', 'the place of imagination in the Montessori method' and other topics which would have gladdened a progressive's heart. Conferences in other years were no different. The progressives had the intellectual initiative and, even when they lost battles, could feel that they might still win the war for it was being fought on grounds of their choosing.

In the training institutions (particularly in the colleges but also in the university departments) the progressives obtained a firm foothold. In 1924, writing his history of teacher training, Lance Jones concluded that the training of the teachers of young children had seen 'more appreciation of new ideas and movements' than any other part of the educational field. He continued: 'Freedom, activity, development, happiness, are the key-notes, the details vary and will continue to vary from college to college and school to school.'[85] The allegiance given to these ideas was sincere but sometimes confused: crowded rooms of would-be teachers often listened to lectures bemoaning the inefficiency of lessons to large classes, and students solemnly copied out notes from lectures which extolled 'activity' methods. Yet even if not acted upon, the progressives' views became the most popular views of the training institutions in the inter-war years.

It is not going too far to say that these institutions were a haven for those who sought to spread progressive ideas and methods. Percy Nunn, Godfrey Thomson, James Shelley, C. W. Valentine, E. P. Culverwell the ardent disciple of Montessori, James Drever who publicized many of the psychologists' findings, J. J. Findlay drawing near to the end of a remarkably active and influential career at Manchester, Millicent Mackenzie earnest advocate of freedom, R. J. Fynne another Montessorian, William Boyd, Susan Isaacs, H. R. Hamley who succeeded Susan Isaacs at London, Olive Wheeler, the then Evelyn Lawrence, John Adams, T. A. Raymont, H. Bompas Smith—all worked for considerable periods at universities. Lillian De Lissa, P. E. Cusden and Grace Owen, leading advocates of the nursery school, and Alice Woods, whose early account of the progressive experiments was of some importance, were among those who worked at the colleges, though some of them were to move to universities. From the colleges and universities came the best known and most widely read educational literature of the period: Nunn's *Education*, of course, certainly the book teachers were most likely to have read; but also (to select but a few) W. G. Sleight, *The Organization and Curricula of Schools* (1922), Constance Bloor, *The Process of Learning* (1930), Nancy Catty, *The Theory and Practice of Education* (1934), Mary Sturt and E. C. Oakden, *Matter and Method in Education* (1928), H. Ward and F. Roscoe, *The Approach to Teaching* (1928), F. Smith and A. S. Harrison, *Principles of Class Teaching* (1937) and A. G. and E. H. Hughes, *Learning and Teaching* (1937)—probably, after Nunn's, the most popular of these books. If we add to these the works of writers already mentioned—Adams, Wheeler or Susan Isaacs for example—the contribution of the colleges and universities is clear—though, of course, only a small proportion of it has been mentioned here. The colleges had begun to play the role of interpreter, spreading the progressives' ideas among the new teachers.[86]

There were others outside these places who wrote and worked for the progressives' cause—for example, Ballard, Kimmins and F. S. Marvin were inspectors, H. C. Dent was teacher, headmaster and freelance journalist during this period, A. J. Lynch who worked to publicize the Dalton Plan was a headmaster and Trevor Blewitt and L. B. Pekin, whose writings on progressive schools were of considerable value, were practising teachers. The training institutions (and especially the colleges) gave the lead but they were not alone.

Further evidence of the extent to which progressive ideas had been absorbed into the educational atmosphere came from that group who have no specific educational expertise (at least in the sense that they have made no systematic study of educational theory or practice) but who are listened to on educational matters because their prominence in other fields gains them attention: the people asked to be chairmen of committees or commissions set up by Parliament or political bodies, school managers, the drafters of statements on the educational policy of political parties, business or professional men asked to advise the government on educational issues. Usually such people cannot be called educationists (and often they do not wish to be) yet they often exert a great influence on a wide range of people. Throughout the twenties and thirties this sort of opinion-maker came, increasingly, to put forward progressive views. For example Sir Henry Hadow and R. H. Tawney were both distinguished academics who can be freed from all suspicion of being professional educationists. Hadow was a music critic, a historian of music (who also composed) and, from the end of the war until 1930, vice-chancellor of Sheffield University. His contribution was made while chairman of the Board's Consultative Committee (from 1920 until 1934); he supervised the publication of a series of vital reports of which *The Education* of *the Adolescent* (1926) is usually thought the most important and the one for which the name 'Hadow Report' is most commonly reserved. Tawney, the distinguished historian, is probably best known for *Religion and the Rise of Capitalism*, but he also helped to form Labour's educational policy and to give it its most telling expression through *Secondary Education for All*.

Neither of these men could be called 'progressive', unless the term is stretched beyond meaning. Hadow's policies were guided primarily by administrative considerations and Tawney's by his political beliefs. Understandably they were both concerned above all with practical problems, but when they did turn to theorizing they adopted the progressive idiom. Hadow, for example, thought that Rousseau had 'shifted the centre of gravity in education, and instead of imposing it on the child as a scheme from above, began with the investigation of the child's mind and worked outwards from that.' He had discovered 'the psychological method in education, which begins by endeavouring to find out what the boy or girl is good for.' Froebel and Pestalozzi also obtain favourable mention.[87] Tawney expressed similar views. The achievements of education, he said

> are to be measured primarily by its success in assisting growth, not in imposing discipline or imparting information; and the problem is not to prepare children to fit into the moulds, or to acquire the formulae, thought desirable by the existing generation of adults, but to enable them, when they are children, to be healthy children, in order that when they are men they may define their own attitude to the world for themselves.

Then, bringing his political convictions to bear on his educational theory, he remarked: 'To an educational system which takes as its point of departure, not the social conventions of adults, but the needs of children, the conventional vulgarities of class and income are merely irrelevant.'[88] Progressive ideas were sufficiently prominent in educational debate to be adopted by men who did not have time to forge their own educational vocabularies but who were not satisfied to mouth the conventional pieties.

Minds more rigid than Tawney's or Hadow's also felt the impact of progressive thought. In the period between the wars the Board's official guide to educational practice, the *Suggestions*, became steadily more sympathetic to progressive theory. The 1927 edition, for example, was full of advice which the progressives would have found satisfactory:[89]

> The latter [the teacher] will aim at a discipline which arises naturally from a mutual understanding between himself and his pupils. Such a discipline is free; it is the children's as much as the teacher's; they have accepted it themselves as a reasonable condition of school life and will be disposed to accept it as a reasonable condition of life after leaving school.

> His [the teacher's] starting point must be no rigid syllabus or subject, but the children as they really are: he must work always with the grain of their minds, try never to cut across it.

> Hence the teacher should be constantly striving to bridge the gulf between school conditions and those of the outside world. He can do this only by so planning and adapting his teaching as to bring into play and gradually develop, direct and refine the children's fundamental interests and instincts.

> ... in recent years it has been more and more clearly recognised that children should be allowed to progress through the school at varying rates suited to their individual capacity.

> The characteristic note of recent educational doctrine or practice has been the insistence on the importance of the individual as distinct from the class.

> Self-education should be the key-note of the older children's curriculum, just as free expression is of the youngest children's; but in neither case is it expected that the teacher will abdicate.

The curriculum discussed in the *Suggestions* was not mandatory, though it was influential—hence its changes in emphasis are of importance. A comparison of the *Suggestions* for 1905 and those published in 1937 show that the simple study of 'English' had grown to 'English language and literature'. Grammar was still to be taught but less formally, emphasis to be placed on oral expression; 'reading' had come to include literature and not just reading books and word recognition; drama was more important. Arithmetic in 1905 had become mathematics by 1937 and there was less interest in speed and accuracy in computation and more in the need to understand the basic processes; observation lessons and nature study were replaced by nature study and science; drawing which aimed at 'enabling the scholar to see correctly and to represent accurately any given object' had, by 1937, become art and craft and it was believed that 'the spontaneity, the freshness and vigour which are characteristic of the free expression of young children's drawing and painting should be recognized as of greater importance than an imitative accuracy'; singing had become music and even where the names remained the same, as in history or geography, there were important changes in emphasis and content.[90]

Not only the various editions of the *Suggestions* but the Hadow study of the primary school, published in 1931, gave evidence that the progressives were penetrating into official circles. The primary school, Hadow's committee concluded, would best serve the children's future

> by a single-minded devotion to their needs in the present, and the question which most concerns it is not what children should be—a point on which unanimity has hardly yet, perhaps, been reached—but what, in actual fact, children are.

But though it shared that uncertainty about ends, which we have noticed was common among the progressives, it took up many of the progressive views with vigour and confidence:[91]

> the central consideration, by which the curricula and methods of the primary school must be determined, is the sum of the needs and possibilities of the pupils attending it ...

> A good school, in short, is not a place of compulsory instruction, but a community of old and young, engaged in learning by co-operative experiment.

> ... primary education would gain greatly in realism and power of inspiration if an attempt were more generally made to think of the curriculum less in terms of departments of knowledge to be taught, and more in terms of activities to be fostered and interests to be broadened.

> Education must be regarded not as a routine designed to facilitate the assimilation of dead matter, but as a group of activities by which powers are exercised, and curiosity aroused, satisfied, and again aroused.

The private papers of the Consultative Committee make clearer still the extent to which the progressives' views had penetrated official educational opinion. From Nunn, Burt, the New Education Fellowship and other predictable sources came evidence deeply coloured by progressive thought; but more recalcitrant bodies (such as a committee of the Board's inspectors and the N.U.T.) spoke of the importance of putting the child first, of 'individuality', 'activity', and so on.[92] Those who give evidence to committees of this kind are no doubt more concerned about educational issues than are the ordinary run of teachers, yet this very concern may make them more likely to influence opinion. And there can be no doubt that the submissions made to the Hadow Committee when it was considering the primary school were very much coloured by the progressives' views.

Perhaps it was in the Committee's report, *Infant and Nursery Schools* (1933) that official acceptance of the progressive ideology was most conspicuous. It was evident in the importance given to the discussion of the physical, mental and emotional development of young children and in the admission that Susan Isaacs had been closely consulted on these matters. It was evident also in the sixth chapter of the report in which the Committee came closest to giving a theoretical justification of their views on infant and nursery school education. It was especially evident in the authorities upon which the Committee professed its reliance: Susan Isaacs, of course, but also Montessori (who attended one of the Committee's meetings to explain her ideas and her material), Dewey, Froebel and Pestalozzi, Margaret McMillan and Gesell. The Committee believed that the principles they supported amounted to the 'no new doctrines'; Wordsworth, they argued, had voiced their ideas when he wrote:[93]

Delight and liberty, the simple creed
Of childhood, whether busy or at rest.

Thus, even if school practice had not been radically transformed by 1939, the progressives had made great gains. They had established a firm foothold in the training institutions, especially the colleges; most of the educational theorists and textbook writers espoused their cause; opinion among influential but non-professional educationists, such as Hadow and Tawney, was swinging their way; the official documents reflected their views. They were making the running.

Of course they had not won the race by 1939. There is no evidence to suggest that there had been a wholesale transformation of school practice, though undoubtedly there had been changes. The most prominent feature of the progressive cause, the pioneer schools, still met with suspicion. In 1934, for example, L. B. Pekin reported that they still represented for many people 'an orgy of noise, dirt, bad manners, idleness, blasphemy, free love and anything else that is calculated to cause an apprehensive flutter in the ordinary parental bosom.'[94] Even the less extreme progressives faced the accusation that they were proponents of a 'soft pedagogy'. Furthermore, especially in the late 1930s as parliamentary democracy took defeat after defeat and the clouds of war gathered, the emphasis shifted slightly from the 'individual' and towards 'society' whose rights, so the critics said, Nunn and the progressives had consistently under-played.[95] This change in emphasis was symbolized by the replacement (on his retirement as director of the London Institute) of Nunn by Sir Fred Clarke in 1936. Clarke is reported to have said of himself that he was 'akin to Joshua, the Son of Nun' but, on this issue at least, he differed from his predecessor.[96] The establishment of an Association for Education in Citizenship and the modification of the N.E.F.'s statement of principles to include greater reference to what W. A. C. Stewart has called 'the threat to free peoples everywhere'[97] were further indications of the change in emphasis.

Yet when all allowances have been made it is clear that in the late 1920s and the 1930s the progressives had gained the initiative in educational discussions. They might not, despite the claims of some of their publicists, have radically altered the practices in primary-school classrooms—though they had certainly made an impact. But they had forced their problems to the forefront of the educational debate. Their views found a haven in the colleges and were there passed on to the new generation of teachers. Official documents such as the *Suggestions* and the Hadow Reports showed marked signs of their thinking. They were no longer on the outside of the educational world trying to make their voices heard.

Of course, it is tempting to view the progressive ideas which gained currency in the 1930s as a diluted version of early progressivism. However, it would be unwise to indulge the temptation too freely for, as we have seen, progressivism was never a firm creed and always contained various shades of opinion and practice : it was, so to speak, diluted from the very beginning. Yet documents such as the *Suggestions* or the writings of the Consultative Committee do draw attention to the less radical of the progressive demands—Neill's abrasiveness, Lane's disregard for the conventions, or Montessori's intense dedication are certainly less evident.

But that is to be expected. By the 1930s progressive views were no longer confined to a small ardent group; they had become a semi-public property. The college lecturer who put them forward believed in them—but he was not a missionary obsessed with his gospel, he was a preacher expounding a text.

Like all missionaries the progressives found that in converting the world they transformed themselves.

5
Progressives and the classroom teacher, 1926-1939

In 1918 Caldwell Cook might have symbolized the progressive cause. The war was over, the Perse School was ready to welcome him back, his book had been applauded, his ideas favourably received, he could work in hope. By 1933 the war belatedly claimed him—he suffered a nervous breakdown due in part to shellshock. He never taught at the Perse School again but gradually removed from it the few possessions he had left there and locked himself away in solitude. The man who had hoped by his art 'to get others to bring their imaginative powers into play, to make them gods of their own'[1] now trembled when he heard footsteps approach his house and would admit only a few friends. He died in 1937, broken and disillusioned.

Obviously Caldwell Cook cannot symbolize the progressivism of the 1930s. Yet, despite their success (upon which we concentrated in the last chapter) the progressives shared some of his disappointment and, in a milder way, experienced the pangs of disillusionment. In 1926 Nunn stated that reform in educational matters requires 'a certain social temperature' and noted that, in comparison with 'the generous heat which made possible ... the passing of Mr. Fisher's Education Act, we must admit that during the last years the atmosphere had grown perceptibly cooler.'[2] H. E. Boothroyd, in his history of the inspectorate (1923) was more depressed:[3]

In 1918 we Inspectors stood upon the mountain-top, looking down into the Promised Land which we expected, shortly, to enter: our old men dreamed dreams and our young men saw visions. Now, however, we must sojourn for a while longer in the wilderness; and, for some of us there will be no entry into the Promised Land.

And F. C. Happold, looking back sadly in 1953, expressed his regret that the hopes built up during the World War I had been disappointed: 'the leaders did not come, and many of us slept. The city was not built. Let us leave it at that.'[4] It could not be left at that—throughout the twenties and thirties the complaint was constantly sounded of hopes that had been dashed, promises broken and sacrifice made void.

This complaint was, of course, widespread. Educationists had been buoyed up by the Fisher Act and many had come to believe that reforms which had long been sought in vain were now to be accomplished. Yet the continuation schools, introduced in this period of determined optimism, rapidly withered in the financial drought which followed the war. By April 1919 the Board had embarked on a policy designed to confine the activity of the L.E.A.s to 'the provision of minimal statutory services'.[5] Two years later Sir Eric Geddes's Committee on National Expenditure recommended raising the school admission age to six, reducing free places, increasing class sizes, and cutting teachers' salaries, school meals and medical inspection. The schemes for expansion and development which the Fisher Act had asked the local authorities to submit to the Board were suspended; local expenditure was meticulously examined, programmes inordinately delayed and building economies made the order of the day. While the 'Geddes axe' chopped savagely away even optimistic reformers were forced to take shelter.

Teachers, first cheered by the acceptance of the Burnham scale, were forced in 1922, after Geddes, to accept a 5 per cent cut; some authorities tried to drop salaries further in 1923 and only after a series of strikes, one lasting eleven months, was the scale retained. In 1924 the local authorities, knowing that the first agreement reached by the Burnham Committee was soon to run out, tried once more to reduce salaries—at first by 15 per cent, later by 10 per cent. Eventually they obtained a 1 per cent reduction. In 1931 efforts to reduce salaries were again made and, while the authorities and the teachers bargained, the Committee on National Expenditure, now under Sir George May, intervened. It recommended drastic economies in the education service, including a 15 per cent cut in salaries. Eventually a 10 per cent cut was made and though this was restored by 1935 the constant haggling and the willingness with which governments and local authorities pared down their education budgets had severely damaged the teachers' morale.

Similarly, the promise for improvement in secondary education made in the Hadow Report, *The Education of the Adolescent* (1926), was not redeemed. The building of the new post-primary schools envisaged by this Report was painfully slow; so was progress in raising the school-leaving age to fifteen: it was frequently discussed, once almost achieved (in 1931, when the House of Lords rejected it) and eventually achieved in appearance (by the 1936 Education Act which made fifteen the leaving age from 1 September 1939). However, even if war had not broken out and finished all talk of further reform, the loose exemption clause would have reduced the effectiveness of the 1936 Act. At the other end of the child's educational career, the nursery school, promises were also made and not fulfilled: sixteen years after the passage of the Fisher Act, despite Hadow's *Infant and Nursery Schools* report, there were only seventy-two nursery schools offering accommodation for 5,440 children.[6]

Of course, the promised land which opened out before the educationist in 1918 and was denied him in the twenties and thirties was also denied to many other Englishmen. Many of the heroes who came home to the land which was to be made fit for them were already disillusioned and bitter. What remained of their hope that the world was a better place because of their actions was soon dissipated in inter-war England. At the very beginning nature seemed to turn against them: the influenza epidemic of 1918–19 took 150,000 deaths in Great Britain—the war had taken 1,500 civilians, demobilization difficulties led to demonstrations among the troops and even to mutiny. The effort to return swiftly to 'normalcy' led to the abrupt removal of restraints on prices and on the control of raw materials, and soon to inflation which the government was powerless to control. Bitter struggles developed over wages, unemployment and conditions of work. Strikes and industrial unrest followed as the police, and particularly the miners and railwaymen, led the fight. 'Homes for heroes', promised in the 1918 election, did not materialize and by 1923 there was an estimated shortage of 822,000 houses despite the extravagant policies of Christopher Addison: the country for which men had been asked to die now could not offer them a place to live. T. S. Eliot expressed the disillusion and disenchantment of the post-war years, as he expressed its lack of certainty.

> I think we are in rats' alley
> Where the dead men lost their bones.

At times the clouds lifted but on the whole the atmosphere was depressing. After the General Strike of 1926 came the depression; by September 1932 there were 3¾ million unemployed, which meant that six or seven million people were living on the dole. After the depression, war.[7]

The distress, disillusionment and financial stringency probably increased the attractiveness of the progressive cause to those who were bent on educational reform, just as the disruption of the patterns of everyday living increased the appeal of more dangerous contemporary ideologues. But the difficult times had a different effect on the classroom teacher. Even if the progressives' message had reached him (and the track from the official report or Nunn's *Education* or the teachers' college lecture to the classroom was long and strewn with obstacles) the times made it desperately hard for him. His attention was distracted from pedagogical matters by the struggle over salary and status, the curbs on expenditure made the obtaining of new equipment, furniture and supplies difficult, the building of new schools and the improvement of old proceeded slowly. If, for example, he wished to abolish the class lesson, to introduce 'activity' methods or just to let children play, the past's unsuitable architecture and furniture worked against him: the lack of floor space, Dorothy Revel claimed in 1928, 'was the worst deterrent to methods of freedom in the elementary school'.[8] And even if space could be obtained the heavy desks could not easily be moved—and there was no money to replace them with new and light ones. There was little in the depressing educational conditions of the 1920s and 30s which disposed the elementary school teacher to adopt novelties easily and much that discouraged him or made his way difficult. That there were resourceful and courageous teachers who triumphed over the odds is undoubted, but their success only served to illustrate the magnitude of the problems facing the teacher.

Furthermore, several important decisions of the mid-1920s made the introduction of new ideas and methods into the classroom still more difficult. Ironically the most significant of these was made by Henry Hadow's Consultative Committee whose 1931 report,

The Primary School, did so much to popularize progressive thought and make it respectable.

The Consultative Committee and the primary school

The Consultative Committee was formed after an Order in Council in 1900 as an independent advisory body to the Board. According to R. F. Young, the best known of its secretaries, it 'constituted a "microcosm" or a senate of the educational world of England and Wales, containing representatives of the different grades and types of educational institution from Primary School to the University and Higher Technical College.'[9] Because its members, usually about twenty, were well known it could have been a powerful source of criticism but in the first two decades of its existence, though it worked assiduously and produced a number of important reports, it caused the Board few headaches. In part its good behaviour was due to the fact that the Board, and especially its Permanent Secretary (from 1911 to 1925) Sir Lewis Amherst Selby-Bigge, was careful to give the Committee references which limited its chances of causing trouble. And care was taken in choosing its members. Thus in 1914 doubts were expressed about a gentleman who 'has fairly sound educational views, but, as you probably know, his manner of expressing himself, both orally and in writing, is not free from exception.' They were also doubtful about a lady with apparently suitable educational qualifications who had 'recently made a public appearance in some feminist connection which might render her an unsuitable choice'. She was clearly not as suitable as another lady who was a member of 'a very clever' and (better still perhaps) 'distinguished' family.[10] Such care, and such criteria, resulted in the Committee having a deserved reputation for good behaviour. In 1918 the Board was able to say:[11]

> The work of the Committee on each reference is finished when the Report is made : it is not concerned as to what action the Board proposes to take, or consulted upon it, and as a body has never questioned or criticized the Board's action or inaction.
>
> No administrative inconvenience has been experienced in connection with the Committee's work, except that of finding constant employment for it ...

Yet in the troublesome 1920s even so docile a body began to disturb the Board. In 1923, unwilling to continue writing elegant reports on safe subjects, it asked to have some say in choosing the issues it was to investigate. The Board at first refused but after a series of deputations (in which R. H. Tawney and Ernest Barker, the distinguished historian who was then Principal of King's College, London, played important parts) it conceded the right, though with certain safeguards. The issue the Committee wished to investigate was 'secondary education' and the reference eventually obtained was that upon which *The Education of the Adolescent*, published in 1926, was based.

Among the factors which interested the Committee in secondary education was that to which the Board had given expression at the end of World War I: 'The hard discipline of the war has taught the nation how great is the debt which it owes to its schools ... how imperative it is that the public system of education should be generous and comprehensive.[12] By the mid-twenties it was clear that the continuation school experiment had failed (or, really, had barely been tried) and that the greatest gap in the English system was in 'secondary education'. In 1926, 83 per cent of the children between eleven and fourteen were still in elementary school and of these only 5 per cent received 'advanced instruction', that is an education which had any pretence of being secondary.[13] Or, to put things another way, in the mid-twenties only 9.5 per cent of the children who left the elementary school in any one year went to a secondary school, and by the time they were fifteen most of them had left.[14] If the lesson the war had taught was heeded, it was the education of the young adolescent which needed most urgent attention.

Educationists worried by the wastage of talent and the squandering of scarce national resources caused by this gap in the educational system found that R. H. Tawney's *Secondary Education for All* (1922) expressed their views well. Of course, Tawney wanted action for other reasons, but at least he persuaded many that 'in starving the education of the adolescent the nation is sterilising itself': what the nation needed 'for the sake both of economic efficiency and of social amenity' was 'educated intelligence'. Assuming, as Tawney did, that 'capacity and incapacity ... tend to reproduce themselves' and that, in the process of this reproduction, nature did not keep to 'the lines of social and educational divisions which exist to-day', it followed that ability was 'probably dispersed more or less at random over the whole population'. Thus, Tawney concluded, 'the potential scientist or poet or inventor or statesman is as likely to be born in West Ham as in Westminster.' Yet, if he were born in West Ham he would be unlikely to receive equal opportunities for development; so there existed, Tawney argued (borrowing another's words), 'a vast reservoir of intellectual power' which was not being tapped.[15]

Hence the direction of ability into the channels in which it can best serve the community depends upon the existence of such abundant opportunities of higher education that every child can be fitted to the service which it can best render.

'The service it can best render'—the view of the education system as a means of social control, especially as a means of conserving and directing the resources of the nation, a view which we have seen gained popularity after the experiences of war—was prominent in discussions of secondary education. Many believed that there should be such a 'catching of capacity' in the national interest (to use the words of C. W. Bailey[16]),

such a transference of the ablest pupils from the Elementary School to the Secondary School, and from the Secondary School to the University, that our great national resources of native capacity are not wasted by the unthrifty hand of adverse circumstances.

Or as Kenneth Lindsay, whose study of 'educational waste' was most influential, remarked: [17]

No one can say how much trouble, delinquency, blind-alley work, human maladjustment and human waste could be saved by spending more money, and spending it more wisely, on those members of the nation under 18 years of age. We are dealing with imponderables, not with a profit and loss account. But vast fields of labour are at once opened up when we recognize that the capacities, qualities, and desires of the individual are the most precious of all raw materials, and that by guidance and due care we can direct those capacities, qualities, and desires into some channels rather than others, to the benefit of all concerned.

From this desire to reduce 'human maladjustment' and to ensure efficient 'capacity catching' (but also, for men such as Tawney, from a disinterested humanitarian concern) Hadow's famous report, *The Education of the Adolescent*, emerged. According to his committee, 'elementary education', with its overtones of impoverishment and class distinction, was to be called 'primary education' and to be the first stage in an educational process which led all children to 'secondary education' at the age of eleven. Yet though primary education was first in time it remained secondary in importance: Hadow first re-organized secondary education and then, with the guidelines already laid down, started to work on the primary school. As a result when, in 1931, the Consultative Committee came to write *The Primary School* it had to accept the implications of its 1926 decisions.

In fact the critical decision was made in 1923 before the Committee had begun its work. Originally the Committee suggested to the Board its own reference: 'To investigate the different types of curriculum suitable to children between the ages of eleven and sixteen and the means by which these can be provided.' The reference on which it actually worked was written in consultation with the Committee by Selby-Bigge while the Conservative, Edward Wood (later Lord Halifax), was President of the Board, though on the fall of his government it was the first Labour President, C. P. Trevelyan, who gave the reference to the Committee. This second reference was more restricted than the Committee's first proposal because it limited the Committee's investigation to 'schools, other than Secondary Schools'—thus the 'grammar' schools (to use Hadow's terminology) set up after the 1902 Act were exempt from examination.[18]

Despite its previous independence, the Committee accepted the restricted reference unanimously. Once it had agreed not to discuss the existing 'secondary' or grammar schools the Committee was forced to accept them as they stood—it could recommend no change. Since they could not be altered, efforts to secure 'secondary education for all', or to extend secondary education in any way, involved instituting a new form of school. It was perfectly clear even before the Committee had met that it never envisaged 'secondary education for all' as meaning making grammar-school education universal. Tawney, perhaps the most likely to take such a line, had stated that he had no wish to 'sacrifice the peculiar excellence of particular institutions to a pedantic State-imposed uniformity'; he stressed that 'equality of educational provision is not identity of educational provision' and argued for 'the greatest possible diversity of type among secondary schools'.[19] Percy Nunn, who was co-opted to the Committee and played an important part in drafting its recommendations, made a more direct statement: 'To conceive of "secondary education for all" as meaning "the grammar school curriculum for all" would be to make a most serious blunder.'[20] Where the Tawneys and Nunns feared to tread not many fools would rush in.

When the Committee recommended the establishment of 'modern' schools, it stressed that the new institution was '*one species of the genus "Secondary Education"*.' And it was not to be '*an inferior species.*'[21] But, from the beginning, the modern school lacked prestige. It received those children who had not gained entrance to a grammar school, its curriculum in the last two years had a more 'practical' bias, it kept its pupils for a shorter time, its teachers did not need to be as well qualified as the grammar school's. The Committee openly admitted that it could recommend the establishment of modern schools with an easy mind—whereas fifteen or twenty years ago modern schools might have been dangerous to the 'Secondary School', they 'ought not to be so now'. Indeed, the Committee concluded, the modern school might absorb those children who intended to leave school at fifteen thus 'making it easier for "secondary schools" to require, as is generally agreed is desirable, a longer period of school attendance from the pupils entering them.' And the Committee warned against 'anything like competition between "secondary" schools and other forms of post-primary school, which could lead to one attracting to itself pupils better qualified to profit by the other.'[22] This warning was clearly aimed to check modern school ambitions and, taken with the other limitations, showed that, its protestations notwithstanding, the Committee gave obvious preference to the grammar school.

Whatever their intentions, the effect of Hadow's recommendations was to increase the pressure on primary schools. Undoubtedly Hadow hoped that the emphasis which his report placed on the unity of the educational process would assist the primary educator—his school was no longer to offer a distinct and inferior kind of education but was to be the first stage of an educational process through which all children went. But probably as soon as it accepted the restricted warrant (and certainly after it had made its recommendations), the Committee endorsed the hierarchical structure of secondary education. By so doing all primary schools were forced to consider themselves as 'preparatory' schools for, at the age of eleven, the child's results in primary school would largely determine the sort of secondary school he attended. The full workings of the eleven-plus were reserved for the years after World War II but in the late twenties and thirties the pressure on the primary school increased—especially the pressure to obtain the scholarships which opened the prestigious grammar school to primary schoolchildren.

'There is little doubt', said the reliable W. H. Perkins in 1936,[23]

> that the shadow of the examination, which is important only for the minority, still darkens the way of too many children through the last year or so of the primary course. As far as school attainments are concerned, the examinations are commonly limited to the subjects of arithmetic and English, and naturally enough the schools are apt to be driven to deal with these two subjects in their 'testable' aspects.

Six years earlier J. H. Hallam, Education Officer for the West Riding, had made a similar complaint: 'The type of schooling of the vast majority of English children after the age of eleven will continue to be determined by a written test in English and arithmetic, supplemented sometimes in border-line cases by an oral test, less often by an intelligence test also.'[24] And the Director of Education for the Barking Education Committee stated: 'It would be hard to find the head teacher of a junior school who does not believe that the effect of the examination held in the last year is cramping and depressing.'[25] A body set up to study the problem of examinations in the primary school[26] summarized the difficulties as

> overpressure upon the children, excessive homework, the organization of a special scholarship class in which attention is concentrated upon the more mechanical aspects of English and arithmetic, the special coaching of the scholarship candidates both in and outside school hours, and the allocation of the best teacher to the part of the school that contains the scholarship candidates.

From witness after witness the same story came—any teacher who wished to break from the traditional curriculum or methods of the primary school had to combat that most conservative of educational influences, an examination.[27]

It has become fashionable to place the responsibility for this examination on the educational psychologists, especially those interested in examining and the development of intelligence tests. Certainly their views were helpful. 'Intelligence itself is native to the child—a gift, good or bad, at birth, which no means known to us can appreciably improve', said C. A. Richardson, expressing the view then dominant and widely publicized by the most influential English worker in this field, Cyril Burt.[28] Not only was intelligence innate but it could be reliably measured by the new techniques. 'Measurement in education', said one writer, 'is, in general, the same as measurement in the physical sciences and approaches the same order of reliability'.[29] E. L. Thorndike, who visited England in 1936 to address a conference concerned with the problems of examining, said that objective tests had in them 'objective facts which mean the same all over the country, the same in 1900, in 1930, in 1940, in 1950, and are expressed in valid numbers, so that men like yourselves can use them.'[30] These optimistic views no doubt encouraged men who were designing a system which divided children at the age of eleven and sent them to different schools which were supposed to be related to their level of intelligence. It must have been a relief to be told, by experts, that intelligence was innate, unlikely to improve much with age and was easily measurable, and that, therefore, the career of a school child was reasonably easy to predict. (Burt in fact assured the Hadow Committee that 'future scholarship winners can be predicted with some success even while still in the Infants' school at the early age of 6.'[31])

Yet it would be unwise to credit the educational psychologists with too much influence. Their tests, for example, were still controversial—an enlightened writer such as T. A. Raymont was not at all pleased with the intelligence tests' 'big budget of small conundrums', and Bertrand Russell dismissed them as 'an American delusion.'[32] Though some proponents of the new forms of testing were as naïvely optimistic and as arrogant as any reformer could be, there remained some psychologists who warned, more authoritatively than anyone, against their limitations. Despite his commitment and enthusiasm few pointed out the limitations of the new testing techniques as explicitly as Cyril Burt: 'To take a young mind as it is, and delicately one by one to sound its notes and stops, to detect the smaller discords and appreciate the subtler harmonies, is more of an art than a science.'[33] And even though the Consultative Committee's 1923 survey of 'psychological tests of educable capacity' helped to gain the tests some respectability, its approach was cautiously sympathetic, not extravagantly enthusiastic.

In any case the separation of children on the basis of their ability, while supported by psychological findings, preceded them:

the psychologists answered a demand, they did not create one. Thus in 1921 Burt admitted that more needed to be done before the Binet–Simon scale became fully reliable, but, because there was a demand, he urged its immediate use:[34]

> While waiting for the slow and sure we must make shift with the rough and ready. The need is urgent; the field is vast. Throughout the country there is a cry for a practical mental test—for a handy method which can be immediately applied by teachers, doctors and social workers; ... for a pocket rule, which will furnish diagnostic measurements in terms of some plain concept, like the mental year, obvious, moderately exact, and instantly intelligible to a magistrate or jury ... To satisfy such a demand, scientific exactitude may pardonably be postponed for the prompt delivery of an acceptable, workable substitute.

Godfrey Thomson also set himself to answer a demand: 'I have spent a great deal of my life in this effort [the devising of better testing procedures], not because I think the English trifurcation at "eleven plus" a good thing, but because, if it must needs take place, I want it to be done as efficiently and as justly as possible.'[35] The work of Burt, Thomson and their fellow psychologists made selection more efficient, and thus more acceptable, but it did not create the demand.

Selection had been implicit in the Board's policy almost as soon as secondary schools became its concern and especially after the free place system became competitive. And the age of selection, about eleven, had been an important part of the official policy since before World War I, not for psychological reasons but because it was administratively convenient: it was hard to keep students at school after they had turned sixteen and as it was believed that the secondary school needed to hold its pupils for four years if it were to have any effect on them, they had to begin no later than twelve. Indeed by 1924, two years before Hadow reported, 71 per cent of children who moved from elementary to secondary school had done so before turning twelve. Thus neither the psychologists nor Hadow can be said to have been responsible for the system of selection at eleven-plus.[36]

Ironically, however, it was Burt who gave the most lucid statement of the reasoning which led to the demand. Giving evidence to the Hadow Committee, he divided children into five categories according to the school they attended: scholarship children going to secondary schools, children who went to central schools, the 'ordinary' children who remained until fourteen in the elementary school, the dull and backward, and finally the feeble-minded. He assigned an intelligence ratio to each category—thus scholarship children had a mental ratio of 130 or more, the feeble-minded a ratio below 70, and the others were situated at appropriate levels between. Burt then claimed that vocational psychology had produced a classification of vocations: the professional, the clerical and technical, skilled labour, unskilled labour, and institutional life or casual labour. This classification, he stated, dovetailed neatly with the intelligence levels of children. Thus, he concluded,

> from quite early years, the degree of a child's intelligence roughly marks him out as fit for callings of a certain grade. He may show no peculiar qualities or talent or special aptitude, yet his later education, if it is to be adapted however distantly to his after life, will inevitably differ in quality as well as in range of difficulty.

The function of the psychological test was to give a 'scientific statement of his [the child's] special and general qualities ... of intellect and character', so that it was possible to 'find the right place for every man, the right man for every place.'[37]

The education system acted as 'a sieve' which, in Godfrey Thomson's words, separated 'the double cream' from 'the single cream' and 'the skimmed milk'.[38] First came the bright child, the scholarship winner, for whom the grammar school was designed. As D. Caradog Jones wrote in 1930, 'It is the bright children of the elementary schools who are favoured and encouraged to continue their education, while the less intelligent are obliged to look for work as soon as they reach the age of 14.'[39] If the grammar school were offered to all, J. W. Headlam-Morley (who had been a staff inspector of secondary schools) told the Hadow Committee, it would 'almost certainly involve a very serious lowering of the standard of work in secondary schools' and thus threaten 'the crown and object of the whole system'.[40]

The Hadow Committee, it is clear, were not prepared to run that risk. They left the secondary school at the pinnacle of the educational pyramid and altered the substructure. More generous than many of their contemporaries, they objected to holding the majority of pupils in elementary schools and recommended establishing the new 'modern' school. Yet this very recommendation indicated how deeply they were influenced by their estimate of the child's future vocation. Certainly witness after witness stressed how important it was to make such an estimate—the inspectors of schools, for example, advised the Committee on how to help those who were 'unsuitable or unprepared' for the course offered by secondary schools or those 'for whom such a course may not be the best fitting for their social and economic needs'.[41] The Committee responded in kind, arguing that the modern schoolchild was different from the grammar schoolchild. In words which later Consultative Committees were to echo, Hadow's said:[42]

> There is no question that among the pupils of the new post-primary schools the desire and the ability to do and to make, to learn from concrete things and situations, will be more widely diffused than the desire to acquire book-knowledge and master generalisations and abstract ideas.

Thus, though vocational training of the direct kind envisaged by the technical school was to be avoided, the Committee kept the vocations of the modern-school pupils clearly in mind—a 'practical bias' was to be given to the last two years of the modern-school course:

> We propose to use the term 'practical bias' to denote the emphasis laid in the school curriculum on practical aspects of certain subjects without involving work in the technicalities of any one specific trade or occupation. The aim which we suggest is that, while no pupil in a Modern School or Senior Class with a taste for industry, commerce or agriculture should be educated with a view to any one specific calling, he should none the less receive such a training as will make it easy for him to adapt himself on leaving school to any occupation in the group of occupations to which the bias is related.

The simple-minded in these matters, such as J. L. Paton, headmaster of Manchester Grammar, told Hadow that children divided themselves naturally into 'Mentals and Manuals'.[44] More than twenty years before the Hadow Committee met, Michael Sadler, who was by no means simple-minded argued that it was 'a cruel kindness to start boys and girls upon a course of higher education from which they were intellectually unfitted to profit' and warned that it was 'not to the public advantage to encourage by large subsidies the formation of a semi-literate class, educated above their intellectual station and discontented with their lot.'[45] In April 1923 Ernest Barker wrote: 'An educated nation is a good thing; but a nation in which all were educated alike would be a poor thing. It would be a fantastic society in which every member went each morning to a business which did not exist by a train which there was nobody to drive.'[46] Crisply, and probably more clear-sightedly than Barker or the Committee, Burt expressed the vision which guided them:[47]

> It is the duty of the community, first, to ascertain what is the mental level of each individual child; then, to give him the education most appropriate to his level; and, lastly, before it leaves him, to guide him into the career for which his measure of intelligence has marked him out.

Underlying the recommendations of the Hadow Committee was a belief in the contribution to the national welfare a school system could make by channelling children into the right courses.

In its 1931 report on primary education and the 1933 report on infant and nursery schools the Consultative Committee followed the advice of the progressives; it tried to dissolve the formal curriculum of the primary school, to relax its discipline, to reduce competition, to increase the time given to art, drama and music, to make the child the centre of the educational process and to organize the school round his needs. The progressives' advice was, as we have seen, deeply coloured by their reaction to the horrors of war; but, as we have also seen, the war taught other lessons. When, in its 1926 report, the Committee attempted to channel the nation's ability into appropriate channels, it was heeding one of these lessons. Unfortunately, the more thoroughly this last lesson was learned, the more difficult it was to attend to the first. For, however widespread progressive thought became in the colleges, however popular it was in the official reports or among writers on education, it could not easily be put into practice while primary schooling ended in an examination which enshrined many of the values the progressives opposed. Of course, it could have been (and was) argued that 'progressive' methods produced better 'results' in the examination at eleven-plus than the traditional method, though some progressives regarded this argument as a capitulation to values they were determined to resist. In any case it was a vain argument for it is clear that when the work of the primary school was assessed in terms of the performance of children at a traditional examination, teachers who might otherwise have implemented the progressives' practices felt safer working with tried and true methods.

When educationists, and especially the college lecturers and the theorists, discussed what should happen in the primary schoolroom they thought of the child as 'the centre of the problem of education, its alpha and omega ... the one and only indispensable factor'. When the educational administrators (and even some of the theorists) went outside the classroom to look at the educational system as a whole, it was the need to direct the nation's abilities into profitable channels which most concerned them. When war broke out again this conflict had not been resolved: the recommendations of *The Primary School* were still made difficult to achieve by the recommendations of *The Education of the Adolescent*.

Educational cultures and conservatism

Even if the educational system has assisted and not hindered the implementation of progressive practices and even if the primary teacher had been undistracted by the struggles over salary and conditions, the nature of the teaching profession would have presented difficulties to the progressives. Some idea of these difficulties can be gained by comparing the teacher of an English grammar school, an 'old boy' returning to teach a new generation of Etonians, an American elementary schoolteacher and a German kindergartener. They are all teachers, yet they work in very different ways: they have different attitudes to their pupils, to fellow-teachers, to parents, to the person in charge of their educational institutions; they teach different subjects (if they teach subjects at all), they use different methods, have different systems of discipline, are trained in different ways.

One way of summarizing their differences is to say that they come from different educational 'cultures'. 'Culture' is here used of the school and the schoolteacher as an anthropologist might use it to describe the life pattern of New Guinean headhunters: it refers to that set of ideas, attitudes, values, habits and procedures which characterizes a particular group. A teacher facing one of the numerous decisions he must make in his professional life is not a lonely Cartesian who has stripped himself of past beliefs and has nothing to rely on but independent reason. He can be thought of as possessing a 'culture' which will to some extent determine his decisions. A teacher who decided to become a thoroughly rational practitioner, to throw away past beliefs and to try with reason only, his own independent reason, to forge a set of theories and practices—such a teacher would soon become professionally paralysed. Every action would present him with a decision: at what hour should he go to school? should he go to school at all? should schools exist? if so, should the particular schools with which he is acquainted exist? what should he teach? in what way should he teach? what clothes should he wear to school? what clothes should his pupils wear? by what name should his pupils call him? what form of discipline should he employ? is 'discipline' a relevant concept? how long should the hours of instruction last? would his school (if it were a school) be co-educational? how many children in a grade (if grades were used)? what books should be prescribed? Faced with these and a myriad other questions, this thoroughly rational teacher would soon find that his trust in reason was unreasonably excessive—so excessive that a continuation of his efforts would produce a state of neurosis which permitted his employers (if he had been prepared to be employed by anyone) to remove him from their service.

Of course no one is so rational. The neophyte teacher is initiated into an educational culture which answers many of these questions for him. Through its customs, parliamentary law, the lore of the profession, regulations, books, rituals, training institutions and example an educational culture makes available to the teacher procedures for answering questions whose very multiplicity might otherwise overwhelm him. It takes away the necessity for countless decisions and saves a teacher from having continuously to think. He can, if he wishes, reflect on the solutions that his educational culture proposes or on its popular practices and theories, but he can do so at leisure—and meanwhile be supplied with procedures which enable him to conduct his day-to-day work with confidence. To be able to function at all, a teacher must accept without close examination or questioning large parts of his educational culture.

Not only does an educational culture provide a teacher with ways of acting, it also helps to determine his professional identity. What being a teacher consists of, the skills he should possess, the values he is expected to favour, the knowledge he is expected to have, the methods he should use, the attitudes he takes towards parents and children—these vary from educational culture to educational culture, and can vary so greatly that a person adapted to one culture may be unsuitable for another. A teacher who taught in an American liberal arts college might find that Eton raised such strange and new problems that he could not easily cope. Of course, an educational culture cannot be separated from the society of which it is a part, and if the American teacher found problems it would be partly because his society and Eton's have obvious and striking differences. The teasing out of the relationship between the general culture of society and that limited version of it which is expressed in its educational activities is a fascinating study which will not be attempted here. Nevertheless it can be said that the American teacher brought with him professional expectations, habits, ideas and procedures which, however acceptable in his own, appear strange in the new educational culture. In fact the teacher is unlikely to succeed at Eton until he allows himself to be initiated into the new culture; just as the habits, ideas, expectations and behaviour of a New Guinean headhunter would have to be adapted if he were suddenly transported to the asphalted streets of Sydney or Melbourne.

'We are afraid', Edmund Burke said,[48]

> to put men to live and trade each on his own private stock of reason; because we suspect that this stock in each man is small, and that the individuals would do better to avail themselves of the general bank and capital of nations and of ages. Many of our men of speculation, instead of exploding general prejudices, employ their sagacity to discover the latent wisdom which prevails in them ... Prejudice is of ready application in the emergency; it previously engages the mind in a steady course of wisdom and virtue, and does not leave the man hesitating in the moment of decision, sceptical, puzzled and unresolved. Prejudice renders a man's virtues his habit; and not a series of unconnected acts. Through just prejudice, his duty becomes a part of his nature.

It is not necessary to draw the same political conclusions as Burke drew, nor need the provocative term, 'prejudice', distract attention from the essential argument. For it is not a matter of being *afraid* to put men out to work with their own private stock of reason; it simply cannot be done. To attempt to be at all times rational, to think before acting, always to weigh the pros and cons of an issue (even in a restricted field such as education) is to give oneself an impossible task, to commit oneself to intellectual frustration. Probably the most important function of an educational culture is that it *restricts*, limits freedom of choice, reduces the options. By providing sanctioned answers it enables security and confidence to develop, by providing accepted methods of procedure it enables teachers to act without having always to justify their actions; it reduces the host of choices to a manageable number. Prediction is possible, so plans can be laid.

An educational culture may be compared to a map. In a map certain features from the multiplicity which any terrain possesses are organized according to conventions which make planning and prediction possible. Because the features are chosen with particular purposes in mind the same area can appear different on different maps—depending, for example, on whether it was mapped to enable cars to drive easily through it, or to permit searches for oil to be begun, or battles to be fought. The use of a map (or the acceptance of an educational culture) means the limiting of activity to a certain area; but it makes possible quick and efficient movement within that area. A person without a map may have unlimited freedom of choice, but often he may not know where to turn. Of course, a person who looks too long at one map may come to believe that the area he studies could be mapped in no other way, or he may even forget the existence of a whole world which is not contained on his map; so also an unreflecting acceptance of an educational culture may lead a teacher to believe that its customs and procedures are beyond criticism or the only possible way of acting. When this happens the restrictions of the culture have imprisoned a teacher instead of freeing him for action.

The map analogy is useful to illustrate how an educational culture can pattern a teacher's activities and produce that security which comes from the thorough realization of what is expected and approved. And, despite the dangers involved in the analogy, it is of value if it makes clear the importance of the restrictions which an educational culture produces. For in certain ways the teacher is in a vulnerable position. Though the decisions he must make are less immediately critical than those faced by (say) a doctor or a lawyer —life or reputation are not so obviously involved—they can be extremely demanding. In the first place, the teacher has many decisions to make; his choices are not defined and limited as are a process worker's, or a clerk's who is assessing insurance forms. Second, in making the decisions a teacher is exposed to conflicting pressures: he must satisfy those he teaches, their parents, his fellow teachers, educational administrators, headmasters, managers of school boards and many others. To satisfy all at any one time is probably impossible, for what a child wants often conflicts with the parents' requirements, or what an administrator wants disturbs the teaching profession. Thus the procedures endorsed by an educational culture are welcomed by the teacher for they free him from the problem of trying to balance one legitimate claim against another. The procedures may not fully satisfy anyone but if many teachers employ them, they will give the individual the safety that comes from numbers.

The teacher's position is further complicated because he is frequently required to make important decisions quickly. Of course, a teacher's error is unlikely to result in a pupil's death or imprisonment (as a doctor's or lawyer's error might), but it can have important long-term effects on the child, and for the teacher it can have immediate consequences. A false step in discipline, a failure to capitalize on an awakening interest, or a decision to take up a matter better ignored, can profoundly effect the relationship between a teacher and his class. Very often, because the class is there in front of him, the teacher has to make important decisions swiftly; and the need for swiftness makes a teacher the more likely to accept the procedures of the educational culture in which he was trained. They offer solutions which permit decisive action in difficult circumstances. 'Prejudice', to repeat Edmund Burke, 'is of ready application in the emergency; it previously engages the mind in a steady course of wisdom and virtue, and does not leave the man hesitating in the moment of action, sceptical, puzzled and unresolved.'

There is another peculiarity in the teacher's position which increases his interest in 'prejudices'. A doctor may form a close relationship with a patient but he will not usually see him daily, and never constantly throughout the working day every day of the week. A teacher gets little respite: there, in front of him, daily, is a class. Every day the behaviour of that class makes a teacher aware of the success or failure of previous lessons, continually throughout his working life he is confronted, in a personal and direct way, with the results of his previous decisions. Many occupations get 'feedback', of course, but few have the immediacy of the teaching profession's: before the teacher's eyes, bored shufflings, restlessness, impertinence, laziness or revolt can emphasize past failures and create future problems. There are few crises in teaching, but many small emergencies—and the certain knowledge that today's class will be back tomorrow bringing with it any defects in knowledge or any unfavourable attitudes which today's efforts to meet the emergencies produced. Once again those procedures which an educational culture identifies as successful, or as likely to lead to success, powerfully attract the teacher.

Thus the conditions of his profession give the teacher a great interest in the established procedures, the methods favoured by his educational culture. By adopting them he is able to do the expected and so avoid criticism; they represent a means of reconciling the conflicting demands of the parties in the education process— parents, teachers, headmasters and the like; they enable action to be taken without the anxiety and delay of calculating the consequences; they carry with them some assurance of success.

Hence to attack the established procedures of an educational culture is to put a teacher's professional security at risk. His first reaction will be to resist the attack, and his resistance will be the more effective because many of the procedures which he uses have not been consciously acquired. Of course, some have been *chosen*, deliberately and consciously, perhaps as the result of convictions formed by instruction, discussion and debate. But many have been simply absorbed from his educational culture, from unexamined habit, or deference to custom, or remembrance of his own school days, or in unconscious imitation of an admired model, and have not issued from a conscious assent to carefully formulated propositions. Thus, for a time the practices endorsed by a particular culture are protected from a confrontation with criticism and can defy challenge.

Sometimes, however, criticism builds up such momentum that it can no longer be ignored. Thus, by 1914, as we have seen, the New Education had made all teachers, who were not mere drudges, aware that the established elementary-school procedures had been seriously challenged. Most of the leaders of educational opinion were dissatisfied with the old ways; the teacher was constantly told that his methods were not satisfactory, that the stern discipline upon which he insisted was unnecessary, that the curriculum he taught was too narrow. The map which his educational culture provided had become confused and ambiguous; security was threatened because no one could be sure of what inspectors or headmasters or parents expected, no one could be certain which skills, knowledge and values were most prized.

By 1939 some (though not complete) stability had returned to the educational culture of the primary school for, as progressive thought was accepted by educational opinion-makers, it offered a security beyond the power of the old to promise. The ordinary classroom teacher might not have been greatly moved by the ideas of Mc-Dougall, Freud or Dewey, and he certainly lacked the passionate conviction of the first progressives; but by the end of the thirties most authorities were telling him the story the progressives had told, less enthusiastically perhaps but nevertheless with feeling. Once the teacher's professional security had best been defended by resisting suggestions of change; by 1939 many believed that it was best served by accommodating the new orthodoxy.

Of course many accommodated the new only slowly and reluctantly and the competitive examination at the end of primary school provided reasons for further delay. It was not until after the war that the new views passed beyond the opinion-maker and entered the classroom on a large scale. Hence in 1939 many primary schoolteachers still found themselves in a state of tension: they were unable to escape the progressives' criticism without discarding some of their old procedures, yet innate conservatism, and the examination, reinforced their old ways. Their reaction to Helen Parkhurst's Dalton Plan gives some indication of the ambiguous position many adopted.

The Dalton Plan

Writing in 1923 F. W. Roman claimed that the Dalton Plan held the 'first place among the new experiments in education in England'. Testimony to its 'remarkable success' came not only from Belle Rennie and C. W. Kimmins (who worked hard to popularize it and in *The Triumph of the Dalton Plan* (1931) claimed that their efforts had been successful), but also from detached observers such as W. O. Lester Smith. Recollecting in tranquillity, he spoke of 'the sudden arrival here from the U.S.A. of the Dalton Plan, and the astonishing vogue that it had.'[49]

The vogue is understandable because the scheme gave practical expression to the progressives' demands. That sacred criterion, 'individuality', was satisfied, for children worked independently on assignments which, theoretically at any rate, were tailored to suit their interests and abilities; and even if the same assignment was given to the whole class (as it usually was) the children could work through it at their own pace. According to Cyril Burt the Dalton Plan was 'perhaps the most thorough-going embodiment of the principle of individual work'.[50] 'Freedom', that other catch-cry of the progressives, also received consideration. According to Helen Parkhurst, freedom was 'the first principle of the Dalton Laboratory Plan': under its arrangements there was no need to tear a child away at a set time from a subject which he found interesting in order to 'chain him pedagogically to another subject and another teacher'. 'Freedom,' Miss Parkhurst said, 'is taking one's own time. To take someone else's time is slavery.' For Lynch, 'freedom' had a different meaning: 'an almost entire absence of repression—the child is free to work, to talk, to think, and to ask questions' and can 'move from room to room if and when he desires'.[51] But, whatever the meaning, the cause of freedom was served.

Moreover an increase in social co-operation and even self-government was said to follow from the Plan. It was, Helen Parkhurst claimed, 'a method whereby community principles and practices can be introduced into the school.' Sir John Adams felt that the Plan 'enters into the very heart of the child's social, as well as his educational, life.' According to Lynch, a Dalton school 'becomes a social unit in ways that could never happen under the old system.'[52] The Plan also permitted breaking down the barriers between subjects so that a more flexible curriculum was produced. Moreover it offered a practical, comprehensible (and not too radical) alternative to the class lesson for if it were put into practice the teacher could retire from the centre of the stage, or at least from the front of the schoolroom, and at least appear less concerned to control the child's educational destiny. The Dalton Plan, said Adams, 'asks the teacher to step aside, and let the children act on their own account.'[53]

Yet the Plan's undoubted popularity was not due simply to a desire to put progressive ideas into practice. In fact the manner in which it was put into practice, as distinct from spoken about, reveals that its attraction was more ambiguous. Staunch advocates of Daltonism such as Kimmins and Rennie acknowledge that in the primary school the Plan was usually confined to the top two or three classes (which was predictable and sensible). They also point out that the subject 'rooms', which the full implementation of the Plan required, had become subject 'corners', and that the pupils' movements 'instead of being from subject room to subject room, can only be from the history corner to the geography corner.'[54] Nunn, writing in 1924, noted that 'after a period of trial', schools had 'settled down to a mode of work and organization which includes the essential features of the plan tempered by a varying admixture of the conventional methods of instruction.'[55]

The problems which teachers discovered when they tried to put the Plan into action show how many of the old attitudes remained in this admixture. A. J. Lynch listed the difficulties teachers raised: first was 'the so-called dull child', next the 'shirker' who, Lynch said, was found in 'any plan of work' and was little affected by 'any fine designs'; then there was the problem of 'copying' which Lynch felt should be checked when it was 'tantamount to cheating' but otherwise ignored.[56] For all the newness of the Plan the teacher was obsessed with old problems—slow children, shirkers and copying.

Again, catering for 'individual differences' was a concern referred to by many advocates of the Dalton Plan. To have put their words into action meant making profound changes in classroom practice, but as the astute Carleton Washburne said after examining the Plan in London schools: 'we see in the effort to make all students cover the same ground in a month or a year one of the weaknesses of the Dalton Plan, as carried out in London and in some schools in the United States.'[57] Old habits remained. The child was free to work at his own pace yet was expected to cover the same work in the same time as he had in the days before his freedom. C. M. Fleming writing in 1934, ten years after Washburne, saw the same problem: 'The assumption is still made that the teacher can predict and prescribe how much ground can be covered in a session's work.'[58] The assumption was perfectly understandable in terms of the old procedures and reflected the very mentality the Plan was trying to defeat.

Equality indicative of the approach of many Dalton Planners is the comment made by Lynch. 'On the administrative side of school practice ... is the advantage that the plan of individual work, honestly and faithfully carried out, produces "more and better" work.' A year's trial has convinced him, Lynch continued, that the ordinary work of the class was better, and so were the results in 'full-dress tests of the conventional type'.[59] Better class work, better exam results—the claim is constant, and when the sacred examination cow can be left to chew its cud in peace, radical changes are unlikely. Lynch often returned to this point. Addressing a conference of the Dalton Association in 1926 he pointed out that the Plan should not be judged by its examination results. 'At the same time,' he argued, 'I feel that we want to assure ourselves that we are not suffering in any way in educational efficiency.' Having surveyed examination results he concluded that 'educational efficiency rather than diminishing is maintained and even vastly improved.'[60] 'The child can only grow', said another advocate of the Plan, 'by her own efforts and by using her own resources, and it is the teacher's task to release potentialities. Because of this, when the child is faced with an examination, she is more or less master of the situation.'[61] Buoyed up by this belief, this teacher also recounted the examination successes her school had achieved.

To a teacher who was worried that the progressives were calling into question the procedures which once had guaranteed him security, the Dalton Plan had a particular attraction. If offered a methodology—a set of procedures, ways of organizing a classroom and conducting discussion. To adopt it, or even to go through the motions of adopting it, meant a certain immunity from criticism, for one could be mistaken for a reformer. Yet it was not too far removed from what had gone before and the old habits, the old expectations (which, we have argued, were of deep emotional importance to the teacher) did not need to be fully discarded. It offered security at a time when the educational culture of the English primary school was uncertain and unstable.

Helen Parkhurst made the offer more powerful by stressing that the Plan could be easily adapted: 'So long as the principle that animates it [the Dalton Plan] is preserved, it can be modified in practice in accordance with the circumstances of the school and the judgement of the staff.' Furthermore, she refrained from 'dogmatizing on what subjects should be included in the curriculum, or by what standards the achievement of pupils should be measured.'[62] This refusal to be committed to a particular curriculum and the willingness to permit a variety of practices increased the Plan's appeal. The advocates of the Dalton Plan can be found discussing the curriculum and the standards by which pupils should be judged, but neither the curriculum nor the standards were rigidly enforced. A teacher could therefore retain much of what he wanted from the past and still be thought a good Daltonian. If you went to Summerhill you had declared yourself unequivocally, you were of the progressives; if you worked with the Dalton Plan your position was more ambiguous.

The part a teacher should play in the classroom was similarly ill defined. Most advocates of the Dalton Plan argued that the teacher should exercise less authority and allow the children to direct their own investigations. In practice, and sometimes in the writings of the Daltonians, the teacher assumed a more familiar and more powerful role. Thus Parkhurst says: 'Under the Dalton Laboratory Plan we place the work problem squarely before him [the child], indicating the standard which has to be obtained'; when that had been done—'he is allowed to tackle it as he thinks fit in his own way and at his own speed.' Clearly the choice of task is the teacher's. Even more explicitly Helen Parkhurst argued that 'we must give him an opportunity to survey the whole field of the task we set.' Hence the student was given a year's programme so that he could obtain 'a perspective of the plan of his education'. With this plan he was in a position to judge how to approach his goal and the rate at which he should proceed.[63] At the same time, the teacher drew up for each form 'a maximum and minimum curriculum' so that control could be exercised over the pace at which the child approached the goal chosen for him by the teacher. The arrangement was symbolized by the contract which pupils were asked to sign: 'I ——, pupil of —— standard (form), contract to do the —— assignment.'[64] Helen Parkhurst can be left to sum up the Plan:[65]

> The Dalton Laboratory Plan is a simple and economic reorganisation of the schools whereby pupils and teachers function to better advantage, inefficiency in pupils and teachers being reduced to a minimum. It does not add to or change the curriculum; it does not involve expensive school plants or elaborate equipment; it precludes the idea that there is any one method of teaching subjects, and approaches the matter from the standpoint of the child. It provides equal opportunities for advancement to bright and slow pupils without any sacrifice of thoroughness.

It seemed, in fact, to be a way of getting the best of both worlds: it offered the shelter of the progressive's umbrella to the uncertain teacher who realized that the old shelters were no longer secure, but it did not require him to forsake all his old ways. He could march with the reformers yet not change his valued habits and procedures too radically.

When Kimmins and Rennie wrote *The Triumph of the Dalton Plan* they rightly, if prematurely and too enthusiastically, celebrated a victory for the progressive cause. But the very victory guaranteed further struggles, for it revealed how thoroughly the teacher was insulated against reform by his attachment to the procedures which his educational culture approved and which gave him professional security. Eventually that attachment was loosened but the loosening was to take a long time and was not completed by 1939.

Shocked by the horrors of World War I the progressive worked to make war impossible—and in September 1939 he watched while his children (or their children) again marched to war. Not only had his wider hopes been disappointed but his less ambitious educational hopes had not been fully realized. Hard times, financial stringency and unsympathetic administrators had drawn the teacher's attention away from the classroom towards more mundane matters of salary and conditions; a determination to make best use of the nation's intellectual resources (a determination fostered, like the progressive's own hopes, by the experiences of World War I) imposed on the primary school an examination which strengthened the forces against which the progressive fought; and teachers were reluctant to abandon procedures which offered them professional security. Thus it seemed to some progressives that their first hopes, their missionary zeal, their conviction that their gospel would remake the educational world had come to nothing, or at least to very little. What had happened to MacMunn's fine enthusiasm for spreading the good news? To Beatrice Ensor's determination to 'go forth and do something to help forward the new era'? What of Caldwell Cook's dream, in his days of hope, that his Play School would remake England? Had the dedication of Neill and Montessori, the Russells and Nunn, O'Neill and Lane produced no better fruit? Had Edmond Holmes's Utopia, that 'what might be' which had fired so many imaginations, turned into a dreary reality where cautious teachers scuttled for cover behind the Dalton Plan?

Certainly by the end of the thirties the bright hopes of the early post-war years had been darkened. In 1918 Nunn believed that the old ways would soon be viewed 'only as prejudices or, at best, conventions'. It was clear in 1939 that they had proved more resilient, for though they had lost much support there were many who still believed in them and in many classrooms they still held sway. Victory had not come swiftly.

Yet, important battles had been won. It was not just that the pioneer schools were firmly established and, by their existence issued a challenge to the conservative, nor was it so important that new educational techniques (of which the Dalton Plan was only one) had moments of triumph, or that the N.E.F. continued to expand. What mattered was that instead of the conflicting set of beliefs, ideas and practices which the New Educationists put before the teacher in 1914, the progressives had, by 1939, produced a reasonably uniform set of ideas and procedures (which owed a great deal to the naturalism made popular by the New Education). By that time a person who was being initiated into the educational culture of the English primary school, who read his textbooks and journals, took part in discussions or listened to the lecturers at his teachers' college—such a person found that he was being constantly confronted with the ideas and practices which have been called 'progressive'. It was not until after World War II that the actual primary-school classroom practices were greatly modified, but before the war broke out those who formed educational opinion were increasingly attracted by progressive ideas.

In 1914 the progressives had been outsiders, a group of missionaries preaching a change and a barely respectable gospel. By 1939, though they had not won all to their cause, they had captured the allegiance of the opinion-makers. In the course of the struggle some of their first enthusiasm had been dulled and some of the sharpness taken from their challenge. But they had persisted and had made a gain vital to any group of reformers—they had become the intellectual orthodoxy.

Notes

Chapter 1

1 *The Autobiography of Bertrand Russell*, vol. 2, p. 42.

2 'England and the war', *Journal of Education*, vol. 46, no. 542 (1914), p. 624.

3 For these details see A. Marwick, *The Deluge*, pp. 13-54; A. J. P. Taylor, *English History 1914–1945*, pp. 1-12, 20 n.

4 Board of Education, *Emergency Measures with regard to Public Elementary Schools* (Circular 855, 8 August 1914).

5 'A letter to teachers in the time of war', *Journal of Education*, vol. 46, no. 543 (1914), p. 693.

6 For these details see Board of Education, *Temporary Restriction of Expenditure on Provision and Improvement of School Buildings* (Circular 903, 8 April 1915); *Occupation of School-Buildings for Military Hospitals and Other Military Purposes* (Circular 859, 17 August 1914); National Union of Teachers, *War Record 1914–1919*, p. 14; Board of Education, *Absence of Officers of the School Medical Service During the War* (Circular 862, 28 August 1914); *Temporary Employment of Members of the School Medical Service in Military Hospitals* (Circular 899, 29 March 1915); and the unnamed Circular 872, 19 October 1914.

7 *Report of the Board of Education for the year 1914–1915*, p. 2.

8 Ibid., pp. 10-13.

9 Board of Education, *Teaching of Thrift in Public Elementary Schools* (Circular 915, 1 July 1915) and the unnamed Circular 949, 5 May 1916. See also *Report of the Board of Education for the year 1915–1916*, pp. 11-12; *Report of the Board of Education for the year 1916–1917*, pp. 1-2; *Report of the Board of Education for the year 1917–1918*, p. 3.

10 National Union of Teachers, op. cit., p. 22; *Report of the Board 1917–1918*, p. 3.

11 Board of Education, *Teaching of Thrift in Public Elementary Schools*.

12 Circular 994, 2 May 1917. For details of the provisions for food control see W. H. Beveridge, *Economic and Social History of the World War: British food control*; J. Burnett, *Plenty and Want*, pp. 214-23.

13 Board of Education, *Economy in Food* (Circulars 917 and 918, both with the same name, were issued by the Board in July 1915); *Public Elementary Schools and Food Supply in War Time* (Circular 944, 1916); Circular 979, 13 January 1917; *Food Production by School Pupils* (Circular 993, 2 May 1917); *Training Courses for Teachers of Gardening* (Circular 1017, 5 October 1917); Circular 1020, 3 November 1917; *Report of the Board 1916–1917*, pp. 2-4, 27; *Report of the Board 1917–1918*, pp. 4-5.

14 Board of Education, Circular 1009, 15 August 1917. The horse-chestnuts could be substituted for grain in certain industrial processes including the making of gas masks. The call for blackberry picking was made in Circular 1056, 30 July 1918.

15 'Schools and food production', *The Times Educational Supplement*, no. 145 (1918), p. 41. With an admirable concern for priorities the same journal warned against forgetting to save a few scraps of food for the birds.

16 For details see Board of Education, *Memorandum: Scheme for training semi-skilled munition workers in Technical Schools* (1915); Circular 951, 2 June 1916; *Report of the Board 1916–1917*, pp. 37-8; *Education: Primary, Secondary, and Technical* (hereinafter *Education*), vol. 25, no. 648 (1915), p. 249.

17 *Final Report of the Departmental Committee on Juvenile Education in Relation to the War* (London, 1917), vol. 1, p. 21; *The Times History and Encyclopaedia of the War: The war and national education*, vol. 14, part 177, p. 287. For details of the system of exemptions see *Report of the Inter-Departmental Committee on Partial Exemption from School Attendance* (London, 1909), vol. 1, pp. 1-2. For the Board's action see its 1914–1915 report, pp. 19-21.

18 Quoted in an enclosure sent by the Board to local authorities with *School Attendance and Employment in Agriculture* (Circular 898, 12 March 1915).

19 *The Times Educational Supplement*, no. 104 (1917), p. 125.

20 For details of the release of workers for agriculture see *Report of the Board 1914–1915*, pp. 19-21; Board of Education, *Children Excused from School Attendance* (Circular 889, 13 February 1915); *Employment of Children in Agriculture Made in Pursuance of 'Robson's Act'* (Circular 890, 13 February 1915); *School Attendance and Employment in Agriculture* (Circular 898, 12 March 1915); *School Attendance and Employment in Agriculture* (Circular 943, 29 February 1916); Circular 1007, July 1917; Circular 1049, 23 May 1918. See also 'Occasional notes', *Journal of Education*, vol. 47, no. 548 (1915), p. 137 and no. 549 (1915), p. 204; and 'The child and the country: Schooling v. agricultural labour', *Education*, vol. 25, no. 637 (1915), pp. 122-4.

21 Board of Education, *Day and Evening Classes Provided During the War for Unemployed Young Persons* (Circular 867, 14 September 1914).

22 *Educational Reform*, p. 32.

23 Ibid., p. 64.

24 *Final Report of the Departmental Committee on Juvenile Education in Relation to Employment after the War*, vol. 1, p. 26.

25 For other examples of this concern see *Education*, vol. 27, no. 688 (1916), pp. 102-3; *Board of Education, Juvenile Employment Committees* (Circular 966, 30 October 1916); B. L. Hutchins, 'The demobilisation of juvenile workers', *Contemporary Review* (1919), pp. 196-201 (Educational Miscellanies [E.M.], Library of Department of Education and Science, London, vol. 69).

26 For details of the bureaux conducted by the Board of Trade and the local authorities see M. Penelope Hall, *The Social Services of Modern England*, pp. 236-7, and H. and M. Wickwar, *The Social Services*, pp. 85-6. Contemporary comment can be found in A. Greenwood, *Juvenile Labour Exchanges and After-Care*; G. A. Armstrong, *Juvenile Employment*; O. B. King, *The Employment and Welfare of Juveniles*, pp. 2-8; and for arrangements in a particular city see A. F. Purvis, 'Juvenile employment and after-care' in J. J. Findlay (ed.), *The Young Wage-Earner*, pp. 135-43.

27 *Interim Report of the Departmental Committee on Juvenile Education in Relation to Employment after the War* (London, 1916).

28 Board of Education, *Juvenile Employment Committees* (Circular 966, 30 October 1916) and Circular 1077, 21 November 1918.

29 For details see H. and M. Wickwar, op. cit., p. 86, and H. C. Barnard, *A History of English Education From 1760*, pp. 282-4. For contemporary comments see W. McG. Eager and H. A. Secretan, *Unemployment Among Boys*, pp. 67-78, 98-107; E. H. Axton, 'The juvenile unemployment centre', *Contemporary Review* (1919), pp. 448-53; E.M. vol. 69; H. C. Dent, *Part-Time Education in Great Britain*, pp. 43-4; V. A. Bell, *Junior Instruction Centres and their Future*.

30 Board of Education, Circular 1072, 12 November 1918.

31 *The Young Delinquent*, pp. 633-4 (first publ. 1925).

32 *The Times History and Encyclopaedia of the War*, pp. 263-4; for other

comments, see 'Occasional notes', *Journal of Education*, vol. 48, no. 563 (1916), p. 311; G. B. Code (ed.), *War and the Citizen*, pp. 115-28; Earl of Lytton, 'Inaugural address', *Report of the Conference on New Ideals in Education 1918* (hereinafter C.N.I., 1918) (London, 1918), pp. 8-9; H. D. Rawnsley, 'Juvenile delinquency: The facts and its cause', *Hibbert Journal* (1917), pp. 651-64 (E.M. vol. 70); W. Clarke Hall, *The State and the Child*, p. 11.

33 Board of Education, Circular 975, December 1916.

34 Board of Education, *Memorandum Accompanying the Regulations for Evening Play Centres for Public Elementary School Children* (Circular 980, January 1917).

35 J. P. Trevelyan, *Evening Play Centres for Children*. See also the Board's reports for 1915–1916 (pp. 4-5) and 1916–1917 (pp. 4-5) and, for a typical comment on the play centres, *The Times Educational Supplement*, no. 120 (1917), p. 301.

36 For details of the Juvenile Organizations Committee see Board of Education, *The Work of the Juvenile Organizations Committees* (London, 1933) and *Juvenile Organizations Committees* (Circular 1137, 2 December 1919). See also *Report of the Board of Education for the year 1918–1919*, p. 1; L. A. Selby-Bigge, *The Board of Education*, pp. 207-8; C. Birchenough, *History of Elementary Education in England and Wales*, p. 183; 'The Wigan welfare experiment: Juvenile employment and welfare work' in E. Young (ed.), *The New Era in Education*, pp. 232-40.

37 E. Hallas, 'Universal service' in G. B. Code (ed.), op. cit., p. 37; *Report of the Board of Education for the year 1913–1914*, p. 64. For typical comments on this issue see the following numbers of *Journal of Education*, vol. 47 (1915): 547, p. 82; 549, p. 205; 550, p. 264; 555, pp. 577-8. See also *Education*, vol. 25, no. 643 (1915), p. 195; *Report of the 85th Meeting of the British Association for the Advancement of Science* (London, 1916), pp. 747-50; P. C. McIntosh, *Physical Education in England Since 1900*, pp. 181-5.

38 See Board of Education, *Memorandum on Methods of Providing Meals for Children in Connection with Public Elementary Schools and on Dietaries Suitable for the Present Circumstances* (Circular 856, 15 August 1914); *Annual Report for 1917 of the Chief Medical Officer of the Board of Education*, p. 128; F. Le Gros Clark, *Social History of the School Meals Service*, pp. 9-10.

39 Quoted in *The Times History and Encyclopaedia of the War*, p. 270

40 See *Annual Report for 1913 of the Chief Medical Officer of the Board of Education*, p. v (this report was published in 1914), and *Annual Report of the Chief Medical Officer 1917*, p. 122. For typical comments supporting Newman's position see H. A. L. Fisher, op. cit., p. 33; Workers' Educational Association, *The Choice Before the Nation*, pp. 5, 19.

41 Board of Education, *Grants in Aid of the Organization and Supervision of the Teaching of Physical Training in Public Elementary Schools* (Circular 976, 10 February 1917) and *Allowances to Teachers attending Vacation Courses in Physical Training* (Circular 910, 4 June 1915); P. C. McIntosh, op. cit., pp. 187-95.

42 Board of Education, *Leaflets Issued by Parliamentary Recruiting Committee* (Circular 875, 2 November 1914); Circular 967, 2 October 1916; *Inadvertent Disclosure of Military Information* (Circular 997, 29 December 1916).

43 'England and the war', *Journal of Education*, vol. 46, no. 542 (1914), p. 623. See National Union of Teachers, op. cit. for an account of the teachers' contribution to the war effort.

44 *Journal of Education*, vol. 46, no. 545 (1914), p. 853; *Education*, vol. 25, no. 646 (1915), p. 225; H. J. Chaytor, 'From a German dug-out', *Journal of*

Education, vol. 50, no. 582 (1918), p. 53; 'The future of German in England', *The Times Educational Supplement*, no. 109 (1917), p. 177.

45 For a discussion of propaganda during World War I see H. D. Lasswell, *Propaganda Technique in the World War*; A. Ponsonby, *Falsehood in War-Time*; A. Marwick, *The Deluge*, pp. 50-3, 140-3, 226-33.

46 R. J. White, 'School music in the light of the war', *Journal of Education*, vol. 48, no. 564 (1916), p. 383; *The Great World War: Infants' Book*; *The Times Educational Supplement*, no. 99 (1917), p. 84 and ibid., no. 111 (1917), p. 204. It is impossible to document fully the activities in the classroom. But for typical comments see *Report of the Board 1914-1915*, pp. 10-15 especially, but also the other reports during the war; *The Times Educational Supplement*, no. 99 (1917), p. 84; A. Clutton-Brock, 'Patriotism and war', ibid., no. 104 (1917), p. 125; *Journal of Education*, 'Occasional notes', vol. 46, no. 543 (1914), p. 699; E. C. Matthews, 'Suggestions for geography teaching in time of war', ibid., vol. 46, no. 545 (1914), pp. 824-6; 'Occasional notes', ibid., vol. 47, no. 546 (1915), pp. 14-15; E. C. Abbot, 'Domestic economy in the school curriculum', ibid., vol. 47, no. 556 (1915), pp. 658-9; E. C. Matthews, 'Geography and Germany', ibid., vol. 50, no. 584 (1918), p. 181; *Education*, vol. 27, no. 692 (1917), p. 153; Earl of Cromer, 'The Teaching of Patriotism', *Nineteenth Century* (1916), pp. 1012-15; *The Times History and Encyclopaedia of the War*, pp. 282-3.

47 *Report of the Board 1914-1915*, p. 13.

48 A. Marwick, op. cit., p. 227.

49 See, for example, *Journal of Education*, vol. 48, no. 561 (1916), p. 197; Board of Education, *Memorandum on Teaching and Organisation in Secondary Schools: Modern European History* (Circular 869, September 1914).

50 For example, see National Union of Teachers, op. cit., p. 22; *The Times Educational Supplement*, no. 104 (1917), p. 125; *Education*, vol. 25, no. 630 (1915), pp. 42-3; *Report of the Board 1916-1917*, p. 1; Board of Education, *Economy in Food* (Circular 918, July 1915); *Inadvertent Disclosure of Military Information*, (Circular 977, 29 December 1916); *Collection and Utilisation of Waste Materials* (Circular 1048, 9 May 1918).

51 I have discussed this more fully in *The New Education 1870-1914*, pp. 102-51.

52 Quoted in P. H. J. H. Gosden, *Development of Educational Administration in England and Wales*, p. 104.

53 *Notes for the Study of English Education from 1900 to 1930*, p. 43.

54 *Report of the Board 1916-1917*, p. 1 and ibid., *1918-1919*, p. i.

55 J. D. M'Clure, 'Presidential address', *Report of the Sixth Annual Conference of Educational Associations 1918* (hereinafter C.E.A., 1918) (Edinburgh, 1918), p. 3.

56 H. A. L. Fisher, *Educational Reform*, p. 65; *The Times History and Encyclopaedia of the War*, p. 255. For other comments see C. W. Bailey, *Steps Towards Educational Reform*, p. 20; Viscount Bryce in the introduction to A. C. Benson (ed.), *Cambridge Essays on Education*, p. x.; Association of Directors and Secretaries for Education, *Towards an Education Policy*, p. 1.

57 L. A. Selby-Bigge, *The Board of Education*, p. 56. For other typical comments on the need for a system of education see Association of Directors and Secretaries for Education, op. cit.; *Education Reform: Being the report of the Education Reform Council*; Workers' Educational Association, *The Choice Before the Nation*; *Report of the 86th Meeting of the British Association for the Advancement of Science 1916* (London, 1917), p. 517; Incorporated Association of Assistant Masters in Secondary Schools, *Education Policy*; *Report of the Proceedings at the Fiftieth Annual Trades Union Con-*

gress 1918 (London, 1918), p. 303; Labour Party, *Labour and the New Social Order.*

58 For discussions of the Act see H. C. Barnard, op. cit., pp. 231-3; G. Bernbaum, *Social Change and the Schools 1918–1944*, pp. 17-25.

59 No. 171 (1918), p. 339.

60 Op. cit., p. 107.

Chapter 2

1 *What Is and What Might Be*, p. 50.

2 This description of the reform movement is based on the conclusions reached in my book, *The New Education 1870–1914*.

3 'The Confessions and hopes of an ex-inspector of schools' in E. G. A. Holmes, *Freedom and Growth and Other Essays*, p. 275.

4 M. W. Keatinge, *Studies in Education*, pp. 151-2 n.

5 See his *In Defence of What Might Be.*

6 *What Is and What Might Be*, pp. 163, 291. Valuable insights into Holmes the man are given by R. W. Macan (in his address of welcome) and E. Sharwood-Smith, 'Edmond Holmes memorial lecture', C.N.I., 1937, pp. 1-16 and 39-48. For an autobiographical sketch see *In Quest of an Ideal* and also 'The confessions and hopes of an ex-inspector of schools'.

7 In discussion at the Conference on New Ideals in Education for 1916. See the report for that year, p. 180.

8 *Sane Schooling*, p. 20.

9 *The Faith of a Schoolmaster*, p. 53.

10 See G. Holmes, *The Idiot Teacher*, pp. 26-7.

11 See W. Boyd and W. Rawson, *The Story of the New Education*, pp. 67-8.

12 A. S. Neill, *A Dominie in Doubt*, pp. 125, 236; H. Caldwell Cook, *The Play Way*, pp. 19-20; N. MacMunn, *The Child's Path to Freedom*, p. 26; A. J. Lynch, *Individual Work and the Dalton Plan*, p. 14; Belle Rennie, 'The Dalton Plan in England, 1920-23' in Helen Parkhurst, *Education on the Dalton Plan*, p. 170.

13 W. David Wills, *Homer Lane*; E. T. Bazeley, *Homer Lane and the Little Commonwealth.*

14 E. T. Bazeley, op. cit., p. 143.

15 *Schoolmaster's Harvest*, pp. 23-4.

16 See J. Adams, *Modern Developments in Educational Practice*, p. 293 for a typical comment.

17 For contemporary comments on Lane see, for example, the dedication to A. S. Neill, *A Dominie in Doubt*; A. Woods, *Educational Experiments in England*, p. 226; H. Caldwell Cook, op. cit., p. 58; J. H. Simpson, *Schoolmaster's Harvest*, pp. 137-51; N. MacMunn, *The Child's Path to Freedom*, p. 64; T. P. Nunn, *Education: Its data and first principles*, pp. 92-5; D. Revel, *Cheiron's Cave*, pp. 25-6; C. A. Claremont, 'Montessori and the new era', *New Era*, vol. 1, no. 1 (1920), p. 13; Earl of Lytton, *New Treasure.*

18 Op. cit., p. 27.

19 Ibid., p. 7.

20 E. M. Standing, *Maria Montessori: Her life and work* gives the biographical details. For Montessori's account of the genesis of her plans see *The Secret of Childhood*, pp. 137-69. See also Board of Education, *The Montessori System of Education* (London, 1912)—the report by Holmes; A. Woods, op. cit., pp. 42-59; E. P. Culverwell, *The Montessori Principles and Practice*; D. C. Fisher, *A Montessori Mother* and R. J. Fynne, *Montessori and her*

Inspirers; W. A. C. Stewart, *The Educational Innovators*, vol. 2, pp. 79-86 is as usual valuable.

21 S. Radice, *The New Children*, pp. xii-xiii.

22 'Occasional notes', *Journal of Education*, vol. 53, no. 622 (1921), p. 270. For other comments see C. Grant, *English Education and Dr. Montessori*, p. xiv; E. R. Murray and H. B. Smith, *The Child Under Eight*, p. 14; C. W. Kimmins, 'Some recent Montessori experiments in England', C.N.I., 1915, p. 55; A. S. Neill, *A Dominie in Doubt*, p. 200.

23 'The Montessori method' in *The Creative Self-Expression of the Child* (London, 1921), pp. 16-17. (This book was a record of the first conference of the New Education Fellowship.)

24 P. B. Ballard, *The Changing School*, p. 192; H. Ward, *Notes for the Study of English Education from 1900 to 1930*, p. 88.

25 'Occasional notes', vol. 47, no. 557 (1915), p. 694. See also A. S. Neill, *A Dominie in Doubt*, pp. 145-8; E. T. Webb, 'Madame Montessori and Mr. Holmes as educational reformers', *Contemporary Review*, April 1916, pp. 578-91 (E.M. vol. 72); G. E. Hodgson, *The Theory of the Primrose Path*.

26 Some indication of Montessori's importance can be gained from J. H. Simpson, *Schoolmaster's Harvest*, p. 15; T. P. Nunn, op. cit., p. 90; J. Adams, *Modern Developments in Educational Practice*, p. 136; C. Grant, op. cit., p. xiv; J. Dover Wilson (ed.), *The Schools of England*, p. 34; Olive A. Wheeler, *Creative Education and the Future*; *Report of the Imperial Education Conference 1923* (London, 1924), p. 76; B. Ensor, 'The schools of tomorrow' in *The Creative Self-Expression of the Child*, p. 185; C. Norwood, *The English Tradition of Education*, p. 232; F. S. Marvin, *The Nation at School*, p. 26; J. J. Findlay, *Foundations of Education*, vol. 1, p. 22; D. Revel, op. cit., pp. 21-2.

27 In discussion at the Conference on New Ideals in Education for 1916. See the report for that year, pp. 179-80.

28 W. Ash (ed.), *Who Are the Progressives Now?*

29 *Memories and Reflections*, pp. 164-5, 170-3.

30 For the Caldecott Community see P. M. Potter, 'The Caldecott Community', C.N.I., 1916, pp. 186-205 and 'The Caldecott Community', *Journal of Education*, vol. 53, no. 629 (1921), pp. 753-4; E. Coggin, *New Foundations: Some aspects of the work of the Caldecott Community* and 'A boarding school for the children of working men : The Caldecott Community' in E. Young (ed.), *The New Era in Education*, pp. 35-42; J. Ransom, *Schools of Tomorrow in England*, pp. 22-9; A. Woods, op. cit., pp. 82-9, 121-4; W. J. McCallister, *The Growth of Freedom in Education*, pp. 509-11.

31 See N. MacMunn, *A Path to Freedom in the School*; *The Child's Path to Freedom*; *Our Educational Aim: Manifesto of the Tiptree Hall Community*; 'Montessorism in secondary schools', *Report of the Montessori Conference at East Runton 1914* (London, 1914), pp. 78-90; 'Unaided dramatic work by boys of 13', C.N.I., 1918, pp. 139-44; 'Unfettered childhood', C.E.A., 1920, pp. 341-4; 'School without a teacher', *New Era*, vol. 1, no. 4 (1920), pp. 109-11; 'The wisdom of educational experiment', *Hibbert Journal* (1920), pp. 740-7 (E.M. vol. 82). See also H. Middleton, 'Class teaching through partnership' in E. Young (ed.), op. cit., pp. 72-9; J. Ransom, op. cit., pp. 116-24; A Teacher, 'School visits', *New Era*, vol. 1, no. 3 (1920), pp. 71-2. For useful comments see W. A. C. Stewart, op. cit., pp. 92-3; W. Boyd and W. Rawson, op. cit., pp. 63-4.

32 See Simpson's books : *An Adventure in Education, Sane Schooling, Schoolmaster's Harvest*. Also N. Wills, 'Rendcomb College, Cirencester', *English Review* (1924), 797-803 (E.M. vol. 86) and W. J. McCallister, op. cit.,

pp. 514-16. The best account of the school is given in W. A. C. Stewart, op. cit., pp. 103-9.

33 There were other theosophical schools established and they, and St Christopher, are discussed in W. A. C. Stewart, op. cit., pp. 50-64. For further details see B. Ensor, 'The schools of tomorrow', pp. 184-90; J. Ransom, op. cit., pp. 1-11; T. Blewitt (ed.), *The Modern Schools Handbook*, pp. 96-112; H. L. Harris, 'St Christopher School' in L. B. Pekin, *Progressive Schools*, pp. 178-97; A. Woods, op. cit., pp. 124-7, 163-7; W. Boyd and W. Rawson, op. cit., pp. 65-6.

34 For an account of O'Neill's work see G. Holmes, *The Idiot Teacher*. See also O'Neill's comments in 'Developments in self-activity in an elementary school', C.N.I., 1918, pp. 110-26; 'Creative education—learning by doing', ibid., 1919, pp. 69-97; 'How the work came about', *New Era*, vol. 2, no. 1 (1921), pp. 128-30. For contemporary comments see A. Woods, op. cit., pp. 143-55, 236-7; H. Middleton, 'Developments in self-activity in an elementary school: Knuzden, Blackburn' in E. Young, op. cit., pp. 20-34; A. S. Neill, *A Dominie in Doubt*, pp. 237-40; C. Washburne, *New Schools in the Old World*, pp. 49-65.

35 A. W. M. Bryant, 'Rural education scheme', C.N.I., 1923, pp. 63-4. See Arrowsmith's 'Physiological education in an elementary school', C.N.I., 1916, pp. 151-63; H. Middleton, 'Physiological education in an elementary school: Mixenden School, Halifax' in E. Young (ed.), op. cit., pp. 11-19; J. Ransom, op. cit., pp. 80-6.

36 For Neill see his 'My scholastic life', *Id* (the Summerhill publication), nos. 2-7 (1960-1) and from his many books, *Summerhill: A radical approach to education*, *That Dreadful School* and the *Dominie* books. For detached yet sympathetic accounts see W. A. C. Stewart, op. cit., pp. 282-302 and *passim*; R. Skidelsky, *English Progressive Schools*, pp. 121-80.

37 See D. E. M. Gardner, *Susan Isaacs*; W. van der Eyken and B. Turner, *Adventures in Education*, pp. 15-67; W. A. C. Stewart, op. cit., pp. 113-27. Susan Isaacs's account of the school is given in *Intellectual Growth in Young Children*, pp. 14-48.

38 Perhaps the best discussion of Beacon Hill is Dora Russell's in T. Blewitt (ed.), op. cit., pp. 29-42; see also *The Autobiography of Bertrand Russell 1914–1944*, vol. 2, pp. 152-6; J. Park (ed.), *Bertrand Russell on Education*; and W. A. C. Stewart, op. cit., pp. 147-53.

39 The best account of the Forest School is in W. van der Eyken, op. cit., pp. 125-44. This book contains a useful bibliography, pp. 185-6. The Order of Woodcraft Chivalry joined the Conference of Educational Associations and the reports of that body contain valuable information. For an account of the Woodcraft Folk, another organization which broke from the main scouting movement, see L. Paul, *The Republic of Children*. For Priory Gate School see T. J. Faithfull, *Psychological Foundations* (London, 1933) and *A Liberal Education for All* (London, 1928). Dorothy Revel's *Cheiron's Cave* and *Tented Schools* are based on the work at Priory Gate.

40 For comments (of varying value) on the new schools see the works by T. Blewitt, E. Young, J. Ransom, L. B. Pekin and A. Woods to which reference has already been made.

41 See Craddock, *The Class-Room Republic*; 'The newer discipline', C.E.A., 1920, pp. 27-40; 'Self-government and the growth of character', *The Creative Self-Expression of the Child*, pp. 117-27; 'The school commonwealth', *New Era*, vol. 1, no. 2 (1920), pp. 47-51.

42 H. Caldwell Cook, *The Play Way*. D. A. Beacock, *Play Way English for*

Today (London, 1943), gives biographical details. For typical reactions to Cook's work see T. P. Nunn, *Education: Its data and first principles*, pp. 89-103; J. Adams, *Modern Developments in Educational Practice*, pp. 205-26; A. S. Neill, *A Dominie in Doubt*, pp. 115-16.

43 For details see H. Parkhurst, *Education on the Dalton Plan*. Typical English commentaries were C. W. Kimmins and B. Rennie, *The Triumph of the Dalton Plan* and A. J. Lynch, *Individual Work and the Dalton Plan*. Evelyn Dewey, *The Dalton Laboratory Plan* gives examples of its use in England. For Ballard's comment see *The Changing School*, p. 197; for Sadler's, 'The Dalton Laboratory Plan at the University of Colorado', *University of Colorado Bulletin*, vol. 24, no. 10 (1924).

44 W. H. Kilpatrick, *The Project Method*: this was first published in *Teachers' College Record*, vol. 19, no. 4 (1918). For English interpreters see E. R. Boyce, *A Record of an Experiment Based on the Project Method of Education* and H. K. F. Gull, *Projects in the Education of Young Children*.

45 See R. S. Bourne, *The Gary Schools* (Boston, 1916) and C. L. Spain, *The Platoon School* (New York, 1925). For English comments see J. Adams, 'The school as a social centre', C.E.A., 1918, pp. 119-28; and also his remarks in *Modern Developments in Educational Practice*, pp. 185-204.

46 C. W. Washburne, 'Burk's individual system as developed at Winnetka' in National Society for the Study of Education, *Twenty-Fourth Yearbook, 1925*, Part 2: *Adapting the School to Individual Differences*, and 'Winnetka —An educational laboratory', *New Era*, vol. 7, no. 27 (1926). See also L. A. Cremin, *The Transformation of the School*, pp. 296-9 and for a typical English account A. G. and E. H. Hughes, *Learning and Teaching*, pp. 388-90.

47 See A. Hamaide, *The Decroly Class*; 'Freedom through method', *New Era*, vol. 8, no. 32 (1927), p. 153. For the Howard Plan, see M. O'Brien Harris, *Towards Freedom*.

48 Ballard reports Montessori's comment in *Things I Cannot Forget*, pp. 251-2. For Mackinder see her *Individual Work in Infant Schools*, and 'Freedom for young children,' C.N.I., 1923, pp. 66-76. Washburne gives an account of her school in *New Schools in the Old World*, pp. 40-8. For further details (and for comments on some of the other materials) see *New Era*, vol. 8, no. 32 (1927), pp. 154-6.

49 See *The Eurhythmics of Jacques-Dalcroze* (first publ. in 1912); P. C. McIntosh, op. cit., pp. 195-6; W. Boyd and W. Rawson, op. cit., pp. 51-2. The Dalcroze Society met under the auspices of the Conference of Educational Associations whose reports should be consulted. The quotation is taken from the report of the 1928 Conference, p. 106. W. Boyd and W. Rawson, op. cit., and W. Boyd (ed.), *Towards a New Education*, contain comments on this and other new schemes.

50 In the introduction to J. Mackinder, *Individual Work in Infant Schools*.

51 See C.N.I., 1918, p. 9. For the first conference, see *Report of the Montessori Conference at East Runton, July 1914*. The decision to widen the warrant and set up the New Ideals group is given in C.N.I., 1915, p. 2. The statement of aim, which was repeated practically unchanged throughout the period, is taken from the same source.

52 J. Adams, *Modern Developments in Educational Practice*, p. 22; J. J. Findlay, *The Foundations of Education*, vol. 2, p. 269.

53 W. Boyd and W. Rawson, op. cit., 67-73; W. A. C. Stewart, op. cit., pp. 217-20.

54 *A Hundred Years of Philosophy*, p. 258. For details see J. W. Tibble, 'Sir Percy Nunn: 1870–1944', *British Journal of Educational Studies*, vol. 10, no. 1 (1961), pp. 58-75.

55 'The development of educational thought in the United Kingdom, 1920–35', *The Year Book of Education 1936* (London, 1936), pp. 272-3. See also H. C. Barnard, op. cit., p. 312; P. B. Ballard, *The Changing School*, p. 201; W. O. Lester Smith, *Education: An introductory survey*, p. 27.

56 'Montessorism in secondary schools', *Report of the Montessori Conference at East Runton, 1914*, p. 78.

57 C.N.I., 1915, p. iii and *The Creative Self-Expression of the Child*, pp. v-vi.

58 *Talks to Parents and Teachers*, p. 192.

59 'Unfettered childhood', p. 343.

60 *A Dominie in Doubt*, p. 41.

61 Quoted in G. Holmes, op. cit., p. 187.

62 C. A. Claremont, op. cit., p. 17.

63 'Self-government and the growth of character', p. 124.

64 H. Parkhurst, op. cit., p. 17.

65 *What Is and What Might Be*, pp. 163-4.

66 *Our Educational Aim*, p. 6.

67 Op. cit., p. 352.

68 'Developments in self-activity in an elementary school', p. 117.

69 See J. M. Mackinder, *Individual Work in Infant Schools*, pp. 8-9; A. J. Lynch, *Individual Work and the Dalton Plan*, p. 26; J. Adams, *Modern Developments*, pp. 136-61; P. B. Ballard, *The Changing School*, pp. 183-4; J. H. Simpson, 'The failure of our class-teaching', *Educational Times*, vol. 2, no. 1 (1920), pp. 15-17 and vol. 2, no. 2, pp. 63-5; J. Arrowsmith, op. cit., p. 157; H. Parkhurst, op. cit., p. 11; W. H. Perkins, 'Educational development in 1924, England', *Educational Yearbook 1924* (New York, 1925), p. 210.

70 E. F. O'Neill, 'Learning by doing', p. 84.

71 P. M. Potter, 'The Caldecott Community', p. 196.

72 'The relation of the school to the home in "Egeria's" village', C.N.I., 1918, p. 18.

73 *Sane Schooling*, p. 177.

74 *That Dreadful School*, p. 31.

75 *Education: Its data and first principles*, p. 101.

76 *The Autobiography of Bertrand Russell 1914–1944*, vol. 2, p. 155.

77 *That Dreadful School*, p. 47.

78 *Sane Schooling*, p. 154.

79 'An enquiry into the true meaning of freedom in the school', C.E.A., 1918, p. 257.

80 'Mathematics and individuality', *Mathematical Gazette*, vol. 9, no. 134 (1918), p. 197.

81 *Educational Experiments in England*, p. 221.

82 T. P. Nunn, op. cit., p. v. Ballard's comment is in *The Changing School*, p. 201.

83 'Self-government and the growth of character', p. 125.

84 N. MacMunn, *Differentialism: A new method of class self-teaching*, p. 9; O. Wheeler, 'New views on human personality and their bearings on educational practice', C.E.A., 1920, p. 77.

85 See Sir Robert Blair's comments in the *Report of the B.A.A.S., 1920*, p. 199.

86 N. MacMunn, *Differentialism*, p. 9.

87 A. Robinson, 'Individuality' in *Psychology in Education* (London, 1922), p. 83.

88 See N. MacMunn, 'The wisdom of educational experiment', p. 745; A. Robinson, op. cit., p. 81.

89 For examples of the move from theory to practice see N. MacMunn,

'The wisdom of educational experiment', p. 745; P. M. Potter, 'The Caldecott Community', pp. 186-7; A. Robinson, op. cit., pp. 81-2; Child Study Society, op. cit., pp. 10-11.

90 'Self-government and the growth of character', p. 122.

91 Discussion in C.E.A., 1918, p. 138.

92 *Give Me the Young* (London, 1921), p. 64.

93 *Sane Schooling*, p. 181.

94 Discussion in C.E.A., 1918, p. 146. See also A. Robinson, op. cit., p. 82; H. M. Mackenzie, *Freedom in Education*, p. 45.

95 'Mathematics and individuality', p. 190.

96 *In Defence of What Might Be*, p. 141.

97 *Educational Experiments in England*, p. 221.

98 *In Defence of What Might Be*, p. 131.

99 *The Montessori Method*, p. 28.

100 'Learning by doing', p. 74.

101 *Education on the Dalton Plan*, p. 16.

102 *Sane Schooling*, pp. 140-80.

103 *Education: Its data and first principles*, p. 9. For similar comments see C.N.I., 1915, pp. 53-5; A. S. Neill, *That Dreadful School*, p. 10; H. Lane, *Talks to Parents and Teachers*, pp. 130-1; H. M. Mackenzie, *Freedom in Education*, p. 15; B. Ensor, 'The schools of to-morrow', p. 184.

104 'The wisdom of educational experiment', p. 740.

105 A. S. Neill, *That Dreadful School*, pp. 12-13; M. Montessori, *The Montessori Method*, pp. 15-20; H. Parkhurst, *Education on the Dalton Plan*, p. 16. See also E. G. A. Holmes, *In Defence of What Might Be*, pp. 128-9; P. B. Ballard, *The Changing School*, pp. 68-70.

106 St George Lane Fox Pitt, *The Purpose of Education*, p. 15.

107 Olive Wheeler, 'New views on human personality and their bearings on educational practice', p. 77; H. M. Mackenzie, *Freedom in Education*, p. 26.

108 H. M. Mackenzie, op. cit., p. 26.

109 *The Montessori Method*, p. 104.

110 'What do we mean by freedom for the child?', C.E.A., 1919, p. 178.

111 'Freedom and discipline', C.N.I., 1915, p. 147.

112 *In Defence of What Might Be*, p. 129.

113 Ibid., p. 27.

114 'The making of the teacher for young children', C.N.I., 1918, p. 36.

115 For typical cases see M. Montessori, *The Montessori Method*, pp. 94-5; T. P. Nunn, *Education: Its data and first principles*, pp. 106-7; H. Parkhurst, *Education on the Dalton Plan*, p. 24; H. M. Mackenzie, *Freedom in Education*, p. 27; Lord Lytton in the presidential address, C.N.I., 1917, p. 2; J. H. Simpson, *Sane Schooling*, pp. 181-2; H. Lane, *Talks to Parents and Teachers*, pp. 84-6; H. C. Miller, *The New Psychology and the Teacher*, pp. 26-9; E. F. O'Neill, 'Developments in self-activity in an elementary school', p. 126; J. Arrowsmith, op. cit., p. 152; C. Grant, op. cit., p. 40; J. A. Green in discussion, C.E.A., 1918, p. 133-4; T. C. Tibbey, ibid., p. 147; O. Wheeler, 'New views on human personality and their bearings on education', pp. 76-7.

116 For the work of these philosophers see R. S. Peters, *Ethics and Education* and *Authority, Responsibility and Education*. See also two books edited by Peters: *The Concept of Education* and *Perspectives on Plowden*; and I. Scheffler, *The Language of Education*; C. D. Hardie, *Truth and Fallacy in Educational Theory*; R. D. Archambault (ed.), *Philosophical Analysis and Education* and R. F. Dearden, *The Philosophy of Primary Education*.

117 Perhaps the best discussion of this issue is P. H. Hirst, 'Philosophy

and educational theory', *British Journal of Educational Studies*, vol. 12, no. 1 (1963), pp. 51-64.

118 See pp. 23-4 above; also Selleck, *The New Education 1870–1914.*

Chapter 3

1 *Freedom and Growth and Other Essays* (London, 1923), p. 286.

2 Montessorism in secondary schools', p. 84. See also J. H. Simpson, *An Adventure in Education*, p. 168; E. Coggin, op. cit., p. 4; H. Caldwell Cook, op. cit., p. 353; A. J. Lynch, op. cit., p. 264; E. A. Craddock, 'Self-government and the growth of character', p. 127.

3 'The schools of to-morrow', p. 190.

4 S. Radice, op. cit., p. x.

5 The dedication to *A Dominie in Doubt.*

6 Op. cit., p. 143.

7 'Developments in self-activity in an elementary school', p. 110.

8 *A Dominie in Doubt*, p. 244.

9 'The confessions and hopes of an ex-inspector of schools', p. 286.

10 W. D. Wills, op. cit., p. 23.

11 *The Montessori Method*, p. 349.

12 *A Dominie in Doubt*, pp. 237-8.

13 C.N.I., 1915, p. 193.

14 Op. cit., p. x.

15 'The biological principles of education', C.E.A., 1928, p. 95.

16 'Mathematics and individuality', p. 193.

17 *Talks to Parents and Teachers*, pp. 115-16.

18 *The Montessori Method*, p. 37.

19 'Montessorism in secondary schools', p. 87.

20 *A Dominie in Doubt*, p. 238.

21 Op. cit., p. 9.

22 *What Is and What Might Be*, pp. 294-5.

23 Op. cit., p. 53.

24 *What Is and What Might Be*, pp. 50-1.

25 *The Montessori Method*, p. 37.

26 *The Child's Path to Freedom*, p. 25.

27 'Self-government and the growth of character', p. 120.

28 *Individual Work and the Dalton Plan*, p. 25.

29 *Cheiron's Cave*, p. 89.

30 C.N.I., 1919, p. 180.

31 'Mathematics and individuality', pp. 193-4.

32 D. Watford, 'Handicrafts in schools and colleges', C.E.A., 1914, p. 135.

33 *Our Educational Aim*, p. 5.

34 'Outlook tower', *New Era*, vol. 8, no. 29 (1927), p. 5.

35 *The Montessori Method*, p. 14.

36 *The Changing School*, pp. 67-8.

37 *What Is and What Might Be*, p. 108.

38 *A Dominie in Doubt*, p. 27.

39 For a useful discussion of ideology see Nigel Harris, *Beliefs in Society*, pp. 1-67; C. Geertz, 'Ideology as a cultural system' in D. Apter (ed.), *Ideology and Discontent*, pp. 47-76.

40 Carleton Washburne, *New Schools in the Old World*, p. 61.

41 'The abolition of authority' in *The Creative Self-expression of the Child*, p. 63.

42 *Talks to Parents and Teachers*, p. 166.

43 *A Dominie in Doubt*, pp. 240-3, 250-2. For a comment on Reich's influence see R. Skidelsky, op. cit., pp. 172-80.

44 *The Montessori Method*, pp. 36-42.

45 The paper read by Lane to the Little Commonwealth Committee after the Rawlinson enquiry. Reproduced in W. D. Wills, op. cit., p. 255.

46 *Our Educational Aim*, p. 7.

47 *The Montessori Method*, p. 42.

48 *What Is and What Might Be*, p. 154.

49 Ibid., pp. 163-4.

50 'Learning by doing', p. 75.

51 *Talks to Parents and Teachers*, pp. 130-1.

52 *The Montessori Method*, p. 28.

53 *Sane Schooling*, pp. 20-1.

54 See Homer Lane, *Talks to Parents and Teachers*, pp. 95-9; Mrs Harriett Weller, 'The dramatic instinct in elementary education', C.N.I., 1922, p. 181; E. G. A. Holmes, *What Is and What Might Be*, pp. 174-7; J. Mackinder, *Individual Work in Infant Schools*, p. 15; N. MacMunn, 'Montessorism in secondary schools', p. 79; H. Caldwell Cook, op. cit., pp. 1-8; T. P. Nunn, *Education: Its data and first principles*, pp. 68-103.

55 Quoted by Foster Watson in discussion, C.E.A., 1918, p. 135.

56 Mrs Hutchinson, 'The Montessori principle in the elementary school', C.N.I., 1915, p. 83.

57 H. Wilson, 'The creative impulse and its place in education', C.N.I., 1919, p. 5.

58 *Labour and the New Social Order*, pp. 3-4.

59 In the introduction to *After-War Problems*, p. 11.

60 *Final Report of the Departmental Committee on Juvenile Problems in Relation to Employment after the War*, vol. 1, p. 2.

61 'What do we mean by freedom for the child?', C.E.A., 1919, p. 175. For a typical comment see M. L. Jacks, *Modern Trends in Education* (London [1948]), p. 117.

62 *An Unfinished Autobiography*, p. 103.

63 *The Choice Before the Nation*, p. 28.

64 Op. cit., pp. 12-13.

65 No. 148 (1918), p. 64.

66 *The Child's Path to Freedom*, p. 54.

67 *Education: Its data and first principles*, p. 3.

68 'Learning by doing', p. 80.

69 Presidential Address, *Report of the 86th Meeting of the British Association for the Advancement of Science*, p. 523.

70 Sir James Yoxall, 'Our schools and the trenches', *Chambers's Journal*, July 1916, p. 430 (E.M. vol. 70).

71 'The training colleges and the war,' *Journal of Education*, no. 547 (1915), p. 124.

72 *Individual Work and the Dalton Plan*, p. 16.

73 In discussion, C.E.A., 1918, p. 134.

74 J. Ransom, op. cit., p. 116.

75 *What Is and What Might Be*, p. 154.

76 J. Ransom, op. cit., p. 22.

77 *The Montessori Method*, p. 161.

78 'What do we mean by freedom for the child?', p. 180.

79 From a selection of Lane's thoughts reproduced in the Earl of Lytton, *New Treasure*, p. 28.

80 'Developments in self-activity', p. 110.
81 'The schools of to-morrow', p. 189.
82 *Tented Schools*, pp. 38-9.
83 *A Dominie in Doubt*, p. 132.
84 'The value and importance of handicraft in education', C.N.I., 1916, p. 34.
85 Quoted in W. van der Eyken and B. Turner, op. cit., p. 104.
86 'New projects in educational and social reform', C.E.A., 1920, p. 245.
87 H. Bompas Smith, 'The problem of urban continuation schools', C.N.I., 1917, p. 31.
88 *What is and What Might Be*, pp. 275, 279.
89 'What do we mean by freedom for the child?', p. 179.
90 'New projects in educational and social reform', p. 246.
91 'Right and wrong', *New Era*, vol. 2, no. 4 (1921), p. 216.
92 *The Montessori Method*, p. 51.
93 'Learning by doing', p. 81.
94 'Self-government and the growth of character', p. 119.
95 'The creative impulse and its place in education', p. 5.
96 *Freedom and Growth and Other Essays*, p. 175.
97 *The Autobiography of Bertrand Russell*, vol. 2, p. 17.
98 'The wisdom of educational experiment', p. 744.
99 Op. cit., pp. 356-7.
100 *Education: Its data and first principles*, p. 219.
101 M. O'Brien Harris, op. cit., p. 3.
102 J. Clarke, *The School and Other Educators*, p. 40.
103 For typical comments see J. Ransom, op. cit., pp. vii-viii; J. Adams, *Modern Developments*, pp. 14-16; H. Wilson, 'The suppression of the creative instinct', p. 11; 'The difference between the old and new type of school', *New Era*, vol. 7, no. 16 (1926), p. 51.
104 Op. cit., p. 3.
105 'Physiological education in an elementary school', p. 156.
106 N. MacMunn, *Our Educational Aim*, p. 4.
107 J. Shelley, 'What do we mean by freedom for the child?', p. 180.
108 'The faults and misdemeanours of children', p. 40; for similar comments, J. J. Findlay, 'An inquiry into the true meaning of freedom in the school', p. 256; E. A. Craddock, 'Self-government and the growth of character', p. 120; A. J. Lynch, *Individual Work and the Dalton Plan*, pp. 13-14.
109 'Developments in self-activity', p. 126.
110 L. de Lissa, 'Recent developments in infant education and their connection with the work of elementary schools', *Report of the Imperial Education Conference*, 1923 (London, 1924), p. 83.
111 *The Right To Be Happy*, p. 210.
112 S. Radice, op. cit., p. 147.
113 *The Changing School*, pp. 80-1.
114 *The Tragedy of Education*, pp. 4-5.
115 *A Dominie Dismissed*, p. 19.
116 *Freedom and Growth and Other Essays*, p. 294.
117 A comment in discussion, C.E.A., 1918, pp. 142-3.
118 *Our Educational Aim*, p. 7; 'The wisdom of educational experiment', p. 747.
119 *The Children of England*, p. 188.
120 See, for example, I. Scheffler, op. cit., pp. 49-50; R. F. Dearden, op. cit., pp. 25-49.

121 'Self-government and the growth of character', p. 122.
122 'Learning by doing', p. 95.
123 *Give Me the Young*, p. 43.
124 *The Montessori Method*, p. 87.
125 'The dramatic instinct in elementary education', p. 181.
126 The title of an article in *New Era*, vol. 2, no. 2 (1921), p. 155.
127 *Lectures on Teaching* (Cambridge, 1881), p. 95.
128 *The Montessori Method*, p. 377.
129 *On Education* (London, 1926), pp. 248-9.
130 *Education: Its data and first principles*, p. 5.
131 'How the work came about', *New Era*, vol. 2, no. 1 (1921), p. 128.
132 Op. cit., p. vii.
133 'The Caldecott Community', p. 187.
134 Op. cit., pp. 14, 19.
135 *What Is and What Might Be*, p. 163.
136 *The Montessori Method*, p. 367.
137 *A Dominie Dismissed*, p. 19 .
138 Op. cit., p. 68.
139 *Reflections on Violence* (New York, 1967), pp. 124-5. I am indebted to my friend Don Miller, Political Science Department, University of Melbourne, for bringing this statement to my attention.

Chapter 4

1 *Near the Brink*, p. 73.
2 In a review of Wilson's book, *Forum of Education*, vol. 6, no. 3 (1928), p. 281.
3 'The new education', C.E.A., 1932, p. 145.
4 L. De Lissa, 'Nursery schools and infant schools' in J. Dover Wilson, *The Schools of England*, p. 34; F. H. Spencer, 'The public elementary schools', in ibid., p. 55; C. W. Bailey, *Joyous Wayfarers*, p. 101; P. B. Ballard, *The Changing School*, p. 14. See also O. Bolton King, *Schools of To-day*, p. 6; M. Sadler in his presidential address, C.E.A., 1928, p. 4; T. P. Nunn, 'The problem of method', pp. 494-6; F. W. Roman, op. cit., pp. 61-7.
5 H. Ward, *The Educational System of England and Wales*, p. 84; C. Birchenough, *The History of Elementary Education in England and Wales*, p. 450; W. O. Lester Smith, *Education: An introductory survey*, pp. 20-59; H. C. Dent, *1870–1970—Century of Growth in English Education*, pp. 98-112.
6 W. H. Armytage, *Four Hundred Years of English Education*, pp. 226-31; G. S. Osborne, *Scottish and English Schools*, pp. 101-8; P. W. Musgrave, *Society and Education in England since 1800*, p. 100; R. D. Bramwell, op. cit., pp. 127-32; S. J. Curtis, *History of Education in Great Britain*, pp. 367-70.
7 *An Introduction to Social Psychology*, pp. 2-3.
8 Ibid., p. 44.
9 Ibid., p. 379.
10 Ibid., p. 21.
11 For example, Robert Thomson, *The Pelican History of Psychology*, pp. 179-80.
12 *An Introduction to Social Psychology*, p. 29.
13 Ibid., p. 44.
14 Psychology and education', *British Journal of Psychology*, vol. 10, parts 2 and 3 (1920), p. 172.

15 'Educational psychology in the United Kingdom', *The Year Book of Education 1936* (London, 1936), p. 294.

16 *An Introduction to the Psychology of Education*, pp. 42-3.

17 C. Burt, *The Backward Child*, p. 539; Godfrey H. Thomson, *Instinct, Intelligence and Character*; R. B. Cattell, *Your Mind and Mine*, pp. 96-105; Olive Wheeler, *Creative Education and the Future*, pp. 76-90; R. R. Rusk, *Experimental Education*, pp. 141-6.

18 *An Outline of Psychology* (London, 1923), p. 72.

19 M. Sturt and E. C. Oakden, *Matter and Method in Education*, pp. 76-90, 110-12; A. G. Hughes and E. H. Hughes, *Learning and Teaching*, pp. 7-24; Board of Education, *Report of the Consultative Committee on the Primary School* (London, 1931), pp. 48-9, 269. See, for other examples, I. Saxby, *The Education of Behaviour*, p. v and *passim*; N. Catty, op. cit., pp. 1-24; B. Dumville, *Child Mind*, pp. 84-92.

20 *Essays in the Politics of Education*, pp. 12-13.

21 *Modern Educational Psychology*, p. 42.

22 H. Ward and F. Roscoe, *The Approach to Teaching*, p. 24.

23 *An Introduction to Social Psychology*, p. 11.

24 *Educational Experiments in England*, p. 242.

25 The title of a book written by Neill and published in 1945.

26 Op. cit., p. 8.

27 *A Dominie in Doubt*, p. 246.

28 *Education: Its data and first principles*, p. 139.

29 T. P. Nunn, 'The problem of method', p. 497.

30 *Education: Its data and first principles*, p. 146.

31 *Modern Developments*, pp. 251-2. The report of the Conference of Educational Associations for 1921 is one example of a conference which concerned itself with the 'new psychology'.

32 Typical discussions were H. Crichton Miller, *The New Psychology and the Teacher*; J. Adams, *Modern Developments*, pp. 249-76; J. Drever, *An Introduction to the Psychology of Education*, pp. 118-25; G. H. Green, *Psycho-analysis in the Classroom*; G. Thomson, *Instinct, Intelligence and Character*, pp. 157-69.

33 J. Drever, *An Introduction to the Psychology of Education*, pp. 123-4.

34 *Children's Dreams*, p. 119.

35 Robert Graves and Alan Hodge, *The Long Week-End: A social history of Great Britain, 1918–1939*, p. 103.

36 'The unconscious mind' in C. Burt, E. Jones, H. Crichton Miller and W. Moodie, *How the Mind Works*, p. 71.

37 B. Dumville, *Child Mind*, p. 244.

38 Op. cit., p. 218.

39 Vol. 2, no. 2 (1921), p. 155. For other examples see J. Adams, *Modern Developments*, pp. 257-8; M. Mackenzie, op. cit., pp. 28-37; Child Study Society, op. cit., pp. 14-15; O. A. Wheeler, *Creative Education and the Future*, p. 349; G. Thomson, *Instinct, Intelligence and Character*, p. 159.

40 *The Child's Path to Freedom*, p. 16.

41 *Education: Its data and first principles*, p. 55.

42 'New views on human personality and their bearing on educational practice', C.E.A., 1920, p. 77.

43 'Asceticism and education', C.E.A., 1935, p. 318.

44 J. Adams, *Modern Developments*, p. 61.

45 'Psychology and education', p. 170.

46 'How the mind works', p. 33.

47 *Research in Education*, p. 70.

48 For details of the work done in the first part of the twentieth century see R. R. Rusk, *Research in Education*; L. S. Hearnshaw, *A Short History of British Psychology 1840–1940*, pp. 254-75; E. G. S. Evans, op. cit.; R. J. W. Selleck, op. cit., pp. 273-94.

49 'The progress of research in education', *Forum of Education*, vol. 3, no. 3 (1925), p. 210.

50 T. P. Nunn, 'The problem of method', p. 497; R. R. Rusk, *Research in Education*, pp. 79-80.

51 For some idea of the topics covered see R. R. Rusk, *Introduction to Experimental Education* (London, 1912)—reprinted as *Experimental Education* in 1919; C. W. Valentine, *An Introduction to Experimental Psychology*.

52 In the introduction to M. Sturt and E. C. Oakden, *Modern Psychology and Education*, p. xxii.

53 *The Psychology of Everyday Life*, p. 9.

54 *Intellectual Growth in Young Children*, p. 1.

55 Ibid., p. 26.

56 Ibid., p. 1

57 These statements are taken from 'The educational value of the nursery school', written in 1937 and reprinted in her *Childhood and After*, p. 48.

58 The definitive study of the American movement is L. A. Cremin's, *The Transformation of the School*.

59 Op. cit., p. 205.

60 See W. H. Burston, 'The influence of John Dewey in English official reports', *International Review of Education*, vol. 7, no. 3 (1961), pp. 311-25. This article shows that many of the report's statements can be paralleled by similar statements from Dewey. This could, of course, result from the direct influence of Dewey on the report's writers; but it could also be explained in other ways—for example, that the report was drawing on the ideas of people such as Froebel, who influenced Dewey. The article is confined to showing that the statements are similar, and does not investigate the reasons for the similarity.

61 *A Modern Philosophy of Education*, p. 78.

62 *On Education*, p. 10.

63 *The Philosophical Bases of Education* (London, 1956), p. 6 (first published 1928).

64 See, for example. T. P. Nunn, *Education: Its data and first principles*, pp. 1-2; M. Garnett, *Knowledge and Character* (Cambridge, 1939), p. 296; G. H. Thomson, *A Modern Philosophy of Education*, p. 62; Fred Clarke, 'The conflict of philosophies', *The Yearbook of Education 1936, passim*; J. J. Findlay, *The Foundations of Education*, vol. 1, pp. 9-30; O. Wheeler, *Creative Education*, p. 23; B. Wright, op. cit., p. 8.

65 *Full Stature* (London, 1936), p. 31.

66 *Foundations of Education*, vol. 1, p. 28.

67 *Education: its data and first principles*, pp. 1-2.

68 *Short Journey* (London, 1942), pp. 124-5.

69 *Science and the Modern World* (Cambridge, 1932), p. 13.

70 'The relativity of freedom', *New Era*, vol. 8, no. 32 (1927), p. 119.

71 In a comment on H. A. Miers, 'The choice of what is good for others', C.E.A., 1927, p. 10.

72 Sidgwick's statement comes from his *A Memoir* (London, 1906), appendix 1; the other statement is from R. S. Peters, *Ethics and Education*, p. 15.

73 *Patterns of Culture*, pp. 5, 278 (my italics).

74 *Ideology and Utopia* (London, 1936), p. 2.

75 Op. cit., p. 132.

76 Op. cit., p. 21.

77 'The unconscious mind', p. 76.

78 H. Crichton Miller, op. cit., p. 162.

79 For valuable studies of this period see Charles Loch Mowat, *Britain Between the Wars, 1918–1940*, especially pp. 201-58, 480-531; H. Stuart Hughes, *Consciousness and Society* (London, 1967), especially pp. 336-431.

80 'Education : Ideals and experience', C.E.A., 1929, p. 195.

81 *The Autobiography of Bertrand Russell*, vol. 2, p. 160.

82 'Freedom and authority in education', C.E.A., 1935, p. 76.

83 In discussion in P. Monroe (ed.), *Conference on Examinations*, p. 69.

84 'The human aspect of the Dalton Plan', C.E.A., 1927, p. 34.

85 *The Training of Teachers in England and Wales* (London, 1924), p. 157.

86 See, for example, the comments in 'The development of the study of education' in J. W. Tibble (ed.), *The Study of Education*, p. 15; P. W. Musgrave, *Society and Education in England Since 1800*, p. 88.

87 *Collected Essays*, pp. 299-301.

88 *Education: The socialist policy*, p. 5.

89 Board of Education, *Handbook of Suggestions for the Consideration of Teachers and Others Concerned in the Work of Public Elementary Schools* (London, 1927), pp. 12, 13, 14-15, 33, 53, 57.

90 A very valuable discussion of the detailed changes in the course of study can be found in R. D. Bramwell, *Elementary School Work, 1900-1925*. The direct quotations in this paragraph come from *Suggestions 1905*, p. 65 and 1937, p. 223.

91 Board of Education, *Report of the Consultative Committee on the Primary School* (London, 1931), pp. xvi, xvii, xxii-xxiii, xxiv.

92 See, for example, the 'Report on the aims of the junior school' prepared by a committee of the Board's inspectors—Paper no. s. 2, Ed. 10, Box 147, P.R.O., London. Many submissions and memoranda from individuals and groups are contained in Box 147.

93 *Report of the Consultative Committee on Infant and Nursery Schools* (London, 1933), p. xvii. The introduction to the report contains a number of statements which reveal the extent of the Committee's debt to progressive thinkers.

94 Op. cit., pp. 18-19.

95 The dispute as to the weight education should accord the individual as against his society continued throughout the period. See, for example, the discussions of Nunn and H. Bompas Smith in C.N.I., 1915, pp. 137-61. E. T. Campagnac consistently raised the issue—for instance in *Education in its Relation to the Common Purposes of Humanity*. For Sir Fred Clarke's contribution see the next footnote.

96 For Clarke's self-description and for his work generally, see Frank W. Mitchell, *Sir Fred Clarke, Master-Teacher 1880–1952* (London, 1967), p. 92. For his views, see for example, 'A review of educational thought: The conflict of educational philosophies', *The Year Book of Education*, 1936; *Essays in the Politics of Education; Education and Social Change*.

97 For examples of the Association at work see J. I. Cohen and R. M. W. Travers (eds), *Educating for Democracy* (London, 1939). For the N.E.F. document see W. A. C. Stewart, op. cit., pp. 225-6.

Chapter 5

1 Op. cit., p. 19.
2 Introduction to MacMunn's *The Child's Path to Freedom*, p. viii.
3 A History of the Inspectorate (private circulation, Board of Education Inspectors' Association, 1923), p. 111.
4 *Towards a New Aristocracy*, p. 42. For other examples of this often expressed mood see P.M.G., 'The educational outlook', *Educational Times*, vol. 3, no. 2 (1921), p. 69. D. Grundy, 'The new education', *English Review*, July 1923 (E.M. vol. 81), p. 118; Educational Workers' International (British Section), *Schools at the Cross Roads*, p. 7.
5 W. H. G. Armytage, *Four Hundred Years of English Education*, pp. 219-20.
6 The details in this and the preceding paragraphs are based on W. H. G. Armytage, op. cit.; A. Tropp, *The School Teachers*, esp. pp. 213-28; H. C. Barnard, *A History of English Education from 1760*, pp. 231-9; C. Birchenough, op. cit., pp. 201-8; S. J. Curtis, *Education in Britain Since 1900*, pp. 84-107; T. A. Raymont, *A History of the Education of Young Children*, pp. 336-40.
7 For details see C. L. Mowat, op. cit., especially pp. 79-143; A. J. P. Taylor, op. cit.; David Thomson, op. cit.
8 *Cheiron's Cave*, p. 28 (footnote).
9 Statement regarding the eight vacancies on the Consultative Committee (as from 1 December 1930), Ed 24/1224, P.R.O. Box 68/4/2. Fuller details of all workings of the Committee (and of all the matters discussed in this section) are given in my article 'The Hadow Report: A study in ambiguity' in *Melbourne Studies in Education 1972* (Melbourne, 1972).
10 These comments can be found in minutes (addressed to Selby-Bigge) by officials of the Board on 26 June and 1 July 1914, Ed 24/1224, P.R.O. Box 68/4/2.
11 Memorandum on the Consultative Committee and other standing advisory committees of the Board of Education, 23 July 1918, Ed 24/1227, P.R.O. Box 71/4/5/ii-iii.
12 *Report of the Board of Education for the year 1917–1918*, pp. 7-8.
13 *The Education of the Adolescent*, pp. 48-9.
14 K. Lindsay, *Social Progress and Educational Waste*, p. 7.
15 *Secondary Education for All*, pp. 70-1.
16 *Steps Towards Educational Reform*, p. 20.
17 Op. cit., p. 29.
18 The reference is given in *The Education of the Adolescent*, p. iv. A discussion of the consultation which led to the changes is given in 'The Hadow Report: A study in ambiguity'.
19 *Secondary Education for All*, pp. 30, 66-7.
20 'The Education of the people', in B.A.A.S., *Report of the 91st Meeting, Liverpool, 1923* (London, 1924), p. 270.
21 *The Education of the Adolescent*, p. 131.
22 Ibid., pp. 80-2.
23 'England', *Educational Yearbook 1936*, p. 279 (Perkins was secretary for elementary education, Lancashire Education Committee).
24 'The expansion of secondary education, England', *Educational Yearbook 1930*, p. 205.
25 J. Compton, 'The junior school, from the point of view of an administrator', *The Year Book of Education 1937*, p. 365.
26 *Examinations in Public Elementary Schools*, the report of an enquiry

undertaken by the Joint Advisory Committee of the Association of Education Committees and the National Union of Teachers (London, 1931), p. 131.
27 See for example, Valentine Davis, *The School Idea*, p. 56; E. B. Warr,
The New Era in the Junior School, p. 3; H. V. Usill, 'A critical survey of
elementary education in England and Wales: The senior school', *The Year
Book of Education, 1933*, p. 208; H. Bompas Smith, *The Nation's Schools*,
pp. 103-5; G. Thomson, *A Modern Philosophy of Education*, p. 60; P. B.
Ballard, 'The special place examination' in International Institute Examinations Enquiry, *Essays on Examination*, p. 110; R. B. Cattell, *Your Mind
and Mine*, p. 395.
28 C. A. Richardson, *Methods and Experiments in Mental Tests*, p. 16. For
similar comments see Burt's *The Subnormal Mind* (London, 1935), p. 11; V.
Hazlitt, *Ability; A psychological study*, p. 2.
29 C. H. W. G. Anderson, 'Measurement in education', *New Era*, vol. 6,
no. 1 (1925), p. 10.
30 For this comment see P. Monroe (ed.), *Conference on Examinations*,
p. 129.
31 'Post-primary schools, with special reference to the age of transference
from the ordinary elementary to the post-primary school', p. 6. This statement is unnumbered but is contained in the Committee's papers, Ed 10,
P.R.O. Box 147.
32 T. A. Raymont, 'Intelligence tests', *Journal of Education*, vol. 55, no.
647 (1923), p. 361, Bertrand Russell, 'Socialism and education', *Socialist Review*
(March 1925), pp. 124-34 (E.M. vol. 87).
33 *Mental and Scholastic Tests*, p. xv.
34 Ibid., p. 209.
35 'Psychology and the social sciences' in J. E. Dugdale, *Further Papers
on the Social Sciences*, p. 149, see also his 'Intelligence and civilisation' (1936),
reprinted in S. Wiseman (ed.), *Intelligence and Ability* (Harmondsworth,
1967), p. 115.
36 See *Report of the Board 1924–1925*, p. 101, and 1923–24, pp. 20-1.
37 'Post-primary schools ...', pp. 2-3 and 'Psychological Tests for general
intelligence', *Journal of Education*, vol. 52, no. 606 (1920), p. 29.
38 'Psychology and the social sciences', p. 148.
39 In University of Liverpool, *Social Factors in Secondary Education: no.
5, The Social Survey of Merseyside* (1920), p. 35.
40 In Hadow Committee Papers: 'Summaries of evidence', Paper no. P-14
(iii), Ed 10, P.R.O. Box 147.
41 Memo on the organisation of objective and curriculum of courses of
study suitable for children who will remain in full-time attendance at school,
other than Secondary Schools, up to the age of 15 plus. By National Association of Inspectors of Schools and Educational Organisers. Unnumbered
statement in Committee papers, Ed 10, P.R.O. Box 147.
42 *The Education of the Adolescent*, p. 108.
43 Ibid., p. 121.
44 'Summaries of evidence', Paper No. P-14 (ii), p. 107.
45 *Report on Secondary Education in Birkenhead*, p. 80.
46 'Until teachers are kings', *Hibbert Journal*, vol. 21, no. 3 (1923), p. 483.
47 'The mental differences between individuals' in B.A.A.S., *Report of the
91st Meeting, Liverpool*, 1923, p. 228.
48 *Reflections on the Revolution in France* (Chicago, 1955), pp. 125-6.
49 F. W. Roman, op. cit., p. 61; C. W. Kimmins and Belle Rennie, op. cit.,
p. 11; W. O. Lester Smith, *Education: An introductory survey*, p. 50. See
also P. B. Ballard, *The Changing School*, p. 197.

50 C. Burt, *The Backward Child*, p. 623. For other comments on the manner in which the Plan helped 'individuality' see P. B. Ballard, *The Changing School*, p. 183; C. W. Kimmins, 'The Dalton Plan' in *Educational Movements and Methods*, pp. 39-40; M. A. Allen, *Stepping Stones to the Dalton Plan*, p. 3; T. Raymont, *Education*, pp. 216-17; A. J. Lynch, *Individual Work and the Dalton Plan*, pp. 13-27; G. Kendall, *A Headmaster Reflects*, p. 80.

51 H. Parkhurst, *Education on the Dalton Plan*, p. 16; A. J. Lynch, op. cit., p. 79; see also Mrs Heath, 'The Human Aspect of the Dalton Plan', C.E.A., 1927, p. 35; C. Washburne, *New Schools in the Old World*, p. 24.

52 H. Parkhurst, *An Explanation of the Dalton Laboratory Plan*, p. 2; J. Adams in the introduction to *Educational Movements and Methods*, p. 24; A. J. Lynch, op. cit., p. 82.

53 *Modern Developments in Educational Practice*, p. 4. For comments on the other attractions of the Dalton Plan which are mentioned in this paragraph see ibid., p. 149; A. J. Lynch, *Individual Work and the Dalton Plan*, *passim*; C. Washburne, op. cit., pp. 14-26; M. Sturt and E. C. Oakden, *Matter and Method in Education*, pp. 124-5; C. W. Kimmins and B. Rennie, op. cit., *passim*; H. Parkhurst, *Education on the Dalton Plan*, *passim*; C. M. Fleming, *Individual Work in Primary Schools*, pp. 18-21.

54 Op. cit., p. 54.

55 'The problem of method, England', p. 495

56 *Individual Work on the Dalton Plan*, pp. 86-100.

57 *New Schools in the Old World*, p. 22.

58 *Individual Work in Primary Schools*, p. 19.

59 *Individual Work and the Dalton Plan*, p. 76.

60 Talk given to a meeting of the Dalton Association, C.E.A., 1926, pp. 51-4.

61 'Examination results under the Dalton Plan', C.E.A., 1925, pp. 60-1.

62 *Education on the Dalton Plan*, p. 22.

63 Ibid., pp. 18-19.

64 Ibid., p. 29.

65 'The Dalton Laboratory Plan', C.N.I., 1921, pp. 52-3.

Select bibliography

Note: Some books were reprinted a number of times. The publication date given below is that of the edition used in this book. Where the date of first publication is important it has been given in the text. The place of publication is London, unless otherwise stated.

PRIMARY SOURCES

1. *Board of Education publications*
(a) The annual and departmental reports, memoranda, circulars and pamphlets for the period. These documents are most easily accessible at the Library of the Department of Education and Science, London.
(b) Reports of the Consultative Committee:
Psychological Tests of Educable Capacity (1924)
The Education of the Adolescent (1926)
Books in Public Elementary Schools (1928)
The Primary School (1931)
Infant and Nursery Schools (1933)

2. *Reports of various organizations*
British Association for the Advancement of Science (B.A.A.S.), annual, for the period.
Conference of Educational Associations, annual, for the period.
Conference on New Ideals in Education (C.N.I.), for the period. The first report is entitled *Report of the Montessori Conference at East Runton* (1914).
New Education Fellowship conference held at Calais (1921), Montreux (1923), Heidelberg (1925), Locarno (1927), Elsinore (1929), Nice (1932), Cheltenham (1936).

3. *Yearbooks*
Educational Yearbook of the International Institute of Teachers' College Columbia University. Edited throughout this period by I. L. Kandel.
The Year Book of Education (Evans) from 1932.

4. *Books and Pamphlets*
ADAMS, J., *Modern Developments in Educational Practice* (U.L.P., 1922).
——, (ed.), *The New Teaching* (Hodder and Stoughton, 1927).

177

ALLEN, M. A., *Stepping Stones to the Dalton Plan* (Dalton Association, n.d.).

ARMSTRONG, G. A., *Juvenile Employment* (Bradford, 1917).

ASSOCIATION OF DIRECTORS AND SECRETARIES FOR EDUCATION, *Towards an Education Policy* (n.p., 1917).

ASSOCIATION FOR EDUCATION IN CITIZENSHIP, *Education for Citizenship in Elementary Schools* (O.U.P., 1939).

The Autobiography of Bertrand Russell 1914–1944, vol. 2 (Allen & Unwin, 1968).

BADLEY, J. H., *Memories and Reflections* (Allen & Unwin, 1955).

BAILEY, C. W., *Happiness in the School* (Blackie, 1919).

——, *Joyous Wayfarers* (Birch, n.d.).

——, *Steps Towards Educational Reform* (C.U.P., 1913).

BALLARD, P. B., *The Changing School* (U.L.P., 1925).

——, *Mental Tests* (Hodder and Stoughton, 1920).

——, *The New Examiner* (U.L.P., 1936).

——, *Things I Cannot Forget* (U.L.P., 1937).

BAZELEY, E. T., *Homer Lane and the Little Commonwealth* (Allen & Unwin, 1928).

BELL, V. A., *Junior Instruction Centres and Their Future* (Constable, Edinburgh, 1934).

BENEDICT, R., *Patterns of Culture* (George Routledge, 1935).

BENSON, A. C. (ed.), *Cambridge Essays on Education* (C.U.P., 1918).

BLEWITT, T. (ed.), *The Modern Schools Handbook* (Gollancz, 1934).

BLOOR, CONSTANCE, *The Process of Learning* (Kegan Paul, Trench, Trubner, 1930).

BOOTHROYD, H. E., A History of the Inspectorate (Board of Education Inspectors' Association (private circulation, 1923).

BOYCE, E. R., *A Record of an Experiment Based on the Project Method of Education* (Froebel Soc. [1932]).

BOYD, W. (ed.), *Towards a New Education* (Knopf, London and New York, 1930).

BURT, C., *The Backward Child* (U.L.P., 1937).

——, *Mental and Scholastic Tests* (King, 1921).

——, *The Young Delinquent* (U.L.P., 1945).

BURT, C., JONES, E., MILLER, H., CRICHTON AND MOODIE, W., *How the Mind Works* (B.B.C., 1933).

CAMPAGNAC, E. T., *Converging Paths* (C.U.P., 1916).

——, *Education in its Relation to the Common Purposes of Humanity* (Pitman, 1925).

——, *Notes on Education* (Evans, n.d.).

——, *Society and Solitude* (C.U.P., 1922).

——, *Studies Introductory to a Theory of Education* (C.U.P., 1915).

CATTELL, R. B., *Your Mind and Mine* (Harrap, 1934).

CATTY, N., *The Theory and Practice of Education* (Methuen, 1934).

Child Study Society, *Memorandum on The Educational Principles Upon Which Should Be Based All Future School Reform* (1917).

CLARKE, F., *Education and Social Change* (Sheldon Press, 1940).

——, *Essays in the Politics of Education* (O.U.P., 1923).

CLARKE, J., *The School and Other Educators* (Longmans, Green, 1918).
CLUTTON-BROCK, A., *The Ultimate Belief* (Constable, 1916).
CODE, G. B. (ed.), *War and the Citizen* (Hodder and Stoughton, 1917).
COGGIN, E., *New Foundations: Some aspects of the work of the Caldecott Community* (1921).
COOK, H. CALDWELL, *The Play Way* (Heinemann, 1917).
CRADDOCK, E. A., *The Class-Room Republic* (Black, 1920).
CULVERWELL, E. P., *The Montessori Principles and Practice* (Bell, 1914).
CURRY, W. B., *The School and a Changing Civilisation* (Bodley Head, 1934).
DALCROZE, JACQUES, *see The Eurhythmics of Jacques-Dalcroze.*
DAVIS, V., *The Matter and Method of Modern Teaching* (Cartwright & Rattray, Manchester and London, 1928).
——, *The School Idea* (Allen & Unwin, 1931).
——, *The Science and Art of Teaching* (Cartwright and Rattray, Manchester and London, 1930).
DAWSON, W. H. (ed.), *After-War Problems* (Allen & Unwin, 1917).
DEWEY, E., *The Dalton Laboratory Plan* (Dent, London and Toronto, 1924).
DREVER, J., *An Introduction to the Psychology of Education* (Arnold, 1923).
——, *The Psychology of Everyday Life* (Methuen, 1921).
DUGDALE, J. E., *Further Papers on the Social Sciences* (Le Play House, 1937).
DUMVILLE, B., *Child Mind* (U.T.P., 1925).
Education Reform: Being the report of the Education Reform Council (King, 1917).
Educational Movements and Methods (Harrap, 1924).
Educational Workers' International (British Section), *Schools at the Cross Roads* (Lawrence, 1935).
The Eurhythmics of Jacques-Dalcroze (Constable, 1917).
Examinations in Public Elementary Schools, the Report of an Enquiry undertaken by the Joint Advisory Committee of the Association of Education Committees and the National Union of Teachers ... ('Education' Ltd and 'The Schoolmaster' Publishing Co. [1931]).
FAITHFULL, T. J., *Psychological Foundations* (Bale, 1933).
FINDLAY, J. J., *The Children of England* (Methuen, 1923).
——, *The Foundations of Education*, 2 vols (U.L.P., 1925, 1927).
—— (ed.), *The Young Wage-Earner* (Sidgwick & Jackson, 1918).
FISHER, D. C., *A Montessori Mother* (Constable, 1913).
FISHER, H. A. L., *An Unfinished Autobiography* (O.U.P., 1940).
——, *Educational Reform* (Clarendon Press, Oxford, 1918).
FLEMING, C. M., *Individual Work in Primary Schools* (Harrap, 1934).
FOX, C., *Educational Psychology* (Kegan Paul, Trench, Trubner, 1935).
FYNNE, R. J., *Montessori and Her Inspirers* (Longmans, Green, 1924).
GRANT, C., *English Education and Dr. Montessori* (Wells, Gardner, Darton, 1913).
The Great World War: Infants' book (Educational Publishing Co., London and Cardiff [1919]).

GREEN, G. H., *Psycho-analysis in the Classroom* (U.L.P., 1924).

GREENWOOD, A., *Juvenile Labour Exchanges and After-Care* (King, 1911).

GULL, H. K. F., *Projects in the Education of Young Children* (McDougall's Educational Co., London and Edinburgh, n.d.).

HADOW, W. H., *Collected Essays* (O.U.P., 1928).

HALL, W. CLARKE, *The State and the Child* (Headley Bros, 1917).

HAMAIDE, A., *The Decroly Class* (Dent, London and Toronto, 1925).

HAPPOLD, F. C., *Towards a New Aristocracy* (Faber, 1953).

HARRIS, M. O'BRIEN, *Towards Freedom* (U.L.P., 1923).

HAZLITT, V., *Ability: A psychological study* (Methuen, 1926).

HODGSON, G. E., *The Theory of the Primrose Path* (Association of University Women Teachers, 1913).

HOLMES, E. G. A., *Freedom and Growth and Other Essays* (Dent, 1923).

——, *Give Me the Young* (Constable, 1921).

——, *In Defence of What Might Be* (Constable, 1914).

——, *In Quest of An Ideal* (Cobden-Sanderson, 1920).

——, *The Tragedy of Education* (Constable, 1913).

——, *What Is and What Might Be* (Constable, 1911).

HUGHES, A. G. and E. H., *Learning and Teaching* (Longmans, Green, 1937).

Incorporated Association of Assistant Masters in Secondary Schools, *Education Policy* (1917).

INTERNATIONAL INSTITUTE EXAMINATIONS ENQUIRY, *Essays on Examinations* (Macmillan, 1936).

ISAACS, S., *Childhood and After* (Routledge & Kegan Paul, 1948).

——, *Intellectual Growth in Young Children* (George Routledge, 1930).

——, *Social Development in Young Children* (George Routledge, 1933).

——, *The Children We Teach* (U.L.P., 1932).

JACKS, L. P., *Near The Brink* (Allen & Unwin, 1952).

JONES, W. H. S., *Discipline* (C.U.P., 1926).

KEATINGE, M. W., *Studies in Education* (Black, 1916).

KENDALL, G., *A Headmaster Reflects* (Hodge, 1937).

KILPATRICK, W. H., *The Project Method* (Teachers' College, Columbia, New York, 1929).

KIMMINS, C. W., *Children's Dreams* (Longmans, Green, 1920).

KIMMINS, C. W. and RENNIE, B., *The Triumph of the Dalton Plan* (Nicholson & Watson [1931]).

KING, O. BOLTON, *The Employment and Welfare of Juveniles* (Murray, 1925).

——, *Schools of To-day* (Dent, 1929).

KLEIN, M., *The Psycho-Analysis of Children* (Hogarth Press, 1963).

Labour Party, *Labour and The New Social Order* (Labour Party, 1918).

LANE, H., *Talks to Parents and Teachers* (Allen & Unwin, 1928).

LINDSAY, K., *Social Progress and Educational Waste* (George Routledge, 1926).

LYNCH, A. J., *Individual Work and the Dalton Plan* (Philip, 1924).

LYTTON, EARL OF, *New Treasure* (Allen & Unwin, 1934).

MCDOUGALL, W., *An Introduction to Social Psychology* (Methuen, 1923).

——, *An Outline of Psychology* (Methuen, 1923).

MACKINDER, J. M., *Individual Work in Infant Schools* (Educational Publishing Co., 1923).

MACKENZIE, H. MILLICENT, *Freedom in Education* (Hodder & Stoughton, 1924).

MCMILLAN, M., *The Nursery School* (Dent, London and Toronto, 1919).

MACMUNN, N., *The Child's Path to Freedom* (Curwen, 1926).

——, *Differentialism: A new method of class self-teaching* (W. H. Smith (London), Shakespeare Press (Stratford-upon-Avon) [1914]).

——, *Our Educational Aim: Manifesto of the Tiptree Hall Community* (n.d.).

——, *A Path to Freedom in the School* (Bell, 1914).

MARVIN, F. S., *The Nation at School* (O.U.P., 1933).

MILLER, E. W., *Room to Grow!* (Harrap, 1944).

MILLER, H. CRICHTON, *The New Psychology and the Teacher* (Jarrolds, 1921).

MONROE, P. (ed.), *Conference on Examinations* (Teachers' College Columbia, New York, 1931).

——, *Conference on Examinations* (Teachers' College Columbia, New York, 1936).

MONTESSORI, M., *The Montessori Method* (Heinemann, 1912).

——, *The Secret of Childhood* (Longmans, Green, 1936).

MURRAY, E. R. and SMITH, H. B., *The Child under Eight* (Arnold [1920]).

NATIONAL UNION OF TEACHERS, *War Record 1914–1919* (1920).

NEILL, A. S., *A Dominie Abroad* (Jenkins [1922]).

——, *A Dominie Dismissed* (Jenkins [1918]).

——, *A Dominie in Doubt* (Jenkins, 1920).

——, *A Dominie's Log* (Jenkins [1915]).

——, *Hearts not Heads in the School* (Jenkins, 1945).

——, *Summerhill: A radical approach to education* (Gollancz, 1962).

——, *That Dreadful School* (Jenkins, 1937).

NORWOOD, C., *The English Tradition of Education* (Murray, 1929).

NUNN, T. P., *Education: Its data and first principles* (Arnold, 1920).

OWEN, G. (ed.), *Nursery School Education* (Methuen, 1923).

PARKHURST, H., *Education on the Dalton Plan* (Bell, 1922).

——, *An Explanation of the Dalton Laboratory Plan* (Dalton Association, 1926).

PAUL, L., *The Republic of Children* (Allen & Unwin, 1938).

PEKIN, L. B., *Progressive Schools* (Hogarth Press, 1934).

PITT, ST GEORGE LANE FOX, *The Purpose of Education* (C.U.P., 1913).

Psychology in Education (Pitman, 1922).

RADICE, S., *The New Children* (Hodder & Stoughton [1920]).

RANSOM, J., *Schools of Tomorrow in England* (Bell, 1919).

REVEL, D., *Cheiron's Cave* (Heinemann, 1928).

——, *Tented Schools* (Williams & Norgate, 1934).

RICHARDSON, C. A., *Methods and Experiments in Mental Tests* (Harrap, 1922).

ROMAN, F. W., *The New Education in Europe* (George Routledge, 1923).

RUSK, R. R., *Experimental Education* (Longmans, Green, 1919).

——, *Research in Education* (U.L.P., 1932).

RUSSELL, B., *Education and the Social Order* (Allen & Unwin, 1935).
——, *On Education* (Allen & Unwin, 1926).
RUSSELL, B., *see also Autobiography.*
RUSSELL, D., *The Right To Be Happy* (George Routledge, 1927).
SADLER, M. E., *Our Public Elementary Schools* (Thornton Butterworth, 1926).
——, *Report on Secondary Education in Birkenhead* (Philip, 1904).
SAXBY, I., *The Education of Behaviour* (U.L.P., 1921).
SELBY-BIGGE, L. A., *The Board of Education* (Putnam, London and New York, 1927).
SIMPSON, J. H., *An Adventure in Education* (Sidgwick & Jackson, 1917).
——, *Sane Schooling* (Faber, 1936).
——, *Schoolmaster's Harvest* (Faber, 1954).
SLEIGHT, W. G., *Educational Values and Methods* (Clarendon Press, Oxford, 1915).
——, *The Organisation and Curricula of Schools* (Arnold, 1922).
SMITH, H. BOMPAS, *The Nation's Schools* (Longmans, Green, 1927).
SMITH, E. SHARWOOD, *The Faith of a Schoolmaster* (Methuen, 1935).
STEAD, H. G., *Full Stature* (Nisbet, 1936).
STEINER, R., *The Education of the Child* (Anthroposophical Pub. Co., 1927).
STURT, M. and OAKDEN, E. C., *Matter and Method in Education* (Kegan Paul, Trench, Trubner, 1928).
——, *Modern Psychology and Education* (Kegan Paul, Trench, Trubner, 1926).
TANSLEY, A. G., *The New Psychology and its Relation to Life* (Allen & Unwin, 1922).
TAWNEY, R. H., *Education:* The *socialist policy* (Ind. Lab. Party, 1924).
——, *Secondary Education For All* (Allen & Unwin, 1922).
THOMSON, G. H., *Instinct, Intelligence and Character* (Allen & Unwin, 1924).
——, *A Modern Philosophy of Education* (Allen & Unwin, 1929).
The Times History and Encyclopaedia of the War: The war and national education, vol. 14, part 177 (1918).
TREVELYAN, J. P., *Evening Play Centres for Children* (Methuen, 1920).
UNIVERSITY OF LIVERPOOL, *Social Factors in Secondary Education: No. 5, The Social Survey of Merseyside* (1934).
VALENTINE, C. W., *An Introduction to Experimental Psychology* (U.T.P., 1919).
WARD, H., *The Educational System of England and Wales and its Recent History* (C.U.P., 1935).
WARD, H. and ROSCOE, F., *The Approach to Teaching* (Bell, 1928).
WARR, E. B., *The New Era in the Junior School* (Methuen, 1937).
WASHBURNE, C., *New Schools in the Old World* (Day, New York, 1926).
WESTLAKE, E., *The Forest School and Other Papers* (Order of Woodcraft Chivalry, Salisbury, 1930).
WHEELER, O. A., *Creative Education and the Future* (U.L.P., 1936).
WHITEHEAD, A. N., *The Aims of Education and Other Essays* (Benn, 1966).
WHITEHOUSE, J. H., *Creative Education at an English School* (C.U.P., 1926).

——, *A National System of Education* (C.U.P., 1913).

WILSON, J. DOVER, *The Schools of England* (Sidgwick & Jackson, 1928).

WOODS, A., *Educational Experiments in England* (Methuen, 1920).

WORKERS' EDUCATIONAL ASSOCIATION, *The Choice Before the Nation* (1918).

WRIGHT, B., *Educational Heresies* (Douglas, 1925).

YOUNG, E. (ed.), *The New Era in Education* (Philip [1920]).

5. *Journals*
Of the large number available the following are the most useful:
Educational Times
Education: Primary, secondary and technical
Forum of Education
Journal of Education
New Era
The Times Educational Supplement

EDUCATIONAL BACKGROUND

ARCHAMBAULT, R. D. (ed.), *Philosophical Analysis and Education* (Routledge & Kegan Paul, 1965).

ARMYTAGE, W. H. G., *Four Hundred Years of English Education* (C.U.P., 1964).

ASH, W. (ed.), *Who Are the Progressives Now?* (Routledge & Kegan Paul, 1969).

BANKS, O., *Parity and Prestige in English Secondary Education* (Routledge & Kegan Paul, 1955).

BANTOCK, G. H., *Education and Values* (Faber, 1965).

BARNARD, H. C., *A History of English Education from 1760* (U.L.P., 1968).

BERNBAUM, G., *Social Change and the Schools 1918–1944* (Routledge & Kegan Paul, 1967).

BIRCHENOUGH, C., *History of Elementary Education in England and Wales* (U.T.P., 1938).

BONHAM-CARTER, V., *Dartington Hall* (Phoenix House, 1958) .

BOYD, W. and RAWSON, W., *The Story of the New Education* (Heinemann, 1965).

BRAMWELL, R. D., *Elementary School Work, 1900-1925* (University of Durham Institute of Education, Durham, 1961).

CLARK, F. LE GROS, *Social History of the School Meals Service* (National Council of Social Services [1948]).

CREMIN, L. A., *The Transformation of the School* (Knopf, New York, 1962).

CURTIS, S. J., *Education in Britain Since 1900* (Dakers, 1952).

——, *History of Education in Great Britain* (U.T.P., 1961).

CURTIS, S. J. and BOULTWOOD, M. E. A., *An Introductory History of English Education Since 1800* (U.T.P., 1966).

DEARDEN, R. F., *The Philosophy of Primary Education* (Routledge & Kegan Paul, 1968).

DENT, H. C., *1870–1970—Century of Growth in English Education* (Longmans, 1970).

——, *Part-Time Education in Great Britain* (Turnstile Press, 1949).

EVANS, E. G. S., *Modern Educational Psychology* (Routledge & Kegan Paul, 1969).

GARDNER, D. E. M., *Susan Isaacs* (Methuen, 1969).

GOSDEN, P. H. J. H., *The Development of Educational Administration in England and Wales* (Blackwell, 1966).

HARDIE, C. D., *Truth and Fallacy in Educational Theory* (Teachers' College, Columbia, New York, 1962).

HEARNSHAW, L. S., *A Short History of British Psychology 1840–1940* (Methuen, 1964).

HOLMES, G., *The Idiot Teacher* (Faber, 1952).

KAZAMIAS, A. M., *Politics, Society and Secondary Education in England* (University of Pennsylvania Press, Philadelphia, 1966).

MCCALLISTER, W. J., *The Growth of Freedom in Education* (Constable, 1931).

MCINTOSH, P. C., *Physical Education in England Since 1900* (Bell, 1968).

MUSGRAVE, P. W., *Society and Education in England Since 1800* (Methuen, 1968).

OSBORNE, G. S., *Scottish and English Schools* (Longmans, 1966).

PARK, J. (ed.), *Bertrand Russell on Education* (Allen & Unwin, 1964).

PERRY, L. R. (ed.), *Bertrand Russell, A. S. Neill, Homer Lane, W. H. Kilpatrick: Four progressive educators* (Collier-Macmillan, 1967).

PETERS, R. S., *Authority, Responsibility and Education* (Allen & Unwin, 1959).

——, *Ethics and Education* (Allen & Unwin, 1966).

PETERS, R. S. (ed.), *The Concept of Education* (Routledge & Kegan Paul, 1967).

——, *Perspectives on Plowden* (Routledge & Kegan Paul, 1969).

RAYMONT, T. A., *A History of the Education of Young Children* (Longmans Green, 1937).

SELLECK, R. J. W., *The New Education 1870–1914* (Pitman, London and Melbourne, 1968).

SKIDELSKY, R., *English Progressive Schools* (Pelican, 1969).

SMITH, W. O. LESTER, *Education: An introductory survey* (Pelican, 1957).

STANDING, E. M., *Maria Montessori: Her life and work* (Mentor-Omega, New York, 1962).

STEWART, W. A. C., *The Educational Innovators*, vol. 2 (Macmillan, 1968).

——, *Quakers and Education* (Epworth Press, 1953).

TIBBLE, J. W. (ed.), *The Study of Education* (Routledge & Kegan Paul, 1966).

TROPP, A., *The School Teachers* (Heinemann, 1957).

VAN DER EYKEN, W. and TURNER, B., *Adventures in Education* (Allen Lane, 1969).

WARD, H., *Notes for the Study of English Education from 1900 to 1930* (Bell, 1931).

WILLS, W. D., *Homer Lane* (Allen & Unwin, 1964).

SOCIAL AND POLITICAL BACKGROUND

APTER, D. (ed.), *Ideology and Discontent* (Free Press, New York, 1964).

BEVERIDGE, W. H., *Economic and Social History of the World War: British food control* (Humphrey Milford (London), O.U.P., 1928).

BURNETT, J., *Plenty and Want* (Nelson, 1966).

EAGER, W. MCG. and SECRETAN, H. A., *Unemployment Among Boys* (Dent, London and Toronto, 1925).

GRAVES, R. and HODGE, A., *The Long Week-end: A social history of Great Britain, 1918–1939* (Faber, 1940).

HALL, M. PENELOPE, *The Social Services of Modern England* (Routledge & Kegan Paul, 1959).

HARRIS, N., *Beliefs in Society* (Watts, 1968).

LASSWELL, H. D., *Propaganda Technique in the World War* (Kegan Paul, Trench, Trubner, London and New York, 1927).

MARWICK, A., *The Deluge* (Pelican, 1965).

MOWAT, C. L., *Britain Between the Wars, 1918–1940* (Methuen, 1968).

PASSMORE, J., *A Hundred Years of Philosophy* (Pelican, 1968).

PONSONBY, A., *Falsehood in War-time* (Allen & Unwin, 1928).

SCHEFFLER, I., *The Language of Education* (Charles C. Thomas, Springfield, 1966).

TAYLOR, A. J. P., *English History 1914–1945* (Clarendon Press, 1965).

THOMSON, D., *England in the Twentieth Century* (Penguin, 1965).

THOMSON, R., *The Pelican History of Psychology* (Harmondsworth, 1968).

WICKWAR, H. and M., *The Social Services* (Bodley Head, 1949).

Index

Hadow, W. H., ix, 122-3, 126, 133-143
Haig, Sir Douglas, 17
Halifax, Lord, 136
Hall, G. S., 39
Hallam, J. H., 138
Hamley, H. R., 121
Happold, F. C., 130
Harrison, A. S., 122
Headlam-Morley, J. W., 141
Herbart, J. F., 23, 61
Holmes, E. G. A., 23, 24-6, 27, 28, 30, 31, 45, 46, 47, 49, 51-2, 55-6, 58, 59, 60, 63, 64, 65, 66, 68, 69, 70, 72, 75, 78, 79, 80-1, 82, 88, 91, 92, 94, 96, 97, 98, 113, 155
Howard Plan, 43, 57, 65
Hughes, A. G. and E. H., 104, 110, 114, 122

individuality, 29, 44, 53-6, 59, 60-1, 70, 80-1, 82, 87-8, 93-4, 97, 104, 108, 119, 124, 125, 150
Ingham, P., 43, 44
instinct, 80-1, 102-6, 124
interest, 24, 27, 32, 37, 41, 50-1, 59, 80-1, 82, 124
Isaacs, Susan, 37, 56, 57, 58, 69, 106, 107, 108, 109, 111-13, 121, 122, 126
Itard, J., 58, 77, 79, 81

Jacks, L. P., 100
Jacques-Dalcroze, E., 43-4
Joffre, J.-J.-C., 2
Jones, D. Caradog, 141
Jones, E., 106, 107, 118
Jones, Lance, 121
Jung, C. G., 68
juvenile employment bureaux, 10
juvenile employment centres, 10-11
Juvenile Organizations Committee, 12-13

Kilpatrick, W. H., 42
Kimmins, C. W., 43, 45, 107, 108, 122, 150, 151, 154
kindergarten, 30, 55

Kitchener, Lord, 2
Klein, M., 106

Labour Party, 85, 136
Lane, Homer, 25, 26-7, 28, 29, 30, 31, 33, 34, 37, 40, 45, 46, 47, 48, 49, 50, 51, 56, 57, 58, 60, 61, 63, 64, 65, 66, 68, 69, 74, 75, 76, 78, 79, 80-1, 89, 93, 97, 106, 108, 113, 127, 155
Laurie, S. S., 72
Lawrence, E., 121
Lindsay, K., 135
Little Commonwealth, 26-7, 31, 34, 48, 76, 79, 88
Lloyd, George, 2, 9, 97
London Society of Psychoanalysis, 106
Lynch, A. J., 25, 69, 70, 88, 127, 151, 152-3
Lytton, Earl of, 27-8, 45

McDougall, W., 46, 102-6, 107, 113, 150
Mackenzie, H. Millicent, 57, 121
Mackinder, Jessie, 43, 51, 70, 75, 81
McMillan, Margaret, 45, 126
MacMunn, Norman, 25, 31, 32-3, 34, 45, 46, 47, 48, 49, 50, 54, 56, 57, 59, 60, 61, 64, 65, 68, 70, 71, 75, 79, 81-2, 87, 88, 92, 95, 108, 155
Malting House School, 31, 37-8, 111-12, 119
Mannheim, K., 117
Marlborough Infants' School, 43
Marvin, F. S., 122
Mather, Sir William, 66
May, Sir George, 130
Miller, H. Crichton, 106, 108, 117
Montagu, George, 26
Montessori, Maria, 28-30, 31, 35, 41, 43, 44, 46, 47, 49, 50, 51, 56, 57, 58, 60, 61, 63, 64, 65, 66, 67, 68, 69, 70, 72, 74, 75, 77, 78, 79, 81, 82, 89, 91, 96-7, 98, 108, 113, 120, 121, 126, 127, 155
Montessori Society, 44